John Henry Gurney

Rambles of a Naturalist in Egypt and Other Countries

With an analysis of the claims of certain foreign birds to be considered British, and

other ornithological notes

John Henry Gurney

Rambles of a Naturalist in Egypt and Other Countries
With an analysis of the claims of certain foreign birds to be considered British, and other ornithological notes

ISBN/EAN: 9783337243678

Printed in Europe, USA, Canada, Australia, Japan

Cover: Foto ©Andreas Hilbeck / pixelio.de

More available books at **www.hansebooks.com**

RAMBLES OF A NATURALIST

IN

EGYPT & OTHER COUNTRIES.

Rambles of a Naturalist

IN

EGYPT & OTHER COUNTRIES.

WITH AN ANALYSIS OF
THE CLAIMS OF CERTAIN FOREIGN BIRDS
TO BE CONSIDERED BRITISH,
AND OTHER ORNITHOLOGICAL NOTES.

BY

J. H. GURNEY, Jun., F.Z.S.

LONDON:
JARROLD AND SONS, 3, PATERNOSTER BUILDINGS.

PREFACE.

IN the following pages I have endeavoured to describe truthfully the incidents of sundry journeys undertaken in the last half-dozen years, more or less with a view to the prosecution of my favourite study—Ornithology—which is fast striding after its sister sciences in the public favour. If I may presume to think that anything I have written can in any degree help to render Ornithology more popular, I shall be amply repaid for the labour and trouble which it has cost me.

I have added a statement, which may not be wholly without interest, of the claims of certain rare species of birds to be included in the British list. The present plan of placing such stragglers on a level with our native species is to be reprobated; at the same time it is not easy to know what to do with them. They clearly cannot be passed over, for they are too important. The proper course is to submit them to a close scrutiny, and insert such as pass the ordeal in small type, or by indenting them, or some other means make it plain that they are not to be on the same footing with our indigenous species.

It is impossible to write a book which is entirely free from error, but I have done my best to make my lucubrations accurate, and I commit them to the public, trusting that my readers will look leniently on mistakes should they find any. I can only say, may they prove to be few and far between; and in conclusion, let me remark that I have had the assistance of my father, so that the work has had the advantage of a double supervision.

J. H. G., JUN.

CONTENTS.

TO RUSSIA AND BACK,

With an Account of the Birds to be met with at the

principal Markets, and a few

Notes on the Museums and Zoological Gardens.

AT 6.15 p.m., on the 11th of August, 1869, the "Ranger" left her moorings below London Bridge, and steamed rapidly down the Thames. It was a finer night than the weather had given any promise of, and I amused myself with standing on deck and watching the docks, and fields and houses, passing in a continually changing panorama, and a small flock of Gulls* lazily flapping over the water, until the waning twilight made it too dark to see. By day-break next morning we were at Gravesend, where the river is a considerable breadth, and plenty of shipping dotted about presented an animated scene. Here the river-pilot and the officer of customs wished us a prosperous voyage, and went ashore in the boat which brought the captain.

---

* In the autumn of 1871, I sent to the Zoological Gardens a Herring Gull which had strayed as far as Kentish Town, by which time it had got exhausted, and afforded a fine Sunday's amusement to sundry "loafers" who ran it down and captured it. This fellow had a fine appetite, and easily managed three herrings at a meal.

B

When off Harwich great quantities of wasp-like insects *(Syrphidæ)*, and a good many Lady-birds, and a few Butterflies came on board. I thought at the time it might have been in consequence of the sugar which formed part of the cargo; but it seems, according to the *Times* newspaper, that on the same day a marvellous flight of Lady-birds arrived at Ramsgate, where they were shovelled up by spadefuls; and on the 24th of the preceding month, a yacht off Hunstanton passed through a black stripe in the water two or three miles in length, all composed of defunct Lady-birds. (Norfolk Naturalist's Society, 1869, p. 62.)

We sighted Denmark on the 15th of August. When still many miles from shore a common Dunlin *(Tringa alpina L.) en trajet*, flew on board, was speedily caught, and is now in my collection. I could by this time see that the coast presented a succession of islands, good places for birds I dare say, and no doubt inhabited by a fishing population, whose one-storied and black-roofed houses were plainly visible. On the 16th we were steaming slowly up the Kattegat, with Denmark on our right and the bold coast of Sweden on our left. The sky was cloudless. The chopping waves of the North Sea were exchanged for the calmness of the "Narrows." Three formidable forts bar the entrance to Copenhagen—vouchers that the Danes will show their teeth to any second Nelson who shall try to ride in their harbour. The Captain allowed an hour and a quarter, and no more, for walking about the place. The houses look old, but many of the edifices are large, and must have been grand a century ago. In that short time I could not find the regular birdstuffer, but I noticed in a shop window two Goshawks, an old one and a young one. Swallows, Swifts, and Martins were flying about, as welcome and as much at home as in every town in England.

There is one hour difference between Copenhagen time

and that of London. After setting our watches right, we steamed off again and passed to the north of the island of Bornholm, and near to the unpronounceable place called Utkhipporna. No view to be obtained of the Prussian coast at any time.

The following morning, a little before 7 a.m., when the "Ranger" had passed the island of Œland—visited for egging purposes by Messrs. Wolley and Huddleston in 1866—and was off Gottland, on the Swedish side of the Baltic—weather thick and inclined to rain—several Insessorial birds alighted on the rigging. With them was a Hawk, which, according to the report of the man at the helm, was so exhausted that it fell into the sea. When I came on deck, the only bird which remained was a *Phyllopneuste*—I believe *P. trochilus (L.)*. It was joined by another, apparently of the same species, somewhat later in the day. At 2.45 a female Pied Flycatcher (*Muscicapa atricapilla L.*) settled on the ship, which I got a good view of by creeping along under the bulwarks. There was no wind at that time. It had no sooner left us than one of the boys caught a bird which had been about, I believe, all the morning, and which proved to be a Red-backed Shrike. Doubtless these feathered pilgrims were but the vanguard of the great autumnal tide of migration. They must have come from the immense firwoods which skirt the Swedish shore, and extend into the interior. The author of a "Note Book of a Naturalist" mentions, (p. 64) that when he was sailing near the same place, a Long-tailed Titmouse came on board, which is far more remarkable than any of the birds I saw.

As evening drew on, the sea, which before was calm as glass, began to be gently rippled by a passing wind. Quickly the sails felt the breeze. Quickly our good ship ploughed her way onwards, and as she went she left behind her a broad wake of foam, on which there fell the rays of a red setting sun in most transcendent splendour. Gradually we left Œland in the distance, but the sun had illumined the vault of heaven, and there remained a glittering pathway over the waters of the Baltic for many hours, until night shrouded the scene. On that occasion I observed a ship in the ball of the sun, as he dipped to his rest below the horizon.

The day following we entered the Gulf of Finland. On the 20th, when off Hogland island, a Kestrel *(Tinnunculus alaudarius)* paid us a visit, which was the only other bird we saw, for the same evening we anchored outside the bristling batteries of Cronstadt. Thousands of half-wild Pigeons were swarming about the harbour, and I recognised my old friend the Grey Crow, *(Corvus cornix L.)* not often to be seen in our country in August, but here in Russia they are stay-at-home birds, and probably do not migrate at all. Their tameness at St. Petersburg would shock Alexander Selkirk. They stalk about the streets with the air of a landed proprietor, who is kindly permitting the wood merchants to pile their timber on his wharf. It is said they have been even known to seize the sacred Pigeons !

The city of St. Petersburgh is built almost entirely upon piles. Nevertheless, it is on such a low bad site, that if Lake Ladŏga overflowed, and a certain conjunction of wind and tide took place, it would infallibly be swamped; and a good many people expect that this will happen some day.

The finest edifice is the Isaac Cathedral, beyond all question. It is in the form of a Greek cross. Its grand simplicity is very effective. Hemmed in by no houses like our St. Paul's, yet with all the finest buildings in the capital grouped around it, its noble porticos, its colossal proportions free from all meretricious ornament, and its vast gilded dome tower up into the air. It is surmounted by a cross, which may serve the newly-arrived stranger as a landmark from all parts of the city. Pigeons make it their home, semi-wild ones of domestic origin, like those which in London frequent the British Museum, the Houses of Parliament, and Somerset House. Crowds of House Martins had gathered on the Winter Palace. The pert Jackdaw was also there, and the ever-present Sparrow, the same as in England.

Those who are not pressed for time when they have done the principal sights, not forgetting the Hermitage and Peter the Great's House, ought to take steamer to Peterhof Palace. One of the rooms is panelled from skirting-board to ceiling with 368 portraits of girls, all selected for their beauty; besides this singular collection there are other things in the palace worth seeing. A fire had just taken place at this suburb when I was there, and nearly two acres of houses had been burnt down, but the Russians are too much accustomed to this sort of thing to think much of two acres of wooden houses. Great precautions are taken in the city by building lofty watch-towers, from which, by means of a system of hoisting balls, alarm can be given in case of fire.

The streets are spacious but badly paved; they are covered with snow half the year, and I suppose the in-habitants do not think it worth while paving them any better. Many of them are of wood, which is delightfully easy to drive on in your "droski" when new, but wears out very soon, without an upper coating of asphalt. They are well lighted with gas, and there is nothing prettier than to lean on the parapet of St. Nicholas' Bridge, and look up the river at the two long rows of lamps reflected in the water.

There is a garden on the Vassili Ostrof which is used in summer as a market for live birds, rabbits, snakes, lizards, tortoises, shells, etc. Here I saw, besides sundry birds which appeared to have been imported from other countries, Skylarks, young Starlings, the Marsh Titmouse, to which De Selys gave the name *Parus borealis*, Bullfinches *(Pyrrhula europœa, Leach)*, Blue-throated Warblers, and Blackcaps: and in gunmakers' windows, stuffed specimens of the Golden Eagle, Peregrine Falcon, Eagle Owl,* Snowy Owl, Black-throated Diver, Shelduck, and Curlew.

Not far from the Millionaya Street there is a small game market, and at one shop a Whooper or Wild Swan, and a Nutcracker† *(Nucifraga caryocatactes L.)*, were hanging up. An attempt had been made to stuff them, so I dare say they had been suspended there all the summer.

Shooting commences on the 15th (27th) of July, but Capercaillie are not in season so early as that. A freshly-killed young bird is of course far superior to what are brought over and vended in Leadenhall market. Old ones would hardly be considered fit to eat in Russia. The *Teterka* (Blackgrouse), and *Riabchick* (Hazelgrouse), are also capital birds for the table. It is said that considerable numbers of the Grey Partridge *(Perdix cinerea Lath.)* have been turned off in the vicinity of the metropolis. There are a great many stories about the Capercaillie; one is that after death it swallows its tongue. Like many other fables it is founded on fact; for the organ is sometimes retracted so far as to become quite invisible.‡

---

* I find that in a tame Eagle Owl of ours, when exhausted with long incubation, the pupils of the eyes become almost white. I also find that the iris in this species becomes very much lighter with age.

† The middle tail feathers are so abraded at the end in a Nutcracker of mine, killed at Christchurch in Hampshire, as to leave the shafts almost bare, and they are worn in the same way in a specimen of my father's, killed at Rollesby in Norfolk.

‡ The number of Scotch Capercaillie sent up to Leadenhall Market is very large, perhaps 200 in a winter, exemplifying the remarkable hold which this species has again taken in North Britain, particularly in

I must now say something of the Museum, which is at the Academy of Sciences (between the Exchange and the University), and contains the famous Mammoth, whose unfossilized remains were found embedded in ice on the banks of the Lena. Professor Brandt was away, but I was glad to meet Dr. Radde, who drew attention to his *Fuligula baeri*, which would appear to be one of those puzzling hybrid Ducks, (Reisen im Süden von Ost-Sibirien in den Jahren 1855—1859, p. 376,) and to the beautiful specimens of *Anas falcata* and *A. glocitans*, which latter is the species to which by English authors some hybrids were incorrectly assigned under the name of "Bimaculated Duck." I also especially noticed no less than twenty varieties of the Blackgrouse, and several of the Capercaillie, also both sexes of the spurious Rakkelhan Grouse *(Tetrao medius (Meyer) Tem.)*, the female of which appears to be exactly like a small female Capercaillie. Another handsome cross is that between the Black Grouse and Willow Grouse, of which I afterwards saw several, but did not succeed in obtaining a specimen. I had hoped to find a good series of the Red-breasted Goose, but I only saw four; one of them a plain grey bird without a particle of red was marked a female, doubtless immature. The collection of Brazilian species is large; but not being well up in South American birds, I directed my attention to the specimen of the Great Auk. I found that there was no egg of this bird in the Museum, but Professor Newton had told me that he believed there were two in the city, and I set on foot enquiries, but without any result beyond learning that Mr. Champley of Scarborough had been making enquiries before me.

Perthshire. They come earlier and are smaller than the Norwegian, and may be known by having been shot. Numbers are also sent to the Glasgow poulterers, according to Mr. Gray. (B. of Scotland, p. 228.)

I passed some birds in the ante-room recently set up, which I rather think were from Finland. They were the Curlew Sandpiper, Wood Sandpiper, Swifts, etc. Also a Short-eared Owl just brought in and skinned, and a Hen Harrier, which was no doubt killed in the environs. There were specimens of both in the collection marked St. Petersburgh. In another ante-room there was an artist at work painting a Ruff, with Gould's "Birds of Europe" to help him. I must not omit to mention seeing some eggs of the Waxen Chatterer,* with the following testimony to an Englishman's perseverance :—

"In memoriam Johannis Wolley, quem in regionibus Europœ, hyperboreis naturœ arcanorum per multos annos studiosum, fames, frigus, bellum, non deterrerunt, hœc ampelidis garrulœ ova musœo."

On the 3rd I saw the Zoological Gardens, and bought a curious muff made of nine necks of Black-throated Divers in their fullest plumage. The gardens are really very poor for a great place like St. Petersburgh. They are a private undertaking, and the property of a lady. Wild Tree Sparrows were flying in and out among the bushes. By the Rumiantsoff Obelisk I saw a Greater Whitethroat (?).

Going again to the Museum, the taxidermist, Monsieur Wosnessensky, showed me a Honey Buzzard *(Pernis apivo-rus, L.)* just set up. I likewise saw a couple of young Cranes, which had been reared by hand. They were a yellowish brown colour; the crown of the head not bare; the iris dark.

Before going away I paid my respects to another live-bird market, where I saw Redwings, Redstarts, Snow

---

* The Waxen Chatterer goes as far south as Algeria. Professor Newton, in his fourth edition of Yarrell, "B. B.," says indeed that it does not cross the Mediterranean, but both he and Mr. Dresser must have overlooked what Loche says :—"De passage en Algérie de loin en loin." (Cat. des Mammiferes, etc., p. 88.)

Buntings, Pine Grosbeaks, an Oxeye Titmouse, a Long-tailed Titmouse, a Pied Flycatcher, and five Storks. I bought a Sparrowhawk* and a Cuckoo, which I skinned the following day, together with an Oystercatcher, which an English resident had shot on lake Ladŏga. From its brown back, and from the edgings to the feathers, I have no doubt that it is a bird of the year.

On the 8th of September I travelled by a second-class carriage to Moscow. I thought it much more comfortable than an English first-class, and a perfect banquet was provided at the stations where we stopped for refreshment.

The only birds seen on the way were a few Wood Pigeons† and Magpies, a Rook, and an old Buzzard perched upon a pole.

I was unfortunately just too late for a meeting of Zoologists and scientific men, in which I might have heard some interesting questions discussed.

As soon as I arrived I hastened to the live-bird market, where I found for sale the Common Sandpiper, Hawfinch, Crested Titmouse and Shorelark; and the next day at some other shops outside the wall of the "Kitai Gorod," a Golden Oriole, a Missel Thrush, and a Raven; and in the game market the following dead birds—Goshawk (in an interesting state of change), Capercaillie, Hazel Grouse,

---

* On the 31st of August, 1873, a young cock Sparrowhawk was made a prisoner in our bantam-house, having dashed through the top netting, of which the mesh is only two and a half inches in diameter. It must have been a squeeze, but he could have come in no other way.

† November 20th, 1871, a gamekeeper in Norfolk drew my attention to a Silver-fir tree with two leaders, near to a Pheasant-feeder, (a wooden contrivance for corn,) remarking that he knew this deformity and many others like it to have been caused by Wood Pigeons coming after the corn, and settling on the tops of the trees when they were young and breaking them thus.

Willow Grouse* (in part summer plumage), Double Snipes, and Teal.

While I was examining them, a fine Buzzard soared about overhead on the look-out for anything he could pick up. I soon afterwards saw some more, circling at no great height. I have understood that they propagate as well as roost in the steeples and minarets; and that besides clearing up all kinds of refuse, as the scavenger Kite once did in London, they make prey of the Pigeons which infest Moscow.

Pigeons are never shot in the town; they roost and nidify in the Kremlin's gilded cupolas, and are very common throughout the city.

Of course I visited the Zoological Gardens of the Imperial Acclimatisation Society, which are prettily laid out, and with a fine sheet of water. I was informed that the animals had fallen off, but there still remained a fine collection, including upwards of twenty Eagles, and a similar number of Ruddy Shelducks, also one or more of the following species —Caucasian Snow-Partridge, Great Bustard, Coot, Black-tailed Godwit, Green Sandpiper, Capercaillie, Snipe, and Common Sandpiper; altogether there were sixty-five sorts of birds in the Gardens, and the collection was very superior to that at St. Petersburgh.

On the 12th, after glancing over the bird market, where I noticed a Nutcracker, an albinoe Quail, and a Waxwing, I drove with a friend to the famous Sparrow Hills, whence Napoleon first viewed the city. It was a noble stand-point, almost equal to Arthur's seat at Edinburgh. "All this is yours," he is said to have exclaimed, and the shout of

---

* Mr. Yarrell, in 1843, gives the price of Ptarmigan at four shillings a brace, (B. B., 11., p. 327,) but does not say if they were Scotch Ptarmigan or Norway Willow Grouse. The latter is far and away the commoner in Leadenhall market. The price has gone up since his time, Scotch Ptarmigan being twelve and sixpence a brace in October, and Norway Willow Grouse six shillings.

"Moscow! Moscow!" was taken up by the foremost ranks and carried to the rear of his army.

On the 13th I got a Spotted Crake, a Sclavonian Grebe, and a young Ruff;* and took a peep into the celebrated Riding-school, 560 feet in length, supposed to be the largest room in the world. Here in the winter two regiments of Russian cavalry can manœuvre at the same time, when the intense cold does not permit of their going through their exercises out of doors.

I had failed in seeing the birdstuffer at St. Petersburgh, M. Dode, though I made his acquaintance in London in the spring of 1871, but I was more fortunate at Moscow. Taxidermy is not a lucrative trade there, and I cannot say much for the way in which a Dipper and a Little Gull were mounted. The latter was in very complete nuptial plumage, and I believe they breed near Moscow.

On the 14th I bought a Garganey Teal and a Nyroca Duck. For the latter I was charged one hundred "copeks," equivalent to a "rouble" or three shillings in English money. Afterwards the birdstuffer's wife came to me with the following birds—White-breasted Nuthatch (*Sitta europœa, Lin.*), Jay, Golden-crested Wren, Chaffinch, Thrush, Willow Wren, Crested Titmouse, Marsh Titmouse (*Parus borealis*), and Blue Titmouse. The latter was a remarkably pale light-coloured specimen, but several of the best Ornithologists to whom I have shown it consider it to be merely a variety.

September 15th.—A Shoveller Duck at the market.

16th.—A very wet day. Picked out from among a lot of other wild-fowl a nestling Nyroca Duck, not half fledged. The market is a famous place for Double Snipes; basketsful

---

* In 1871, in the early part of the summer, I am informed a drove of sixty old Ruffs were seen at Hickling Broad (in Norfolk), yet there were only two nests, I hear, and, sad to say, the eight young birds were all shot.

of them are brought in every morning. They are very greasy but delicious eating.

17th.—At the market, Corncrake, Tufted Ducks, Pintail Ducks, Blackbird, Thrush, and Golden Plover. I bought a Common Snipe, which had the outer tail feathers elongated. Compared to the Double Snipe it is quite a rarity.

20th.—I got a Smew before breakfast, and in the evening the birdstuffer's wife brought a Jack Snipe, a Brambling, two Siskins, a Whinchat, a Skylark, two Spotted Crakes, a Jay, and a Cuckoo. This Cuckoo, and the one I obtained at St. Petersburgh, were most curious specimens. Both were immature. In the first one the peculiarity consisted in a broad mark of reddish brown like a stain all down the head and back, and two others similar upon the wings. In the second the wings and all the upper surface were mealy-colored.*

21st.—Paid a final visit to the market and got a drake Gadwall. I had been led to expect great things from the Russian markets. Waxwings and Pine Grosbeaks were to be had for a few "copecks" I was told, and heaps of other rare birds ; but this can only apply to the winter, when I have no doubt they would vie with any in Europe.

I must not omit to say that the Zoological Cabinet at the University is particularly worth seeing, containing as it does no less than 73,638 specimens. The birds are fairly stuffed and in good order. I saw a beautiful skin of the rare Red-breasted Goose, and a mounted one which was not so good. One case was full of bottles of various sizes. Each bottle contained a card on which was gummed a bird's gizzard and its contents—gnats, flies, beetles, etc. The Rook, being of special importance to agriculture, the stomachs of no less

---

* The Cuckoo has been stated to have a pouch, but I have not succeeded in finding it, though I have remarked the very gelatinous skin of the neck in some specimens.

than eight were displayed. The preparations were really very neat, and each had a separate label. In the International Exhibition of 1862, there was a very similar series of the dried contents of the gizzards of the chief birds of France.

The University was founded by Elizabeth, daughter of Peter the Great. There are seventy-five professors, and the library contains about 160,000 books.

The line of railway which connects the two chief cities of Russia is straight as an arrow. The story goes, that the Tzar took a ruler and drew a line across the map, and said to the government engineer, " That is how the railway is to go." He made it accordingly, and it is 403 miles long.

On re-visiting the live-bird stalls at St. Petersburgh I saw pretty much the same species as before, and a few additional ones, to wit, the Pied Wagtail, Reed Bunting, Creeper, and Lapwing. In a poulterer's window I saw a stuffed Blackcock most beautifully pied, and a hybrid between that species and the Willow Grouse. I purchased a Green Woodpecker and a Goldeneye Duck, and tried to skin them, but the Woodpecker was almost too stale for the purpose. It is difficult to see what birds the poulterers have, for they keep them shut up in lockers instead of hanging them out.

On the 24th I saw a Waxwing at the Exchange Gardens for sale, and bought a Missel Thrush. On the 25th I dropped on to some fresh birds at the market, three Little Stints, a Dunlin, a Ring-Dotterel *(Charadrius intermedius)*, and a young Grey Plover, which was so yellow that but for its black axillaries it might have passed for a Golden.

The close of the month was wet, and I was not sorry to leave on the 28th of September, after collecting fifty-nine birds, a considerable number for so short a time. St. Petersburgh is wonderfully hot in summer, considering how far north it is ; but the climate appears to suit the English, who muster plentifully there; though indeed where are not our countrymen to be found?

By train to Berlin was about the longest journey without a break I ever made, occupying nearly forty-two hours; and so sparsely furnished with birds was the tract through which we passed, that I saw nothing worth recording.

The Zoological Gardens at Berlin are not equal to ours at London, though I think the grounds are larger. The Society is well off in *Accipitres*, and a pen of fifteen Little Egrets and Squacco Herons was a beautiful sight. A mouse, which my approach frightened into the Crane's enclosure, was caught up in a twinkling.*

The trade in Thrushes, carried on in the open place by the theatre, is quite a business. This was the only market I could find. I saw a Great Bustard *(Otis tarda)* in it, but nothing else worth mentioning.

I thought none of the Berlin sights better worth seeing than the Aquarium. In fish it has now been eclipsed by that at Brighton, but in addition to the fish there were many birds of considerable interest and rarity.

The Museum is too renowned to call for any praise from me. It is in the left wing of the University. In passing through the Thier Garten to see the Royal Necropolis, I had a capital view of a Greater Spotted Woodpecker. I have been told they are rather common.

My next stage was to Hanover. The Zoological Gardens there are decidedly good, and the Raptorial birds well cared for. In one cage was a nearly white Buzzard, and in another two more with a great amount of white.

From my bedroom window at the hotel I observed a

---

* Some years ago my father kept a pair of Purple Herons. Some rats burrowed a hole in the ground at the bottom of their cage. A can of water was poured down to bolt them, and two half-grown ones ran out, but they only escaped drowning to be instantly captured and swallowed by the Herons.

pair of Black Redstarts. They seem partial to bricks and mortar. So is the Crested Lark, which at Hanover will perch freely on buildings. Near the Waterloo Column I had about twenty of the two species in view at once.

Having done the Museum, which contained a Great Auk, I took the train to Brussels. In Brussels' market I have always found good birds, and on this occasion I made the following list of species during the few days I spent there :— Curlews, Hazél Grouse, Serin Finch, Spotted Redshanks,* (easily picked out by their long bills,) Scaup,† Gadwall, Pintail, Shoveller, Grey Shrikes, Hawfinch, Jays, (some of them plucked!) Dunlins, Spotted Crakes, Coots, Water-Hens, Dabchick, Jack Snipes (in plenty), Woodcocks (a fair number), Pheasants (a few), Grey and Red-legged Partridges (about equally common), Quail, Red Grouse, (these at a poulterer's,) Wood Pigeons, Wild Geese, (I forget what species; but on another occasion I saw a small but un-doubted Bean Goose,) Short-eared Owls, Lapwings, Golden Plovers, Green Woodpecker, Magpies,‡ Merlin. The con-sumption of Thrushes is nearly as great as at Berlin, and many birds which we should not much esteem are sold for food, e.g., Thrushes, Redwings, Blackbirds, Ring Ouzels, and an occasional Fieldfare or Missel Thrush, which find patronizers. Nor are there wanting people who have the heart to dine off Bramblings, Larks, and Tree Sparrows; and I even saw a Robin and a Cole Titmouse offered among the more legitimate *gibier:* but my greatest stroke of luck

---

* I have often seen Spotted Redshanks in Leadenhall market. They have been got there in all states of plumage, but the commonest is the adult winter, and the rarest the adult summer.

† In the Exeter Museum there is a curious female Scaup Duck with a white collar, also a white chin, which was shot on the Exe.

‡ On the 23rd of December, 1869, I saw an astonishing number of Magpies in the market at Paris, but nothing else except a great many Squirrels.

was when I detected a knot of people on the staircase handling a splendid Kite, which of course I bought.

At Brussels I met my father, who had been in the town a few days.* On reference to his diary, I observe that he met with some species in the market which I did not, viz., Kestrel, Jackdaw, Greater-spotted Woodpecker, Ortolan Bunting, Corncrake, Water Rail, Teal, and Wild Duck.

Being at the market again in December, 1870, I saw a Starling, some Great and Blue Tits, Linnets, Purple Sand-pipers, Brent Geese,† (plucked all except their wings,) and a Velvet Scoter (plucked also, a choice morsel all ready for the first fasting devotee who came a market-ing): nor have I yet got to the end of my list, for on another occasion I saw several magnificent old drake Smews, Goosanders, and Shelducks, quite a fine ornitho-logical sight ;‡ besides which the late Dr. Saxby enumerates in his "Notes on the Birds of Belgium," (Zoologist, 7537,) Scops Owl, Tengmalm's Owl, Lapland Bunting, Black Grouse, and Red-crested Duck ; to which I can further add Richardson's Skua :§ but I think I have said enough to make anyone's mouth water who is fond of poking about for rare birds in markets.

---

* He had just come from Ghent, where he got four Richard's Pipits from among Larks and Wagtails in the poulterers' shops and eating-houses.

† Willoughby describes "a very heedless fowl" found in Yorkshire, called a *Rat* or *Road*-Goose. "If a pack of them come into Tees it is seldom one escapes away." This is the Brent, and the name of *Road*-Goose is persistent to this day at Tees-mouth.

‡ This was after the very hard weather which ushered in 1871. The same week I saw several adult male Goosanders in Leadenhall market, and about seven magnificent Smews were killed in Norfolk. (Zool. ss., 2600.)

§ I have more than once had Richardson's Skua, from Flamborough Head in Yorkshire, in *July*.

The Museum, of which M. Alf. Dubois is curator, contains 22,500 specimens. The Macqueen's Bustard (killed in the vicinity in 1845,) has a beautiful ruff, equal I think to the finest Houbaras which I obtained in Algeria. It appears that two others were killed with it. The Great Auk seemed (for it was getting dark when I got round to it,) to be a well-stuffed specimen, in summer plumage of course. It was bought of Frank, through whose hands several have passed, twenty years ago, when they were not considered to be extinct, for 150 francs in the skin. As far as I remember, all the Great Auks which I examined had the ribs on the bill white. (cf. Zoologist, 1642).

I must now mention a Goose in the Zoological Gardens which had pink legs, and yet from the length of its bill was an undoubted Bean Goose. Curious as this is, it is not more so than the converse which has happened in Somersetshire to Mr. Cecil Smith. That naturalist has recorded (Zoologist, 3412, 3627, 4333,) Pink-footed Geese of his own breeding with yellow legs, but as they were that colour in early youth, it is not to be taken as any corroboration of Strickland's exploded notion that the Pink-footed Goose was the young of the Bean. Strickland's "Bean Goose" was Bartlett's true Pink-footed Goose. Both these writers agreed that the Geese with black nails to their beaks were divisible into two species, but they differed about the names which should be applied to them. Now that the distinctions are properly understood, it appears clear that the Pink-footed is much the commoner, and that many even of the more recent records of "Bean Geese" must be taken as referring to it. I happened last June to see living examples of both in an enclosure together, and there is no tangible difference in plumage. Practically the best marks to seize on are those originally published, viz., the short bill, smaller stature, and pink legs of the Pink-footed Goose, and also the middle of the beak pink, as opposed to the yellow colour of the same parts in the Bean Goose.   Oddly enough, I could find no specimens of the " Long-billed Car Goose " in Mr. Strickland's collection in the York Museum.

With many apologies for being led into this digression, I will now return to my journal.   At the chief poulterer's at Lille I saw more than a dozen Tufted Ducks, and a beautiful Grey Phalarope.   It is the custom to hang up skins, and at this game-shop there was a Kentish Plover, and at another a Merganser, a Scoter, and a Black-tailed Godwit.

With regard to the Museum of this town I cannot do better than quote my father, as his note is more full than mine.

" There are two collections of birds in the Museum here, one a good general collection, the other a very fine series (in a separate room) of the birds of Europe, which formerly belonged to the late Dr. Degland, author of " Degland's Birds of Europe," who lived at Lille.   In the general collection there are a fine pair of adult Goshawks from the Ural Mountains, which seemed to me to have the transverse bars on the breast decidedly narrower and finer than on the breast of adult Goshawks in Western Europe.

" In the collection which was formerly Dr. Degland's, there is a remarkably fine series of Honey Buzzards, chiefly from the Pyrenees, some specimens of Greyheaded Wagtails killed near Lille, and one similar Wagtail killed there with a head quite black, and in fact the same as the black-headed yellow Wagtail of the south of Europe, and also as Mr. Vingoe's Cornish specimen, except that the latter has, I think, a little white mark near the eye. There were also nearly pure albinoes of the common Yellow Wagtail and the Tree Pipit; two specimens of the Turdus Atrigularis, said to have been killed at Amsterdam; a nestling Golden Oriole, taken from the nest near Lille; a nestling Ring Ouzel, very different from the adult, and spotted almost like a young Blackbird; a Siberian Bunting (*Emberiza chrysophrys, Pall.*), caught near Lille; a nestling Little Gull from the Ural Mountains; and lastly, a Great Auk, bought by Dr. Degland of a dealer at Amsterdam in 1835,

It seems a small adult bird, with the cheek spots quite white, and also the throat, except the chin, which is black."

My next move was to Calais, where, on the 28th of October, I had a good opportunity of watching a Velvet Scoter, which was swimming between the piers. I suspect it had swum there purposely, as the next day there were two, seemingly both females. They were diving in the most unconcerned manner, but I know not whether they were fishing, or whether they were trying to escape the stones with which a gang of small street Arabs were pelting them. A little flock of Purple Sandpipers proved even more interesting than the Scoters. I was watching their quaint actions at the edge of the water, when a man came up and began to stone them also. Stoning seems a favourite diversion of the French. Walking home I saw a Woodcock flying wildly among the chimney tops. A Chaffinch was shown me which had killed itself against the lighthouse, a lofty structure which can be clearly seen from Dover. A wire netting has been found necessary to protect the lantern from the birds which dash against it. The keeper showed me into a room where there were about eighty species of birds set up, all of which he asserted had killed themselves against that light. I can hardly credit it, although he made the same assertion to my father, for there were several which appeared to me most unlikely to be obtained in such a way, e.g., Montague's Harrier, Rock Thrush, Little Bittern, Avocet, Purple Heron, Red-necked Grebe, (full breeding plumage,) Razorbill, and Gulls. The story he told my father was that, in 1855 a Whooper Swan flew against the lantern, and broke the glass and its own wing. This was stuffed, and after that specimens of all the species which killed themselves against the glass had been preserved. The tickets testify that the collection has been long finished. Of late years all the birds have gone to a collector at Saint Pierre, but for the last two years the keeper admits that nothing but Larks and small birds have been got.*

Proceeding to Boulogne, I found that most of the birds in the Museum there had been collected by M. Demarle of Douai, but the rare Capped Petrel bears the name of Lebeau Lonquety as donor. There are local specimens (as indicated by two blue lines upon the ticket) of the Spotted Eagle, Crested Titmouse, King Duck, and Caspian Tern, besides four Purple Waterhens, which may not have been really wild. Only the Eagle and Titmouse are included in the list in Bertrand's History of Boulogne by Demarle, entitled "Oiseaux observés dans le Boulonnais."

And here my notes on this journey terminate. Leaving in a steamer at 6.30 for Folkestone I had a quick passage, but did not see many birds worthy of record. I have, however, once seen Fulmar Petrels about midway in the straits. I mistook them at first for Gulls, until as they came nearer, their buoyant flight attracted my closer attention, and I made out what they really were. I have also sometimes seen great flocks of restless Scoter Ducks, particularly in November, 1870, near Ostend, and parties of Puffins and Gannets prowling along in pairs; and I have known the steamer go so close to a Red-throated Diver as nearly to run it down.

---

* A Wild Duck once flew against Happisburgh lighthouse, in Norfolk, broke the glass and indented the copper; but this is nothing to a story of what happened at the Lundy Island lighthouse. One frosty night a large flock came full tilt against the lantern, the glass of which was 5/16 of an inch thick, which they immediately broke. Seven of the foremost were killed by the concussion, but the rest flew through the breach, and actually smashed the glass on the other side, leaving nine more of their number slain. The relics of this gallant band passed through in safety over the dead bodies of their comrades; and the keeper, as compensation for the smash, netted a haul of eight couple of Wild Ducks.

MY JOURNAL

THE ALGERIAN SAHARA.

Monday, 25th of January, 1870.

A SWARM of low-class Arabs and swarthy negroes pounced upon me as I stepped on to the quay at Oran, and bade me yield my luggage to their care. Pestered with their importunities I fled to the custom house, and while my cases were undergoing a nominal examination, the official in charge drove back the exasperated crowd of mendicant porters, until I could select two less frantic than the rest, to carry my baggage up to the hotel. It was a lovely day. Oran, the westernmost town in Algeria, a French seaport and chief place of the province, lay spread before me. It is no inconsiderable place, having a population half as large as that of Algiers, two hotels, a theatre, a *place*, a market, and sundry large *bureaus;* but it is not much visited by tourists. In this instance it appeared that there were some English there already, for a party of sportsmen who, I heard belonged to our nationality, had been out shooting, and had just brought back three wild boars: stretched upon the pavement they lay with bullet holes in their rugged sides. There is no lack of them in the brushwood on the mountains, but the sport is considered expensive, owing to the number of beaters required. After duly inspecting them, I remembered that I had come to Africa to study birds; and all athirst for unknown species, I ascended to Fort St. Croix.

Having satisfactorily identified some Dartford Warblers, (*Melizophilus undatus*) whose flight was very weak, especially if there was any wind, I worked my way home by another path, noting as I went along the Kestrel (*Tinnunculus alaudarius*), the Black-headed Warbler (*Sylvia melano-cephala*), the Corn Bunting (*Emberiza miliaria*), the Wren (*Troglodytes parvulus*), and the Grey Wagtail (*Motacilla sulphurea, Bech.*), flirting about by a ditch of water. Other birds I saw in the distance, but enough had been identified to show that the avifauna of Algeria was not so very different from that of England; however, on the hillside I listened to a truly African bird (as I believe), the Dusky Ixos (*Ixos obscurus*). Its notes rang through the newly-planted pine groves. There were three in the market, which confirms my impression that the bird I heard was the Ixos. It is said to have occurred in Britain. It is very sombre coloured. I made notes of two species not in-cluded in the late Mr. Drake's "Birds of Eastern Morocco," (Ibis, 2nd series, III., p. 142.—V., p. 147,) the irrepressible Sparrow (*Passer domesticus*), which I thought I had left behind me in England, and the Barbary Partridge (*Caccabis petrosa*), which flies fast and straight with neck outstretched, making as much noise with its wings as our grey one when flushed, and giving utterance to a shrill note or two. I was surprised to see some in the town with their throats *not* cut, which the Arabs generally insist upon doing, for your true Mahommedan conceives himself forbidden by the direct law of the prophet to eat anything which has not died by the knife. I afterwards got eleven eggs of this Partridge.

There was a steamer to Algiers on the 28th, a distance of

about 250 miles, which I preferred to travelling over land. It was a clear day and a calm sea, and we coasted along near enough to observe the verdant hills, in some places sparsely covered, in others clothed with rich foliage. I stood on deck watching some Manx Shearwaters, until the blue bay of Algiers came in sight, and we cast anchor at a short distance from the boulevards, constructed for the French government by Sir Morton Peto. Algiers is one of those places which have been so much written about, that nothing more remains to be said. Piesse's "Itinéraire de l'Algerie," and Bernard's "Indicateur de l'Algerie," give a sufficiently good account of it, and to them I refer the reader. An astonishing number of English make it their winter quarters, the climate being recommended in cases of consumption and lung disease; and some of them hire houses, and have delightful gardens, in the suburb of Mustapha. The Moorish part of the town is highly interesting, while the French part can boast of capital hotels (the Hotel d'Orient is perhaps the best,) and a great number of first-class shops. There is very good society, and plenty to see in the neighbourhood for those who do not go further into the interior.

I copy the following extracts from some correspondence in the "*Field*," which may be of use to anyone intending to go there.

"Houses can be obtained in the suburbs at £20 to £40 per month furnished, and the owners let them generally only for the season of six months, and not for a less period. English furniture would be useless here, or at any rate quite incongruous. The houses, moreover, are let furnished. There are no dependable house agents. It is a good plan to come here early, perhaps in the beginning of October, and stop at an hotel until a selection of a house can be made. There are doctors of all nations in the season. Horses can be bought at all prices, from £8 to £120. The best horses that can be bought (for the Arabs will not sell their best) are to be had for 3,000 francs; any higher price that may be paid is money thrown away. Very fair horses may be hired at £5 per month, the livery-stableman keeping them and providing saddles and bridles. Good servants are very difficult to obtain, especially for short periods. A thorough good cook earns nearly at the rate of £30 per annum.

W. P. B.   (Algiers, April 9th, 1873.)

"For a sportsman Algiers, or rather its vicinity, affords excellent shooting; Snipe and Duck, golden and grey [?] Plover, being the principal winter game; and in spring great quantity of Quail can be got.   I remember killing ten brace of Quail in a few hours.

*   *   *   *   *   *

"Within two days' journey of Algiers there is a large lake called Lac Alloula, where capital sport can be had. It is covered with wild duck in the winter with a good supply of geese and wild swans, and the margin of the lake is full of Snipe—a friend and myself killing forty couple of Snipe and several Bittern in a few hours.   *   *   *   *   *   *

Waverley.   (Oct. 21st, 1872.)

For a graphic account of this lake, and the ornithological treasures to be had there, see the "Ibis" for 1860, p. 149.

I procured from Madame Loche (the widow of the distinguished ornithologist) a Golden Eagle *(Aquila chrysaetos)*, which had been killed at Arba, twenty miles distant from Algiers, about three months before. I also saw another alive. Captain Loche had several, but they, with other *Accipitres* to the number of 180, perished in the following manner. An earthquake occasioned the fall of an immense wall, beneath which was the "fauconnerie," and alas! it buried in its debris the precious birds which it had taken the Captain ten years to collect.

The adventures I had in getting a "permis de chasse" were quite as amazing as Canon Tristram's. It did not cost so much as an English game license, but the number of officials whose signatures were necessary was something awful. The mayor did me the honour to write "my description." From him I obtained the gratifying information that my hair was chestnut, my nose regular, my beard fair, my chin short, my eyes brown, and my complexion red!!

The next day I left early for Mustapha to explore the lanes there. This beautiful suburb is the Richmond of Algiers, and the favoured resort of the best families. My first shot was at a female Black-headed Warbler. Instead of slate colour as in the cock, the back was brown, and the head no darker than a Lesser Whitethroat's. Males of this species would appear to preponderate. After crossing several fields, and losing a specimen of *Chlorospiza aurantiiventris*, the interesting Algerian representative of our Greenfinch,* from which it can scarcely be said to be distinct, I came to a wooded valley, where I had a couple of shots at an Ichneuman. I missed him, and never had a chance of getting another. Here I fell in with a Serin *(Serinus hòrtulorum)*, singing merrily even then, at a period when winter had hushed for a time the notes of most of its congeners. One of the rarer British birds, it may be distinguished at a glance from the hen Siskin, the only one on the list with which it could be confounded, by its thicker beak. Trying to scramble up some sandrocks I disturbed a dozing Barn Owl, which, being brought to bag, proved a very spotted specimen, with the bars of the tail more defined than in English examples. The next bird was a Cirl Bunting *(Emberiza cirlus)*, not an uncommon species in Algeria. Then leaving the valley I gradually worked my way home by the sea shore, and the only bird I procured was the White Wagtail *(Motacilla alba)*, but the blue bay beneath me, and the transcendent scene, made up for the small bag, and I returned well satisfied with my walk.

---

* In the summer of 1871, I saw an Algerian Greenfinch in the Zoological Gardens, supposed to be eight years old.

February 3rd. Bought a cock Sandgrouse (*Pterocles arenarius, Pall.)* at the poulterer's, killed at Aumale, and went to the "Exposition," which is in one of the arches below the "Place du Government." M. Loche's birds are nicely set up and arranged, but the space devoted to them is not very large. The rest of his collection of skins is now dispersed. I saw his eggs at No. 9, Rue Marine, which are very good indeed. There were several drawers of duplicates.

February 6th. Observed a curious pale-coloured variety of the Robin in the market, and also a slightly pied Blackbird. A short time ago I read of a single taxidermist having twenty-nine pied Blackbirds to stuff in about a twelvemonth in Ireland. Surely they are as common there as pied Ring Ouzels are in Alsace and Lorraine. I have never had more than one or two since I began to collect birds.

February 7th, Sunday. Attended service in one of the arches beneath the "Boulevards." The large congregation showed how much need there was for the English Protestant Church, a site for which had been found not far from the Eastern gate, and which was already near completion. I began the new week at Blida, so famed for its delicious oranges, which are exported to Paris where one may see "Blida oranges" advertised in the shop windows. Among its scented groves I daily sauntered, and found the same choristers which we have at home. The familiar garden Thrush was quite common, and so were Redbreasts. Willow Wrens and tuneful Blackcaps seemed to abound everywhere. Starlings, Titlarks, and Linnets were in some numbers, and the sprightly Blackbird was not uncommon. But most beautiful of all were the Buff-backed Herons ; perched on the backs of cattle, they stand like alabaster images, and no herdsman but gladly makes them welcome. Here I shot the rare Dipper, or Pale-backed Water Ouzel, described by Dr. Tristram as *Cinclus minor* (Ibis, 1870, p. 496,) but since assigned in Dresser's "Birds of Europe" (Part 24 and 25, p. 3) to *C. albicollis (Vieill)*. Loche says of it in the "Exploration Scientifique," p. 306—

"Le cincle plongeur, que nous n'avons rencontré que tres accidentellement en Algérie y semble excessivement rare, et il est supposable qu'il ne doit y être que de passage."

But M. Germain, at p. 63, says :—

"Sedentaire—Se recontre sur le cours de l'*oued—Anasseur* (Milianah)."

On the 16th I caught a green Lizard, about a foot and a quarter long, but having nothing to preserve it in, set it at liberty. While I was in the "Tell,"* and afterwards in the Sahara, I had not much time to attend to anything but birds. I however made notes of a Water Tortoise at Miliana, of a Weasel (apparently the same as ours), of some Bats, and of Foxes in the rocks at Boghari, and of a few other things which will be mentioned in the course of my narrative.

On the 17th I took the Diligence to Boumedfa, a village stated to contain about 270 inhabitants, (though I should. have supposed it much less,) and leaving again on the 18th, moved to the fortified town of Miliana. Miliana is a place of considerable importance. Its ornithology has been worked by Monsieur Germain, but I was not aware of the existence of his paper, or I should not have been so much surprised at meeting with *Ruticilla Moussieri*,† a beautiful bird of restricted range, which he makes the subject of a long note ; or at shooting *Parus ledoucii* (Malh.), figured in Sharpe and Dresser's "Birds of Europe," and the only

---

* The "Tell" is the mountainous country of the Atlas, from the sea to the commencement of the Sahara.

† In Captain Shelley's collection I recently noticed a male marked "Blida, 1st of March, 1873."

specimen they could obtain for their work. The latter is very like our English Coal Tit.

From M. Germain's list, printed in the "Nouvelles Archives du Museum d'histoire Naturelle," I., p. 59, (Paris) and entitled "Catalogue Raisonné des oiseaux observés dans la subdivision de Milianah," I cull a few remarks on this species :—

"Commune dans les forêts de chênes du Zaccar, des Beni— Menasser et des montagnes de la rive gauche du Chelif. À Milianah, elle descend quelquefois en hiver dans les jardins les plus éléves. Partout où l'on rencontre cette espèce, on est certain de trouver le Geai cervical *(Garrulus cervicalis)* qui, comme elle, parait ne se rencontre qu'à une altitude determinée, que j'évalue à sept on huit cents mètres au dessus du niveau. de la mer. Je crois aussi que ces deux espèces n'habitent que les regions élevés où la neige est durable en hiver."

Of this species also M. Labonysse, in his " Lettre sur les oiseaux de la partie littorale de la province de Constantine,"[*] says :—

" La Mésange Ledoux pratique en terre, dans le forêt de l'Edough, un trou de *Om* 15, de profondeur, où elle établit son nid. Elle a été observée pour la première fois le 16 Avril, 1842." (Annales de Société d'Agriculture de Lyon, 1853, p. 15.)

Another rarity which I got at Miliana was Cetti's Warbler *(Cettia sericea,* Natt), a tame little bird which ventured quite up to houses on the outskirts of villages. I found it equally in woods and gardens, but always near a ditch. At Algiers I got one, and at Blida three specimens.

On the 25th I moved from Miliana to Boufarik, once a mere morass, but now an important place numbering 4,000 inhabitants. There are a good many Griffon Vultures near

---

[*] About 110 species are included, with some notes of considerable interest, besides a short article on domestic birds in this "letter."

here. Monsieur Jeannot, ornithologist, Hotel du Mazagram, showed me a pair killed with ball in the plain of Metidja. About April he told me some of the cattle generally die, and when the hot weather has made them partly putrid, a score or more of these Vultures will come from the mountains to feed on them, and in this way they are occasionally obtained. I did not get one then, but I bought a ragged skin (nearly adult) of a Zouave at Laghouat, which has since been made presentable by Mr. Burton, of Wardour Street.

At a wood outside the village, as I was sitting on a little bridge, I saw an old Jackal quietly coming up the ditch at a slow swing trot. I watched him with a binocular-glass until he was within twenty-five yards, when probably scenting me, he leapt into the wood.

On the 26th I returned to Algiers, and on the 1st of March I made my start for the Great Desert, having laid in a good stock of things for the journey, including a sovereign's worth of alcohol for preserving reptiles. By train to Blida, and by "diligence" to Medea along a first-rate French road, is the route, passing through the famed gorge of the Chiffa. Here I stopped at the " Ruisseau des Singes" *auberge*, where Canon Tristram tried in vain to obtain accommodation, and saw exactly the same species of birds as he saw, (" The Great Sahara," p. 33) including the Blue Thrush *(Petrocossyphus cyaneus)*. I did not obtain a specimen of it, for I had no opportunity of using a gun, but I bought a female in winter plumage at Algiers. I never saw it again in my Algerian travels, nor did I ever come across the Rock Thrush *(Monticola saxatilis)*.

There are a good many Monkeys on the beetling sides of this verdant, rocky, pass. Two at the "auberge" appeared to be the same sort as I saw at Gibraltar. The Barbary Ape I believe they are called.

The Medea road passes through a line of forest country.

The Arabs burn the bark off the trees, which is as valuable as our oak bark is to us in England, but this practice ruins the picturesque. Beneath many a stately monarch of the forest we passed, now scorched and blackened. I believe these great woods are chiefly composed of oak, ilex, and cork; seven sorts of oaks are enumerated in Piesse's "Itineraire de l'Algerie." They form a safe home for such woodland birds as *Pica mauritanica, Lanius auriculatus*, and *Fringilla spodiogena*, which nest here in perfect security. Perched on one scathed limb, a noble Eagle seemed to keep guard over all around him: he eyed us as we approached him, and it was not until we were almost within gunshot that he condescended to stretch his broad pinions.

After a long drive, Boghari came in view, an Arab village, close to the town of Boghar, and the usual stopping place for travellers as there is an inn there, and to ascend to the town would be much further. Here the traveller may taste "*couscous*," an Arab preparation of barley, milk, meat, and fruits. It is variously called *couscous* and *couscousoo*. He will also see the black nomadic tents of camels' hair, which he is afterwards destined to sleep in. They are very ill-constructed, and so low, that you can barely stand upright in the middle. A partition divides them into two chambers, one for the men, and one for the women where the cooking is done. They are generally made of camels' hair, some-times of goats' hair, interwoven with wool, black or in coloured stripes. They are propped up with sticks, and are grimy in the last degree. To sum up the description of them, they are the reverse of picturesque at a distance, and present a filthy appearance on closer inspection! Half a dozen surly dogs mount guard, and so obstreperous are they that I was several times on the point of shooting them, and only refrained from fear of offending their masters.

After inspecting the Jews' quarter, which is worth a visit for the sake of seeing the Jewesses who dress very gaily, wearing a variety of ornaments, and peeping into a Moorish bath, the inner room of which was intensely hot, and examining the stock in trade of a negro who dealt in jewelry, scent, spurs, purses, and swords, and after collecting specimens of the Black Wheatear *(Saxicola leucura)*, Little Owl *(Athene glaux)*, Rock Dove *(Columba livia*, Lin., *C. turricola* Bp.). and Ultramarine Tit *(Parus teneriffæ*, Less.), I made the discovery that I had seen all that was worth seeing at Boghari, and on the 8th I ensconced myself and my impedimenta in the weekly "Diligence." Six horses drag it. In the "Tell" eight are not considered too many; indeed I sometimes saw ten to a large vehicle, but then admirable as the French government roads are, the hilly nature of the country must be remembered. Mules and horses are yoked indifferently to the same vehicle.

The first *caravanserai* is Bougzoul. It is in the "Hauts Plateaux." A *caravanserai* in Algeria is a one-storied fortified house, enclosing a large court-yard, with chambers on two sides for the accommodation of travellers, and stabling for several horses. The "Hauts Plateaux" is a term for the northern portion of the Little Desert (or Algerian Sahara), which commences where the "Tell" ends, and terminates at Waregla. The water at Bougzoul is nearly unfit for drinking; it comes from the neighbouring marsh where the phenomenon of mirage may be seen. Canon Tristram found a profusion of aquatic birds at this marsh— Flamingos, Ruddy Shelducks, White-headed Ducks *(Erismatura mersa)*, Gull-billed Terns, White-winged Black Terns, Stilts, Purple Gallinules, Great-sedge Warblers, etc. When I was there it was nearly dry. The Sandgrouse, and the Desert Wheatear *(Saxicola deserti*, Rupp.) had supplanted the waders. I obtained however one Flamingo, and was assured by many persons that they are occasionally found dead under the newly-constructed military telegraph, as well as "Ganga" (Sandgrouse) and other birds. The commonest bird at Bougzoul was the English Skylark, next to that the Calandra, and then Reboud's Lark (*Calendrella minor*, Cab. ; *C. reboudia*, Tristram). The Skylarks were still in flocks, but the Calandras had paired.

February 11*th*. Went a twelve-mile drive in the broiling sun with the keeper of the *caravanserai*. At some Arab tents we were entertained with coffee, hot bread, and *Mzab* dates, in return for which we gave our hosts as much powder and shot as we could spare. Coming home we saw eight Cranes (*Grus cinerea*) marching abreast across the plain in the grey twilight. We guided the cart nearly to within gunshot, when they all ran together with their heads up, and without uttering any call, slowly sailed away, to seek safer quarters in the adjoining marsh. There is just enough traffic to mark a road over the desert to Ain-oussera, a lonely *caravanserai* with a muddy stream winding before the entrance. Nothing but a scanty herbage clothes the plain, a coarse kind of grass, to the height of two or three feet, (different from what grows in the *weds*,) forming a bleak retreat for the Desert Wheatear, the Dotterel, and the Tawny Pipit. Well may Dr. Tristram term this place "a genuine piece of desert." In front, behind, and on either side stretches the vast Sahara. Sometimes level, often undulating, like a great sea of sand it stretches away. In some places the soil is soft and sandy (where it is red it is very soft), in some, hard and pebbly; but the herbage is everywhere reduced to a minimum. Every *chott* and *Sebkhra** is coated with a saline incrustation, and the tantalising mirage leads the traveller to suppose that he has in view a magnificent lake. Seen from afar the resemblance is perfect, but as he draws near, the mists are dissipated, and the lake resolves itself into bushes, rocks, or even camels.

As the setting sun sheds its glare over this treeless plain of

---

* Salt lakes of more or less extent.

Ain-oussera, and the shadows lengthen, one feels inclined to speculate on the not distant period when bands of lawless Bedouins roamed over the desert now so completely brought under French jurisdiction. Should the Nomads again break out, a few days will suffice to bring a column from Algiers sufficient to subdue any insurrection. Meanwhile the Barbary states remain at peace, from the palm-shaded oases of Tripoli to the bazaars and gardens of Moorish Tangiers, and not even the reverses in the terrible Franco-German war emboldened the Bedouin to attempt another rising, so deep is their respect for the "chassepôt," and for French military organisation.

February 12*th.* Breakfasted sumptuously off a Houbara Bustard *(Houbara undulata,* Bp.), an agreeable change after the customary meal of goat. This magnificent bird is still common. I saw three at Ain-oussera, and afterwards at Laghouat no less than seven were brought to me. In one old cock the feathers which composed the ruff were seven inches long.

The master of the *caravanserai* killed a pair of Grey-headed Wagtails. I afterwards obtained some brilliant specimens at Laghouat. One had a white throat, dark ear-coverts, and no white line from the eye to the beak. But this variety, generally called *Budytes cinereicapilla* (Savi), merges on one side into *B. flava* (L.), and on the other to *B. melanocephala* (Licht), and has no constant characters to establish its specific difference. Loche obtained the three, and treats them as separate (Catalogue, p. 80) ; but subsequent research has proved that *B. cinereica-villa* at any rate is not a good species.

It was not until the 13th of March that I noticed a Hoopoe *(Upupa epops).* It happened to be Sunday, and I was re-clining on a stack, when at a distance I observed what at first I took to be some great Creeper coming right at me. I marked where he settled, watched his habits a considerable

time, and the next day shot him. Though I have since had
the rare chance of scrutinizing this bird in England,* it did
not afford me so much pleasure as this my first encounter
with it at Ain-oussera. Afterwards I saw a pair at Laghouat
feeding on a path, near to which the commandant had
planted a row of willows, and one of them flew up to rub
its bill against a branch, a very common action in birds to
get rid of soil after feeding. On going to the place I discovered a number of dead locusts under the trees. Now
was the Hoopoe feeding on them ?

The tongue in this species is very small, hence there is no
groove on the inside of the lower mandible.

March 14*th*. Shot a Desert Wheatear, which had lost
seven toes ! It was a female, the only female I obtained.
Saxicola homochroa (Trist.) is stated by Mr. Dresser to be
referable to the female of this species (P. Z. S., 1874, p. 225).
A rather favourite perch of the Desert Wheatear is the
Laghouat telegraph wire, on which the French there pin
their faith, and to cut which would be the greatest crime an
Arab could commit, for it would be tantamount to rebellion.

Guelt-El-Stel. *March* 20*th*. I came here on the 16th,
having passed—novel sight—a clump of trees about forty
feet high. On one was a Moorish Magpie, on another a
Raven, on another a Neophron or Egyptian Vulture.
Doubtless in a month's time each tree would have its nest.
Two armed Arab troopers came to the *caravanserai* with
five prisoners, also Arabs ; they had chains round their
necks. They reminded me of the poor prisoners I have
seen in chains marching through the streets of Moscow.
Among other birds that I collected here were the Stapazine
Wheatear *(Saxicola rufa)* and Tree Pipit ; the latter with
flesh-coloured claws, but precisely like ours in other respects,
and coming north with the migratory tide. By Monsieur

---

* In May, 1874, at Leyton in Essex (cf. Zoologist, 4035).

Taczanouski this Pipit was seen continually, (Zoologist, p. 2584) "from after the month of March."

21st. Our route lay between Zahrez and Sebka Zahrez, great shallow lakes, stated by Canon Tristram to be nearly thirty miles long in wet weather. I could not go near enough to them to see the myriads of Flamingos which he saw, but on one of the streams which flows into them I observed a Tern, probably of the White-winged species. At Rocher-de-Sel the soil becomes more sandy, while a frost-like whiteness coats the plain. After passing the Salt Mountains (from which the *caravanserai* takes its name), the country assumes a more fertile appearance. These mountains are worth a visit. At a little distance they present a blue appearance.

At Djelpha I witnessed an interesting spectacle. An Arab tribe with upwards of a hundred camels and numerous horses were getting ready for an expedition, and were having a grand review before starting. Tearing as hard as they could go over the plain in pairs, they suddenly caused their horses to swerve—one to the right, the other to the left—discharging, as they wheeled round, their long guns at the feet of the spectators. The white burnouses waving in the air, the clouds of dust, and the cries of the combatants, made this wild fantasia the more like a battle, while the eye was arrested by their swarthy visages and the splendid trappings of their horses. Eight gaudy palanquins (each borne by a camel, and surmounted with a bundle of sticks and a tuft of leaves,) contained the wives of the chief *Agha.* Doubtless mounted on his best *Mahri** camels, they in the hour of battle would be kept in the rear, that they might be ready to escape into the wilderness, should the day go against their Bedouin lord.

At this place Roman ruins terminate. None are known

---

* The tall white Dromedary of the Touareg Arabs.

further south, which would seem to attest that beyond Djelpha the Romans never penetrated into the Sahara. As I was in haste to get to Laghouat I did not sleep at Djelpha, but pressed on as soon as dinner was over. Near the "Assassination Rock," so named from several dreadful murders having been committed there, we passed through a small flight of locusts, and that was the only incident worth mentioning, until tired and weary we beheld the banner of France floating over the fortress of El Aghouat, the pearl of the desert, the key of the Great Sahara. Laghouat (Lar'ouât) or El Aghouat, according as we prefix the French or Arab article, is the last French outpost. So far civilization extends and no further; beyond is nominal submission of the "tribus indigènes," men who, like the Chamba and the Touareg, trust to the fleetness of their camels, and own no master. An exception only must be made in the case of the Mzab, who are a peaceful nation and the good allies of the French.

Situated on the right bank of the river Mzi—I should hesitate to say river, for it is only in wet seasons that there is any water—Laghouat is, in fact, the first oasis. Twenty thousand matchless palms encompass the town, forming a noble belt of verdure, beneath which the vine, the fig, the pomegranate, and the apricot interlace their foliage, mingling in rank confusion. About half a mile to the north the "river" forms a small marsh, which I found to be an excellent collecting ground. Nearly all the houses are white, flat-roofed, and made of mud-bricks. The same materials partition off the Arab gardens. In the centre of the town, and half way between the two forts, is the Place de Randon, named after Marshal Randon. It is a neat French square, with a sort of bazaar on one side and the officers' club on the other, embellished by about a dozen palms. Many of the streets are entirely occupied by Arabs, and present a very uninviting appearance. The heat inducing a natural apathy among these gentry, some of them are generally to be seen stretched at full length on the pavement, wrapped in the universal burnous, which approximates so nearly in colour to sand and boulders, that at Boghari I used to find it very hard to distinguish them. Without a burnous you never see an Arab. These garments have no arms, but are open down the middle, so that when the wearer applies himself to manual labour, he must either throw one side over his shoulder or take it off altogether, and the lazy Arabs universally do the former.

Banish from your mind all high-flown sentiment, for there is nothing picturesque about them. The French have improved away the old stock, and the present people are their degenerate descendants. Not so the Chamba and the Touareg, wild tribes of the true desert, who still cherish a deadly hatred towards that people against whom their hardy fathers swore eternal enmity.

There are very few French besides the military, and they lose no opportunity of endeavouring to render themselves more popular ; but it is misspent energy. The old antipathy still exists, and the Arabs are and ever will be jealous of them. By nature a distrustful people, they deem every improvement an innovation. Their masters may strive to ingratiate themselves by acts of kindness, but they cannot put down popular feeling, any more than they can obliterate the remembrance of the severity with which the rebellion of 1864 was met, a severity which perhaps was necessary, but which will ever rankle in the bosoms of a vanquished people.

March 24th. Shot two Aquatic Warblers (*Acrocephalus aquaticus*). The legs are rather whiter than the Sedge Warbler's, and the iris is not red as figured by Dr. Bree, but dark brown. I found them chiefly in the rushes. They are restless little birds, but sometimes they settle at the bottom of a reed, and then is the best chance of getting them. .

April 3rd. I strolled to-day in an easterly direction to a place where I had shot one of a pair of *Galerida macrorhynca* (Trist.), *G. randoni* (Loche. Revue et Mag., de Zool., April, 1860, p. 148, plate XI., fig. 2), and found the other apparently mated again. They are the only ones I have seen here, though Canon Tristram found them "abundant near Laghouat." They were quite tame, and evidently meant to nest if they had not eggs already. While I was watching them, a number of shadows attracted my attention, and looking up I saw a flight of locusts overhead. I have been several times made aware of locusts by first seeing their shadows on the ground. I must not omit to state that I shot a Blue-throated Warbler *(Cyanecula leucocyanea ?)*, with the chest spot partly white and partly red. Unfortunately it was too much shattered for preserving. Loche mentions having shot near Brouage specimens with the chest spot "roussatre" (Exploration, Sc. V., p. 224).

Every evening, almost before the sun went down, I used to hear the hooting of the Little Owls *(Athene glaux*, Sav.), and again at daybreak I could hear them. The ear in this species is nearly round, and not large for an Owl. One day I observed a Black Wheatear *(Saxicola lencura)* on some rocks in the town. As the eye wanders over the dreary landscape, it is a relief to see one of these handsome fellows spreading his tail on a grey rock, and displaying himself to advantage as the pairing season approaches. I have found on this Saxicole a formidable white-bodied tick with eight legs. The Frenchmen at Laghouat call them "Merle de Roche," a name applied by Buffon to the Rock Thrush. On another occasion I saw a Goldfinch *in* the town. This common species yields in beauty to none. To my mind, if you see them in the sunshine, they are brighter than the brightest butterflies; but African specimens of many birds surpass English in richness of colouring. Loche adds that as a rule they are smaller, but this is certainly not the case with the Tawny Owl *(Strix aluco,* Lin.), of which there are two very large specimens in the Algiers Museum, and which the late Mr. Verreaux proposed to describe as a distinct species, and name after my father.*

On Sunday, happening to be out for a stroll, I observed twelve Vultures at a distance, circling round a mountain; and having nothing to do, I determined to cultivate their nearer acquaintance. When however I got to the foot I counted them again and there were were only eleven, but the twelfth, while I was wondering what had become of him, leisurely turned out from behind a boulder, not fifty paces from me, and displaying the huge body and pinions of a stately Griffon *(Gyps fulvus)* slowly sailed away to where his mates were still performing their aerial evolutions. That he had been gorging I have no doubt, which would account for his tameness, for on no other occasion did I ever get so near one, though I often saw them at a distance.

I will only mention the Swallow for the sake of saying that it is a mistake to suppose that this bird, or any of the European *Hirundinidæ* (except *Cotyle rupestris,* the most stay-at-home of all the family,) pass the winter in Algeria. It was not until the end of February that I observed Swallows, and I am convinced that few, if any, remain throughout the year. On the 26th and 27th of March we experienced a very cold wind at Laghouat, and so be-numbed were they that hundreds might have been killed with stones. The poor birds were to be seen sitting about in all directions. I shall not forget one affecting incident of which I was a witness. I found a Swallow lying dead in the town with its mate beside it, and although the poor creature had been some time dead, she would not leave it. Constant to her post beside its head, she sang (if their notes

---

* Specimens of this Algerian race are preserved in the Norwich Museum.

can be called anything more than a twitter,) and heeded not my approach until I could almost have touched her; and before I had gone three yards she was back again. I quite felt for the unlucky little bird, as I watched her trying to restore her partner to life by every means in her power, and wailing out her lamentations at her vain efforts. The House Martin was so far affected by the same cold wind of March 27th, that I found many in the early morning upon the sand, and others clinging to the mud-brick walls which partition off the gardens. I caught some with my hat, which will give an idea of their extreme feebleness.

While enumerating the principal birds, I wish also to make some mention of other animals. Once I shot what I suppose to have been a Short-tailed Marmot, and occasionally I could have shot Hares, but did not, as they would have been too much trouble to carry home. I brought back to England a Panther's skin, a brace of Boar tusks, a fine head of Gazelle, *Gazella dorcas*, (of my own preparing) and several curiosities in mythellated spirits, including a Chameleon exactly like one of my father's, which he had alive and kept a long time by feeding it on meal worms. In every direction are to be seen the singular footprints of the Jerboa, or jumping mouse, whose holes perforate the plain. I got one and kept it alive some days. I found two huge frogs at the foot of a garden wall, on the edge of the marsh. Large Lizards were often brought in. Concerning them and Serpents I shall have something to say in another place. On the brink of the stream which feeds the small and half-dry marsh, there are a good many water tortoises. When one gets near them they slip into the deep water like English flounders. I do not remember having ever seen any Butterflies, but Beetles of every size and shape swarm. The Ant of the desert digs a curious structure, though not on the scale of magnitude of its more southern relatives, as described to us by many African travellers.

I left Laghouat on the 9th of April for the Mzab. For this expedition I had engaged by way of a Dragoman an Arab named Mahommed Belhuri, and another to act under him, named Mzoud. We bestrode two mules, and behind us came Mzoud on a camel, beneath· whose belly slung a goat-skin containing our water for three or four days. I had also a joint of meat, a keg of wine, a dozen new loaves, six boxes of sardines, a German sausage, a supply of cheese, a paper of cigars, the first and second volume of Sclater's "Ibis," and a new journal-book. Thus armed and equipped I proposed to explore the Mzab country, and see if the inhabitants were the fiery sons of Ishmael which they had been represented to be. By ten a.m. we sallied out of the south gate, breathing all manner of slaughter against rare birds, and began our journey. As we rode along I shot two new to me, the Bifasciated Lark (*Certhilauda desertorum*), and the Bleached Shrike (*Lanius lathora*). I never got the former again in Algeria, but I saw the latter daily infesting every Mzab garden. A favourite perch is the bottom of a Palm's crest, where the fronds are broken short, whence they dart off to snatch the passing beetle, or rise into the air after the more high-flying locust. But what are my guides looking at so intently? A great thick snake. One of them jammed its head off with a pole. It was, as near as I remember, about three feet in length, but thick in pro-portion, with beautifully marked coils, something like our common Viper's. Only on two other occasions did I see snakes. There is one sort that the French are very much afraid of, called the "Vipére à corne." An English tourist is said to have encased his feet in tin boots as a protection against them.

Though viewed from the highest rock in Laghouat, the Southern Sahara had appeared to be a boundless plain, we soon descried *dayats** ahead, and halting beneath their welcome shade, consumed our frugal lunch. Attentive Mohammed had provided a repast of roasted locusts, which tasted something like shrimps. The remains of a fire and the horns of a Gazelle showed that some travellers had been there before us.

When the sun sank to her rest, our first day's journey was ended. We had reached more clumps of trees— Jujubes, Terebinths, Olives, etc. ; all the larger ones had Ravens' nests on them; and I may here remark that the Ravens of Algeria appear to be much smaller than English ones. They moreover breed in society. In 1867, L. Tacza- nouski, of the Warsaw Museum, was so struck with this difference in size that he refused to catalogue them as *Corvus corax* (Zoologist, p. 2587) ; and Lieut-Col. Irby has since bestowed the name of *Corvus tingitanus* on this variety (Ibis for 1874, p. 264). Ravens are proverbial for their shyness, and I never had the luck to shoot one. Though glad to find other's carrion, or to make carrion of them if he can do it with impunity, as some writer has observed, the Raven takes good care that none shall make carrion of him. I have seen one pursue a bird of prey for a quarter of a mile, and on one occasion I witnessed a sharp fight between a Kite and a Raven, in which the blows of their wings could be plainly heard like distant pistol shots.

Early next morning we descried some tents, where we were treated to dates, sheep's milk, and the staple dish *couscous.* This, their favourite repast, is served on a carpet, which is always spread on the arrival of strangers, for no Algerian would invite you to sit upon the ground. I ob- served several pairs of Bushchats (*Saxicola mæsta,* Licht., *S. philophthamna,* Trist.), hopping about it. They are pretty

---

* *Dayats* are miniature oases where there is no constant supply of water, and consequently no palms, though other trees grow there.

birds. Mr. Dresser, in the "Birds of Europe," part XVII., says :—

"One of the least known of the Chats; this species has a very restricted range, and has hitherto only been met with in North-Western Africa, Palestine, and Persia, not having as yet been recorded from any portion of the large intervening tract of country."

He states that in summer the cock is much brighter than in winter, and figures the former plumage from a specimen obtained by Loche, who appears to have got them about the same time as Canon Tristram, but to have considered them the same as *Dromolæa isabellina* (cf. Ibis, 1859, p. 299).

Hanging in the tent we had come to were the head and foot of a Griffon Vulture *(nis'sr)*, whilst several kids were tethered to a cord inside, and outside others gambolled, and occasionally got upon the roof. Not far off two Egyptian Vultures, an old one and a young one, were discussing the skeleton of a defunct animal. They are most effective scavengers, never, I believe, leaving a carcass while a bone remains unpicked. The young one permitted a very near approach, but the old one was more wary. Well known are they to the Arabs by their name of *Rackma*. Here I had opportunity of looking at the women, who in general are so jealously guarded by their masters as to be invisible to the stranger's inquisitive eye. They are short and bent, probably from carrying heavy waterskins. They appear to be kind to their children, and give them bracelets and earrings made of shells, beads, and bright pieces of tin. But the Arab himself has few ornaments to deck his shabby tenement. In flocks and herds his wealth consists. If there be enough tents to form a circle, these are driven in and folded at night, and are guarded by dogs of a savage breed against the Hyenas and Jackals which are lurking in the *weds*. The Arab is his own cobbler, and a rough sort sort of (laced) boot he makes, but I suppose he thinks it better than walking barefoot over the soil, which in some places is covered with pebbles, and in others with small bright stones. On the sand he prefers to go barefoot. Socks are not worn by the poorer class. Every man carries a knife, professedly for eating, but also for defence when occasion requires, and I fear for offence also, the "piping times of peace" being not much known in those dark lands. It is slung round his waist, and kept in its sheath by a piece of string passed through a hole in the handle. All classes tattoo themselves more or less, and *henna* is in great request among them, for staining their nails pink.

Having added to our party an Arab named Ateya Banateya, whose local knowledge for the next few miles would be a great assistance to us, we now began to pass through a vast plain, slightly undulating, interspersed with *dayats*, each a mile or half a mile apart. Ateya inveighed against the French for imprisoning his son at Marseilles, who had joined in the revolt; while Mohammed beguiled the time with an account of how when a boy he had gone to war with his father, and killed a man by spearing him in the back; which was no doubt very plucky, but some rough unhewn stones by the wayside had a deeper tale for me than the exploits of either of them. I judged them to be the graves of wayfarers who had in all probability perished of thirst. They may have been the very cairns which Canon Tristram and Mr. Peed reverently contributed a stone to. Meanwhile I was on the "qui vive" for everything. [This region has been visited by only two ornithologists, while the route from Waregla to Gardames is still a "terra incognita" to naturalists; for if the unfortunate M. M. Dupéré and Joubert, who were murdered near that city, made any collections, they perished with them. I am convinced that an expedition there would repay any naturalist, for he would infallibly meet with forms of desert life unknown to science, and I would recommend him to pay particular attention to the Chats and Larks.]

I saw Ravens, Kestrels, Pigeons, Turtle Doves, and Hoopoes, and other birds which I did not know, but we were pressed for time and could not collect many. I shot one small bird not unlike a Whitethroat, which I have no doubt was a Spectacled Warbler *(Sylvia conspicillata)*. Canon Tristram calls it "the common and characteristic Warbler of the whole Sahara" (Ibis I., p. 417); but I only shot one other, and that was a female at Laghouat. Nearly every Terebinth of any size carried several nests, and the ground beneath them was white with the droppings of birds. As we rode along, the Desert Horned Lark *(Otocorys bilopha)* ran before us, and twice I saw a benighted Wryneck crouching on the plain. Here was indeed a glorious country for a collector. I kept a look out for Ostriches, but never had the good fortune to see any. "The capture of the Ostrich," says Dr. Tristram, "is the greatest feat of hunting to which the Sahara sportsman aspires: and in richness of booty, it ranks next to the plunder of a caravan." To this I may add, that the feathers and the eggs are so highly prized, that they are worth more at Laghouat than in London. "A skin in full plumage is worth on the spot from 40 to 100 Spanish dollars," i.e. £22. Step by step civilization is driving this brevipennate southwards. Like the Garefowl of Geir fugla drángr *(Alca impennis)*, its ancient haunts know it no longer; like that flightless bird, its appearance, its actual name will be forgotten, and in process of time its existence will become a matter of tradition to be talked about over the camp fire with the Roc and other legendary birds. So surely as the advancing hunter substitutes his express rifle for the firelock of the Arab will the Ostrich forsake the desert's fringe and seek an asylum far beyond the country of dates. Does not its impending extinction in the country I passed over typify the decay of the Nomad in the Northern Sahara?

About noon on the second day we came to water, the

first we had seen since we started; it was dirty, but my guides pronounced it drinkable. A Gazelle (*Gazella dorcas*), which was quenching its thirst, suffered a near approach, but bounded over the plain when we were within sixty yards. I often saw these graceful animals, but they were generally very shy. When browsing at a distance they look like herds of sheep, though a practised eye can distinguish them in a minute. Once I was offered a lovely fawn alive, which I surmise had been caught in a trap set for Bustards in the *Lalpha* grass. I have seen them in confinement, but I have heard that they are very difficult things to rear successfully.

We were obliged again to sleep in the open air. The Arabs kindled a fire, but it was bitterly cold. The wind had got up during the day, and at 9 p.m. it rained in torrents: of course our fire was speedily extinguished. The gusts now howled over the Sahara, vivid lightning shot across the sky, and terrific peals of thunder shook the firmament. In vain we shifted to the other side of the bush, under the lea of which we had endeavoured to obtain shelter: everything was completely soaked. We were in the saddle again before daybreak, but my wet burnous hung on me like a dead weight. The heavy rains of the preceding night seemed to have converted the Sahara into an expanse of mud. At length the Mozabite town of Berryan hove in sight, and leading our mules up a somewhat steep ascent, we beheld the panorama of her Palm gardens, all of which had been laid under water by the recent rains. A carpet was quickly spread in an unoccupied house called the guest house, and the chief, with about thirty other Arabs, squatted round us in a circle. While Mohammed detailed our adventures I produced the credentials which had been furnished by the "Commandant superieur" at Laghouat, and which were of the greatest possible service to us. Let me here thank that gentleman, and everyone also who contributed to the success of the expedition, for their courtesy to a stranger—a courtesy more stamped on the French than on any nation in the civilized world.

Calling for a pipe *(sebsi)* and some tobacco, I had an opportunity of seeing the way the Mzab smoke. They brought me the bone of a sheep, about six inches long, with a bit of black leather fastened at the end. It was hollowed out, and in this makeshift for a bowl was inserted about half as much tobacco as one would put into an ordinary briar-root. The tobacco was quite green* and very strong, but fatigued as we were with the journey it was very acceptable, and had a soothing effect.

It was a two-storied court where we were located. In the rafters I observed a pair of House Buntings *(Fringillaria saharæ,* Bp.). As this desert species is so little known in Europe, and as I was the first to bring the eggs and young to England, I shall be excused for copying in detail the account of it contributed by me to the " Ibis."

" *Emberiza Sahari* (Levt.) " Exploration Scientifique de l'Algerie." Plate IX., Bis. fig. 2. House Bunting of Tristram.

" I think every house in Gardaia is tenanted by a pair of House Buntings. They are equally common in the other Mzab cities. A nest in the inner court at Berryan was upon some plaster in a large square hole. It contained one young one, yellow about the gape, and covered with a whitish down. It was a shallow nest made of the thin twigs of firewood, and lined with hair. The hen generally flew to it from the edge of the opposite wall. As I afterwards found other nests, I was able to make further observations. I think the eggs must be deposited in March, as in most instances the young had been hatched off. Judging from the one at Berryan, which had flown when I returned to that place on the last day of the month, the young remain in the nest at least twenty-one days. On the 23rd of April I saw a nestling full grown and able to feed

---

* The tobacco smoked by the *fellaheen* of Egypt, which they call *Sieedy,* is green.

itself, which must have been hatched about the 1st. The eggs are rather like Sparrows' eggs, but rounder. I only got three. Dr. Tristram did not get any, and there are none in the Museum at Algiers. The nest is generally, but not always, placed in a hole, and is composed of twigs or little sticks, and lined with hair, with sometimes the addition of wool or a bit of cotton. On one occasion two were found together, which probably belonged to the same bird, as one of them was unfinished. The young are less noisy than Sparrows : the female brings them food about every ten minutes ; and they never chirp except when they see her. I never could detect anything in her beak, or see on what she fed them, although I watched the operation often ; so I do not doubt that she reproduces what she has eaten for the benefit of her callow offspring. Until the young leave the nest the male takes no share in feeding them. The female bears away the fæces. The males sing much the loudest, indeed the females never do more than twitter ; but the cock pours forth a lively strain during the season of incubation. They are as tame as Robins. Frequently one would hop upon our carpet, to search for fragments of *couscous*, scrutinizing us within a few feet with his dark brown trustful eye. They are nearly omnivorous. I caught one in a trap baited with grain, and saw another nibbling green carrot leaf; and once the female at Berryan made her appearance with a large fly, which was not swallowed without a great effort and after much mastication. They drank out of our goatskin, fluttering and clinging to the wall for the moisture which had oozed through. For a few seconds before settling down for the night I used to see them "hovering" perpendicularly, with quivering wings and tail brought forward. Half circles of accumulated droppings under the rafters showed where they roosted."

Near this town I saw examples of the Woodchat, and White-headed Rock Chat *(Saxicola leucocephala)*, now united with *Saxicola leucopygia;* while the Egyptian Turtledove *(Turtur egyptiacus*, Tem.) was so common, that I had only to take my stand in a garden and load and fire until as many had been killed as I required. Directly one falls the

Arabs rush up to it to cut its throat *before it dies*, and I soon found out that they would never cook any which did not die by the knife. Of course they ruin everything for stuffing. A splendid Golden Eagle, which Dr. Tristram shot, was served in this way. The natives do not shoot the Doves, simply because they do not think them worth powder, which the French traders are not allowed to sell them under any pretence. They come among the houses and peck and walk about the tents exactly like tame pigeons. They were not then paired. Neither were the lovely Bee-eaters *(Merops apiaster)*, many of which I saw irradiating the landscape by their beautiful colours. In their buoyant and graceful flight, Bee-eaters are not unlike Martins. Few birds surpass them in beauty as they glide nearly motionless through the air (except when a momentary rapid beating of the wings is necessary to gather impetus). Like a meteor they glitter in the sunlight for a moment and are gone.

Berryan is a town of some 400 houses, surrounded by a mud-brick wall with a good many small towers. They are pierced for musketry, and have been used on various occasions for defence against the Chamba. The wall is surmounted by a fence of thorns, which serves as a favourite perch for the Pallid Shrike *(Lanius lahtora*, Sykes ; *L. pallens*, Cass.; *L. dealbatus*, De Filippi). Messrs. Sharpe and Dresser say they have never seen nestlings of this species. I got one on the 25th of April just able to fly. All the upper surface, which is grey in the adult, is ashy brown, faintly barred, the lore and ear-covets are very faint, as well as the other parts which are black in an adult, but the breast and underparts are the same, the beak in my skin is yellow.

The loftiest building in the town is the Mosque; its tower is in the shape of an obelisk ; but what interested me most was the wells. In my paper read on my return to the

Norwich Naturalists' Society, I endeavoured to describe the method of drawing water; but Canon Tristram's description is so much better, that I will quote it.

"But the machine for drawing water from the well is both original and ingenious. There is a double pulley and a large leathern bucket slung by pulleys across the beam. The water-drawer holds two ropes, one of which draws up the bucket, which has a leathern funnel at the end of it, to which the second rope running on the other pulley is attached. This second rope, when the bucket reaches the top, turns the tube into the cistern,* on the same principle which we see adopted in some English mines." (l. c. 134.)

The drawer is generally assisted by a camel, or sometimes a brace of mules pull the cord. There is always an inclined pathway for them to run down, which materially lessens the labour. There is no garden without its well, and some of them are very deep. The wheel reaches to at least ten feet above the ground. Little trenches convey the water all about the garden, as the sand would soon soak it up; these trenches, says Canon Tristram, are "beautifully formed of hard lime, and branching in all directions from the well, so that the precious fluid could be conveyed without the slightest waste through the grounds." He considers the cultivation in these gardens "far superior to that of Laghouat," but the southern oasis is capable of greater things. The water is limpid and tasteless. All day long the Mzab haul it up. "The Mzab work always" has become a saying. Men, women, and children toil in the gardens, even in the noontide hours when no European could venture out of doors.

There are two cemeteries, one with a row of common earthenware urns on each grave, and the other without. Canon Tristram gives a woodcut of the urns in his work. A *Marabout*, or Sheik's tomb, was distinguished by some

---

* Generally a stone tank, sometimes two.

flags, but not by any Ostrich eggs as some of those at Gardaia were.

On the 14th news came that the Touareg—a lawless tribe of robbers—were assembling in force on the Waregla route; and the following day a letter was brought to me (in Arabic) with tidings of a great camel "razzia" at Zergoun, (which though not in our road, lay to the north of us,) in which 2,000 camels had been carried off, and it was said six men killed, but I did not place much reliance on this latter statement. The "Spahis," Arab soldiers in French pay, were in hot pursuit, but with little chance of coming up with the fugitives. Trusting that they would not come on our way, we on the 16th left Berryan and travelled to Gardaia, which is the chief city of the Mzab confederation.

Our road lay through a dreary tract of country—stony, brown, and mountainous—save at rare intervals, where the dull prospect was suddenly broken by a patch of green, formed by the rain collecting in a hollow; but these fresh spots were few and far between. In this ride Canon Tristram got Dupont's Lark, a species I never met with.

And now by narrow defiles our cavalcade drew near the capital. I could not help thinking, as often as I reined in my mule, what awful havoc the long guns of the Arabs would make with an invading army in such a place; and no doubt for them many a winding pass teems with historic interest. That the city has figured in more than one sanguinary conflict the bullet marks on the walls testify. But who will forget the first view of Gardaia? Standing upon a gentle eminence, crowned by the never-failing Mosque—her flat-roofed houses rising tier over tier above the evergreen Palm trees, the ancient Arab city bursts upon your view.

It is too hot to go out in the middle of the day, her gardens therefore should be visited in the cool of the morning, or in the red blush of sunset. Then the woods resound with joyous carols, while the sparkling Bee-eater, the painted Roller, and the gilded Oriole flicker in the foliage—a veritable naturalist's paradise!

Nothing can exceed the fertility of the oasis. Vines, surpassing any which I ever saw in size and luxuriance, were bent with many an unripe cluster, trained from Palm-stem to Palm-stem, and all the Figs, and Pomegranates, and Apricot trees were loaded with green fruit, while high overhead there towered six-and-fifty thousand Date Palms. I saw the last red rays of the setting sun as they shed a golden pathway through the trellissed stems, grander than the grandest palace.

I had now come, as I calculated, about 430 miles from the sea, in a nearly direct line due south from Algiers—only one or two Englishmen have to my knowledge ever penetrated further.

An inquisitive mob gathered round us in the market place—brawny men and *henna*-stained children pressed forward, or mounted on the bench of justice with cries of surprise. Doubtless many of the latter had never seen a white face before. The Guest house was in the market place; it had two doors, and three apertures which did duty for windows. As it was three-storied I used the bottom part for the mules, received guests on the second floor, and kept the top story for skinning and writing. Canon Tristram gives a picture of it (l. c.). How strange to be quartered in the same room of the same house where he and Mr. Peed were, fourteen years before!

While we awaited the arrival of a negro with a ponderous iron key, I could not help noticing how many there were in the crowd who were blind. Alas! ophthalmia is only too prevalent among them. When we had washed and taken coffee, which is an indispensable ceremony among the Arabs, the chief led the way to the Jews' quarter. We entered the house of a wealthy Hebrew. The Rabbi, as I suppose him to have been, was reading in the doorway. He rose on the entry of Simhamed Betoumi (that I believe to have been the name of my conductor,) with many genuflections. As he seemed anxious to show me everything, we walked all over his house without any ceremony. There were texts upon the walls, and printed books which appeared to be portions of the Old Testament. The man was a silversmith. Before leaving I was invited to partake of the thin Jews' bread, and some absinthe, the most dangerous of all spirituous liquors.

I found that the Mzab sheiks knew the name of London, and some very curious questions were asked me through the interpreter about its extent; also about the Queen and our navy—whether we had more men-of-war than the French, etc.? I catechising them in return about their manners and customs. They evidently supposed that I had come to inspect the products of the country with a view to commerce.

I had often asked my attendant to get me an opportunity of seeing the Mosque, but knowing the prejudices of the Arabs, and that he was himself a Mahommedan, it was quite unlooked for when the chief's sanction came one morning, and a Christian and a stranger I passed up the slippery ascending passage, by which the faithful draw near the sanctuary at Gardaia; but I was not to be permitted to enter. From the top of the roof only might the Christian dog look down upon the worshippers. In an inner open court, some forty feet square, about a dozen devotees are chanting, in a low monotonous tone, the prayers which Mahomet commanded. No verses from the Koran, no gilded lamps, no mural decorations, only the same reiterated wailing chant. But my attendant hints that we are there by stealth, so after briefly noticing that they keep the *haik* on, (for their heads are shaven) I slip away from the precincts and return to the Guest house, glad to have seen the Moslem devotees, and to have had a glance into the interior of their Mosque. There are two towers, one perfect, the other leaning; the court alluded to is not directly beneath either of them.

We stayed until Friday for the weekly market, which is one of the most important in southern Algeria, being far larger than that at Berryan. It was formerly held outside the walls, no doubt that tribes from a distance might trade without seeing the internal arrangements of the city, but now it is in the market place near the south gate. The buyers sit, and the sellers walk about among them, calling over the wares, which consist of woollen stuffs, burnouses, butter, desert potatoes, and dates of all sorts, as well as live stock—camels, goats, and sheep—which are brought up by merchants to be conveyed into the *Tell.* Jews vend silver bracelets, and cracked date stones are sold as food for camels! It is a mart for everything brought by the caravans, which are constantly going and arriving. Yet it does not last above three hours. The merchants began to come about eight o'clock, mounted on *Mahri* or *Mahara* camels, from Waregla, and by eleven it was all over.

We were now nearly into May, and though my health had been wonderfully preserved hitherto, I was anxious, with the summer coming on, to get back to the coast. If before I feared the rain and the cold nights, I now dreaded tenfold more the unendurable mid-day sun. Accordingly on the 22nd we moved to Mellika, determined to make our visits to the other towns as short as possible. The next day, strolling out with my gun, I collected specimens of the Pied Wheatear (*Saxicola leucomela*, Pall.), a male in moult, with the under tail-coverts as nearly white as possible, and a good deal of grey on the crown, (the gizzard contained a thick white grub about three quarters of an inch long), Rock Pigeon, (generally observed in pairs on the rocks, and not in the palms where the Doves were,) Egyptian

Turtledove, Common English Turtledove, Pied Flycatcher, Wood Wren, Willow Wren, House Bunting, and Rock Chat (*Saxicola leucopyga*). These Rock Chats are quite the handsomest birds in the oases. They are very common about the *weds*, (i.e. dry rocky water-courses,) and on the wells, where I suspect they breed, as I saw some fly down them. I saw a boy with one which he had doubtless caught on its nest, tied to a long string which was passed through its nostrils! On the 25th I shot a Roller (*Corracias garrula*, Lin.). Its stomach contained four of the largest beetles. As might be expected, so rich an oasis affords food and shelter for many beautiful birds unknown in other lands; and one, which from its gay colours has attracted the notice of all travellers, is the Roller. Accordingly M. M. Peysonnel and Des Fontaines, in their "Voyages dans les régences de Tunis et D'Alger," say:—

"On voit aussi le long des rivières un bel oiseau qu'on nomme *cher agra*. * * * * C'est un espèce de Geai : il se nourrit de sauterelles. Cet oiseau est de passage; il parait en Barbarie vers le mois de Mai, et y séjourne jusqu'en automne. Il y niche dans des trous le long des rivières ; son cri est : *gra, gra, gra*."

This work was published in 1838, five years after Des Fontaines' death. What few birds Des Fontaines collected are in the Paris Museum. His life was so much taken up with the study of flowers, that he seems to have only had time for one ornithological "brochure," entitled "Memoire sur quelques espèces nouvelles d'oiseaux des cotes de Barbarie." (Mem. de l'Acad. des Sc. (1787), p. 496.) It contains figures and descriptions of seven species—*Otis Hobara* (*Houbara undulata*), *Turdus fulvus* (*Crateropus fulvus*) *Turdus barbatus* (*Pycnonotus barbatus*), *Tetrao sylvaticus* (*Turnix sylvatica*), *Tetrao fasciatus* (*Pterocles arenarius*), *Falco cœruleus* (*Elanus cœruleus*), *Upupa alaudipes* (*Certhilauda desertorum*). For a sight of it I am indebted to

Professor Newton. The name *alaudipes* for the Bifasciated or curve-billed Lark, takes precedence I presume of *C. desertorum*, Stanley, being twenty-four years older; and in that case five of Des Fontaines' specific names would be adopted.

Often in my rambles I intruded on the haunts of the cunning *Crateropus fulvus*, a bird first made known to science by Des Fontaines. It is exactly the colour of sand, like so many other birds in these arid regions.[*]

The venerable Kadi Bouhammed, who was chief of Mellika in Dr. Tristram's time, is doubtless gathered to his fathers; the present man is Salki Benadulla. Barbaaisa Bembamen is Kadi of Bou-Noura, and Adown of Benisguen. All these towns are in the same oasis, and the dry course of the Wed N'ca winds between them. Bou-Noura is a heap of ruins; half the town has been dismantled, and the crumbling, unroofed, long-deserted houses have grown brown like the rocks which surround them. El Ateuf and Benisguen are in better preservation, and contain some shops or magazines, the principal wares, says Canon Tristram, "being leather, dyed cloths, and all sorts of materials for tanning and dyeing." Benisguen has long been the rival of Gardaia, and that its inhabitants still aspire to the chieftainship of the oasis was proved by a new wall which we found them constructing, and which affords an instance of the intestine rivalry which has rendered every stand against the French abortive. The day is far distant when the burnous will vanquish the tricolor flag.

We did not start upon our return journey until the last day of the month. Then bidding a hearty farewell to the Sheiks, and giving them at their request a certificate of our

---

[*] I should think the species observed by Mr. W. T. H. Chambers in Tripoli (Ibis, 1867, pp. 101 and 104) is more likely to have been this species than *C. acaciæ.*

thorough satisfaction with our entertainment, to be followed by a more tangible present of silk burnouses when we got to Laghouat, we trod once more the inhospitable desert. One of them was good enough to say he would accompany me, and I further availed myself of the convoy of two *Spahis*, who had been sent with letters from Laghouat. The first day's journey was performed in a sharp sirocco wind, and the only rare bird seen was a Houbara Bustard. I noticed however a Lizard, about two feet long, running over the stones in the barest part of the sterile *chebka*. I had one brought to me at Laghouat which was more than three feet long. Berard, in his "Indicateur," says, "On trouve le Pleitiondon Aldrovandi ou Scinque Cyprien, gracieux lézard à bec de poisson qui plonge dans le sables comme un poisson dans l'eau." Perhaps this was the species I saw. The next morning I shot *Ammomanes regulus*, a pretty little sand-coloured Lark, described in 1857 by Prince Bonaparte (Canon Tristram terms it "a very scarce bird," and I believe justly,) and *Saxicola erythrœa* (Ehr), *S. halophila* (Trist.), erroneously given in my list in the "Ibis" as *S. homochroa*.

When the Chebka Mzab was passed, I had further opportunity of examining the *Dayats*. It was now the period of migration (May 2nd), and where there was water they were teeming with life. It was as if all the spring migrants of Southern Europe had been compressed into fifty acres. Beneath every jujube tree—at every thicket—were massed and congregated all manner of rare birds :—Pied Flycatchers, Hoopoes, Doves, Rollers, Woodchats—Warblers without end, seeking shelter from the burning midday sun. The Neophron *(Neophron percnopterus)* and the hoarse croaking Raven perched upon the taller Terebinths. Different sorts of Sandpipers flew before us, mingling with noisy Shrikes, while dozing Little Owls, awakened by our approach, dashed out from the deep foliage and hid themselves again. The

shores of France and Albion's white cliffs are the migrants'
goal. Like a great tidal wave they press on, dropping I
suspect a few laggards here and there, who, tempted by the
water and rich foliage, remain and rear their progeny in
these glorious *Dayats.*

This is the country to which the Arabs apply the term
"*Sahara.*" I know it is the Great Desert which is so
marked in maps, but this is the true "*Sahara*"—the habit-
able country which ends where all regular supply of water
fails. Of course I worked hard with note-book and scalpel.
Inter alia I procured examples of the Orphean and Subalpine Warblers, Abyssinian Crested Lark, and Short-toed
Lark. Canon Tristram and Mr. Salvin did not meet with
the Subalpine Warbler, but M. Taczanouski seems to have
encountered it freely in Constantine. Loche in his catalogue
(p. 69) gives as its habitat—"Le cercle de Milianeh;" but
it appears not to be included in Germain's "Birds of Miliana,"
a catalogue comprising 162 species. It is an elegant little
species. A cock and hen, shot at Bou-Noura on the 25th of
April, were in perfect plumage.

Mr. Dresser unites *Galerida Abyssinica* (Bp.) the Abyssinian Crested Lark, with *G. cristata* (Birds of Europe, Part XX.),
but I am sure that my bird is not the same as the common
Crested Larks I shot in the "Tell." I noticed the difference
directly I shot it; it is a much lighter bird, with a longer
beak. Possibly it may be *G. arenicola* (Trist.), but it signi-
fies little, as Mr. Dresser with a sweeping hand has united
them both with *G. cristata.* Matters are not helped by a
discrepancy between Canon Tristram's account of *G. arenicola*
and M. Taczanouski's. The former says, "This bird may be
at once distinguished from its congeners by its bill, which is
extremely elongated" (Ibis, 1859, p. 426); but the latter
remarks—"Like the preceding species *(G. cristata),* this one
is short-beaked" (Zoologist, 2582).

My Short-toed Lark, *Calendrella brachydactyla* (Leisl.),

C. hermonensis (Trist.), has the crown of the head slightly rufous. In the "Birds of Europe," Part XXII., it is stated that "M. Taczanouski observed it in the winter in Algeria;" but in his list, translated in the Zoologist, that naturalist says, "*Not seen during the whole winter.* In the beginning of March we caught sight of a small flock for the first time." (Zool., 2581).

With thankful hearts we rode into Laghouat on Thursday morning. It was nearly a month since I had seen an European, and I was not sorry to get back to the comforts of a bedroom at the hotel. On all hands I heard of the Camel "razzia" at Zergoun. I might almost say it had created some uneasinesss. I was very glad to take the first "courrier," and return to Algiers as quickly as possible. I did not attempt to shoot any more, but at Ain-El-Ibel I was given a Red-necked Goatsucker (*Caprimulgus ruficollis*) in fine plumage. The next day being Sunday, I slept at Guelt-El-Stel, and saw three more of the same species, apparently attracted by the young locusts with which the ground was perfectly black in places. It is not included by either Tristram, Salvin, or Taczanouski. Near Medea I got the finest Golden Oriole (*Oriolus galbula*) I ever saw. The coach stopped to bait at a roadside public-house, the landlord of which had shot it on a fruit tree in his garden. Its stomach contained a mass of hair, apparently that of hairy caterpillars.

Nothing else worth mentioning occurred until I reached Algiers. There I saw two more new birds, the Yellow-legged Herring Gull (*Larus leucophœus*), and the Purple Heron (*Ardea purpurea*), the former in the harbour, the latter in a barber's shop apparently just set up. In crossing to Marseilles I observed Stormy Petrels (*Thalassidroma pelagica*) at the Balearic Isles, and Cinereous Shearwaters (*Puffinus cinereus*), both of which may be included in the Algerian avifauna. Indeed in May, 1856, Dr. Tristram shot eight

Cinereous Shearwaters in the bay in three days. One of
these—the specimen figured by Dr. Bree in his " Birds of
Europe "—through his kindness now enriches my collection.
In addition to these I saw the Cream-coloured Courser
(Cursorius gallicus), as I firmly believe, running and flying
before the heads of our mules in the Tibrem country ; Manx
Shearwaters (as already mentioned) when I went by sea
from Oran to Algiers; and Kites so often in the course of
my wanderings, that I think I may at least include *Milvus
ictinus* and *M. migrans.* Skins of the Greater Spotted
Cuckoo *(Cuculus glandarius)*, and Cisalpine Sparrow *(Passer
cisalpinus)* I bought in Algiers before I went into the
interior, which had been killed in the vicinity. Jays *(Garrulus cervicalis*, Bp.*) I often saw in cages, though never
wild, and once a dainty Stilt *(Himantopus candidus)* shut
up in a rabbit-hutch at Laghouat, and fed by Zouave soldiers
on bread, meat, fish, insects, and rice. At the same place
two Lanner Falcons *(Falco lanarius)*, taken young from
the nest, were offered to me. I bought one, and on my
return to England deposited it in the Zoological Gardens,
but it only lived three years, probably owing to the pernicious
habit of feeding it on butcher's meat, instead of rats and
rabbits.

Including all the above (except the Stormy Petrel), and
deducting *Dromolæa leucocephala* as not a good species, the
total number of birds identified by me in four months was
152. I refrain from including the Lammergayer, though
often in the Atlas I saw large birds of prey which I should
think could scarcely have been anything else, neither do I

---

* Mr. Dresser states in his " Birds of Europe " that I saw the Jay
at Tibrem and Medea, but there he slightly misquotes me. It was the
Moorish Magpie, not the Jay, which I saw at those places. The eye in
G. cervicalis is exactly the bluish colour of the British Jay's, with an
inner ring of brown.

reckon the Garganey Teal; albeit, I flushed a brace of Ducks on April 4th, which looked uncommonly like them.

ADDENDUM.

In the Ornithological Journal—the "Ibis"—edited by Salvin, and published by Van Voorst, I have given at pages 68, 289 of the 1st vol. of the 3rd series, an extended account of all the species I positively identified. The following slight rectifications require to be made.

No. 31. *Cinclus aquaticus* should be *Cinclus albicollis* (Vieill).

No. 36. *Dromolæa leucopygia* is to be united with No. 37, *D. leucocephala.*

No. 43. *Saxicola homochroa* should be *S. erythræa* (Ehr.) *S. halophila* (Tristram). The only specimen obtained was a female at Berryan, on the 30th of April, 1870.

No. 59. *Sylvia hortensis.* "Only shot one," add "in the Gardaia oasis, 26th of April."

No. 63. *Sylvia conspicillata.* "Tibrem;" add "and Laghouat."

No. 72. *Anthus arboreus.* "Common in Summer," should be "Common in Spring."·

No. 80. *Calandrella brachydactyla.* "Once seen at Laghouat," should be "one shot at Laghouat, May 4th, 1870."

No. 86. *Galerida abyssinica.* The only one obtained was a female between Tibrem and Laghouat, May 3rd.

No. 87. Two lines from the bottom. For "*Galerida abyssinica* is found on the hills," read "*Galerida cristata.*"

No. 95. *Passer salicicola.* For "ten near Blida," read "three near Blida."

No. 104. *Pica mauritanica.* This Magpie was seen at Tibrem and Medea.

No. 106. *Picus minor.* Only met with in the wood of Oued El Alleg (in the Tell), February 14th, 1870. Figured in Part XI. of Sharpe and Dresser's "Birds of Europe."

No. 123. *Œdicnemus crepitans.* "A fine specimen in the Algiers market about the end of February," should be "on the 5th of February."

No. 135. *Crex pratensis.* "I found one about the end of February," should be "on the 3rd of February."

No. 138. *Anas clypeata.* For the "Market at Algiers," read "The markets at Algiers and Oran."

No. 140. *Anas acuta.* One in the market at Algiers about the 7th of February.

NOTE.—The white variety of the Corn Bunting, so common in England, is occasionally met with in Algeria. Canon Tristram obtained one, April 21st, 1856; and Germain observes that pied specimens are frequently seen (l. c.).

NOTES DURING

THE FRANCO-GERMAN WAR.

FEELING very strongly for the French peasantry, who
had lost their all during the ravages of the Franco-German
war, I joined a body of delegates for their succour; and I
think that some memoranda from a journal kept during
that memorable time will be found interesting. Of course
I had other things to attend to than Natural History, but I
contrived to put together a few ornithological notes. Our
head quarters were at Metz.

December 2nd, 1870. Starting from Luxembourg, at length
we reached the French frontier. The people at the village
stations said they had had 300 Prussians billeted on them.
Some were kind to the women and children, some were not.
They had had sufficient to eat, and the only thing they
complained of was having their tools taken away. Presently
we passed some more small villages, whose inmates had
deserted them, and then Thionville came in sight. No one
who has not witnessed its effect can realize what war is.
Some of us were looking forward with a strange curiosity,
for in Thionville we had learnt that we should see a dire
sample of the dreadful scourge. Before its calamity fell
upon it, the town must have stood in a wood. Desolate
enough it looked now; all its trees felled. Everything—
sheds, shrubs, and walls—levelled for a cannon-shot all

round. But it was worse inside. There its split walls, rent roofs, and ruined houses, presented a spectacle never to be forgotten while memory last. Upwards of twenty-five houses were totally destroyed, and one hundred others rendered uninhabitable. All this was the work of the sugar-loaf shells,* one of which had pierced the face of the old church clock, stopping its hands at twenty minutes after one. The bombardment had begun on the 20th of November at six o'clock in the morning, and continued, with one short interval of rest, for two days. The victors marched in on the 26th, and immediately hastened to extinguish the flames, but two houses were smoking still when we arrived. The ability displayed in managing the assault was very great. Before beginning, the Germans divided their artillery into three batteries, so placed as to be about equidistant. From each of these was hurled, no round shot, but the much more effective shell—oblong and conical—which bursting into fragments jeoparded alike life and property, while at the same time the petroleum inside ignited, quickly kindling all that it might happen to come in contact with. No sooner was a house perceived to be in flames than the guns were compressed into a focus on it, and all the efforts of the artillerymen were directed to spreading the conflagration. This was the mode of warfare, and the gutted town bore awful testimony to its success. We did not see a French soldier; they had been all sent away into Germany. They were chiefly the " Garde Mobile." Very few of them were killed or wounded. Only the poor inhabitants were made to suffer, for the enemy did not fire at the ramparts. This explains why the town did not surrender sooner. In spite of the confusion we got a capital dinner, but the people were afraid to light a fire, dreading lest there might be an unexploded bomb in the chimney. However, I believe it

---

* 20,000 were thrown into this devoted town.

was a needless alarm, for the Prussian shells were much better than the French ones, which very often did not go off when they were meant to. The landlady was most polite and obliging, though she had two officers billeted upon her, and the upper part of her " Hotel de Luxembourg " was in ruins. There was only one chamber intact, so some of us had perforce a draughty night of it.

December 3rd. Utter disorder prevailed at the railway station. German guards, porters, drivers, stokers, had been substituted for French ones, and the people could not or would not make themselves understood. Even the ticket-clerk did not know French money when he got it, or a *bonâ fide* traveller when he saw one !

Arrived at Metz. Three prisoners, recaptured runaways, were chilling themselves and their guard on the platform until they could be taken off prisoners into Germany. Wretched-looking objects ! How different from the smart uniforms in the " Grand Place," where were being drilled a moiety of the five and thirty thousand Prussians who now garrisoned Metz, as was currently reported. The flower of France went down before these broad-shouldered fellows.

December 5th. Walked to the village of Woippy ; noticed Crested Larks in small flocks upon the snow. Just before we got to the village, we met the Curé, who sent for the " Maire," who sent for the Sergeant of the Police, who conducted us to the farm of St. Agathe. The Prussians had taken it and held it, and the " chassepôt " had left its mark on the walls in many places. I picked up in the grass several bullets shaped liked a miniature shell, barring the ribs. He then took us to Chateâu Ladonchamps, which was held by both parties and twice bombarded. It is a square castellated building in a wood, surrounded by a moat. We found outhouses, extensive stabling, a chapel, etc., and altogether it must once have been—before its investment—as nice a residencè as any country gentleman could wish to live in ; but chance, or its castellated character, had cost it dear. The lead was wrenched off the chapel roof; the beautiful stained-glass window was broken ; the altar was a shapeless wreck. Even an antique folio missal had not escaped the rancour of an incensed soldiery, and I picked up and brought home as relics some of its leaves which were strewn on the floor. One shell, after boring through two roofs and a granary, had buried itself deep in the founda-tion. Another had smashed right into a costly mirror, which had probably been too large to take away. Every-thing had gone to rack and ruin. Plaster had crumbled, lead was curled, slates displaced, wood shivered into pieces. But perhaps the most singular sight was the trees on the road pitted with bullet marks, as if the " franc-tireurs " had sheltered behind them, and here and there a large bough riven by some fragment of shell. A little to the right were two mounds surmounted by a simple cross, but thousands of brave men were placed beneath the sod with no sign to mark their graves. We heard some revolting stories of bodies which were not buried deep enough, but I think my readers will spare me the recital. The regulation depth was only two feet. The sergeant gave me a few brief par-ticulars of the fight. It was commenced, he said, on the 7th of October, by the " franc-tireurs," at half-past three in morning. The constant firing lit up the horizon, while the rattle of the musketry so terrified the Hares and Partridges, that they allowed the soldiers to catch them with their hands. Bazaine's troops made several sorties, and at first drove the Prussians back ; but running short of ammunition were repulsed in their turn, and defeated with the loss of a general. The nearest Prussian post to Metz was the " Bois de Woippy," near Saulny. The French were finally worsted, but not until they had left 4,000 of their foes dead on the field.

6th. As I was passing through the streets, I saw some

waggons at the head of Rue St. Marcel, full of rusty, dirt-begrimed French rifles. I suppose they were what Bazaine's warriors had thrown into the Seille, and had been fished up and just come in.

8th. A horse came to our depôt which had had its mane and tail eaten off by another horse during the siege; but this does not give an idea of what they were reduced to. One of the most shocking sights I ever saw, was one poor skeleton brought up into the "Place" which had been found in a cellar. It was simply sickening; but it excited no pity in the lookers-on, for what time have men who are engaged in butchering one another to think of the sufferings of dumb animals? The poor wretch had been shut up many days without food and forgotten by its inhuman master. The trees inside the fortifications of Metz were in many places completely barked by the famished horses; while outside whole groves of them were felled whenever they could interfere with a cannon's range. Round the Redte. du Paté the desolation was something extraordinary. Fortunately the face of the country, far and wide, was wrapped in a mantle of snow. This in a great measure concealed what had happened, hiding up for the time being the dreary spectacle.

9th. Saw six of the captured mitrailleuses and their carriages. The guns are brass, with centrepieces of steel pierced for twenty-five bullets. They were not as effective as was expected. I believe the principal fault found with them was that they drop their shot.

Hitherto I have said nothing about ornithology, but I had been wishing to see the Metz specimen of the Great Auk, and was very glad when I found time to get to the Museum. It proved to be not in good condition, and but indifferently stuffed, standing on its toes, with loose leg wires and long neck (which appeared to have been cut open); its attenuated frame was suffering much from mould

on the back and ear. Its head was chafed by the shelf
above, and no care seemed to be taken of it whatever.
There were eight white ribs on the upper mandible, and
eleven on the lower. Perhaps the principal birds of local
interest are a White's Thrush—the first killed in Europe,
two young Sea Eagles, and a Pelican *(Pelecanus onocrotalus)*,
which was shot at Remilly in 1835.

On the 13th I was deputed to accompany a lady who
was leaving our party to return to Carlsruhe. We had
hardly started and got clear of Metz station when we ran
into a train of trucks, and broke the buffer of a waggon.
We proceeded again, but we had not gone very far before we
were once more brought to a standstill by an accident to a
train just in front of us. This announcement filled some of
the passengers with consternation, but after sitting still
about an hour we were all ordered out. It was now quite
dark. There had been a rapid thaw, and nobody relished
a walk of two hundred yards in the slush and melting snow
into the heart of a deep wood, where the cutting took us, to
a place where sixty men, with flaring laths dipped in pitch,
were working against time to repair the loosened line. It
was a wild sight. Three of the carriages had fallen over
the embankment, but whether many people had been
wounded I could not hear. My only wonder is that the
trains ran at all, considering how disorganised everything
was. I have no doubt it was the passage of the heavy
artillery which had displaced the metals.

There is rather a nice Museum at Carlsruhe. I remarked
a curious variety of our common Nuthatch, in which
the throat and crown of the head were pure black, and
another specimen pure white. I never heard of but
two other white Nuthatches; the first killed in August,
1834, in Suffolk (Mag. of Nat. Hist., VIII., p. 112); the
second at Lyng in Norfolk, in 1846, presented to me by
Mrs. Clarke. I also remarked a Great Titmouse with

crossed mandibles, which immediately reminded me of one picked up in a street at Faversham, and figured as a frontispiece by Mr. Lewin to the first volume of his "British Birds;" and I noticed a young Brent Goose with a very dark breast. The very great differences in the colour of the underparts of the Brent will be fully entered into in the third volume of the "Birds of Norfolk." The birds were very fairly stuffed, and the European series good. Many specimens were varieties, the most remarkable deviations being an extraordinary *lusus* of a Blackbird, a very singular Bullfinch, and the Nuthatches already mentioned.

The Zoological Gardens possess a good many interesting birds for so small a place; but I will only mention one of them, which was a white Magpie with pink eyes. Albinism, not leucotism. Flitting about in the bushes were Marsh Tits, Tree Sparrows, and Yellow Hammers. The Tree Sparrow is certainly a very common bird on the continent of Europe. In Lorraine I consider it was the most numerous of all small birds, which assuredly could not be said of it in any county in Great Britain. It is an inhabitant of the country. I only once saw one in a village.

The "iron road" makes a considerable *detour* before entering Strasbourg. The point where the train enters the walls appeared to have been made a special mark, if one might judge from the numerous dints with which the bricks were pitted. The drawbridge was also burnt, and some brass guns on the ramparts had met with very severe usage; but the oddest sight was a long train of empty trucks which had been drawn up three deep, and which had come in for their full share of the knocking about.

One or two holes had been made in the Museum, but nothing of any consequence was lost. It is in the Rue de l'Académie. The birds are in first-rate preservation with the exception of the Great Auk, which is unhappily a wretched specimen. Part of its neck is bare, its lower mandible is without a sheath, and its breast is spotted with grease. The tongue appears to be still in the mouth. In a cursory glance through, I noticed an adult *Haliaetus pelagicus;* and a Red-breasted Goose, not the specimen recorded by Vieillot as killed near Strasburgh, of which Krœner makes no mention ("Apperçu des oiseaux de l'Alsace et des Vosges"); also a separate collection of Alsace birds, containing many rarities of local interest, e.g., four adult (grey-visaged) Honey Buzzards, and an example of the white variety, which is rarer than the white or whitish Common Buzzard, a Hawk Owl, killed in 1842 in the forest of Brumath, and a Tengmalm's Owl. Of this last the editor of the fourth edition of "Yarrell" says, "occasionally occurs on the Vosges." He might have gone further, since, according to M. Krœner (l. c., p. 5), it is sedentary (though very rare) nesting "dans les hauts vallons de la vallée de Munster."

I brought away two relics from the house of the taxidermist. Perhaps some will remember an account of the havoc which the bursting shells played among his insects and stuffed birds. One was a piece of a Middle spotted Woodpecker, which had originally been stuffed, but having had the misfortune to be hit again, was instantly torn in pieces. The other was a Water Ouzel, which had had a similar hard fate of being shot twice over.

A venerable pile is the ancient Minster of Strasburg, and very sorry I was to see that on one side its long buttressed nave had suffered a good deal. Though not a mark itself for the Prussian artillerymen, except when used as a lookout, it would appear that some of the houses in its immediate vicinity were selected to suffer. Of one called the Maison Ohlmann, which is but divided from the Cathedral by the breadth of the street, only the bare walls remained. The shoemaker who tenanted it may well have envied his neighbours, for the houses on either side of it were untouched.

It seems that the major part of the bomb-shells which were pitched into this unlucky town were not filled with petroleum as at Thionville, but with bullets, which however well suited to a field of battle, are not intended for streets and houses where the object is not the taking of life, but the destruction of property. It was these which had chipped the fretwork of Strasburgh Cathedral and her stately sculptures, and dotted so many holes in the grand old stained-glass windows of the fourteenth century. Although there was every likelihood of the war not being finished for some time, and in the opinion of many, Strasburgh stood a fair chance of being besieged again, the sanguine townspeople were busily mending their cracked roofs and broken houses. The effect of putting bright new tiles into old roofs was very absurd, for it made the town look as if an epidemic of red spots had broken out.

21st. Shortly after my return, a friend and I ascended the heights of St. Quentin. On this lofty hill, at a short distance from Metz, has been built an almost impregnable fort, for it was obvious that if this hill was once taken, and cannon placed upon it, Metz would be at the mercy of the invader. But the Prussians had no thought of trying to take it. They knew an easier way of getting into the town; and so far as I could see not a shot had been fired at its walls, though I believe it took part in the affair of St. Privat. It is also stated on the 9th of September to have shelled St. Blain and Ars, and perhaps some of the shells we saw in Chateâu Ladonchamps came from hence. In every direction were strewn about, caps, cartridge-cases, straps, cleaning cases, fusees, sand bags, and all those small munitions of war which a retreating soldiery leave behind them. The trees were gnawn, and the ground trodden wherever horses had been picketed. Bridles were hanging in some of the boughs; and here and there a good steed's skeleton was given over to the Carrion Crows and Rooks, whose sable flocks with loud caws flew overhead, or picked the bones half hidden by the deep snow.

22nd. An eclipse of the sun from 11 a.m. to 1 p.m. At twelve it took the form of a crescent. The disk was not perfect at three.

23rd. Drove to Gravelotte, but it would be impossible to see the whole field of battle in one day. In fact it was a three days' engagement, reaching from Ars to St. Privat. In every direction I could perceive graves; some with crosses, some without. On one I saw four helmets. Others were the graves of horses and cattle. The latter had died by hundreds; the former were shot by thousands. The recent heavy rains had washed away the mould, and I had to give a wide berth to all carcases partially exposed. It is a marvel they did not breed a pestilence, The deep ruts of wheels could be seen in those heavy soils in every direction where the field artillery had been dragged by the straining horses; and a piece of the army telegraph was still hanging on a tree, which the fugitives had not tarried to cut down. The peasants had gathered up the scabbards, etc., which were now lying in heaps around the village, and the conquerors had carried off the swords and guns, and everything which could be used again, even to the brass tops of the helmets which were lying on the road by hundreds; but many small articles were still lying about, some of which I particularly remember, such as a silk handkerchief which had been used to staunch a wound, a sleeve cut off at the elbow, a nosebag, pegs of tents, and an empty mitrailleuse cartridge. The schoolmaster who, terrified out of his life, had seen it all from the tower of the church, showed us from the brow of the hill the wood which sheltered the Prussian cavalry, and the place where the mitrailleuses had stood which worked such fearful execution among them.

24th. Visited Nouilly, Noiseville, St. Barbe, and Vremy. It was a strange sight to see the people getting ready an altar for Christmas eve in their wreck of a church. The churchyard had apparently been attacked, for many of the tombstones were wrenched up and thrown across the gateway to barricade it. We saw the ground all trampled and trodden, haversacks tossed about, a dead horse in an entrenchment not buried yet, and all war's ghastly symptoms.

25th. Towards evening firing heard: supposed to be letting off of cannons which had been loaded by the French at the forts, and abandoned without being discharged. Our Christmas was one of the coldest days I ever experienced. The keen frost, which had lasted with little intermission since our arrival, had bound everything in its icy fetters; but this rigorous weather, while it increased the suffering of many poor people, was a most valuable check to the spread of infection. Typhus, Dysentery, and Small-pox were rife. No less than five members of our small society took the last, and one, who had come out to do all she could for the sick and impoverished people, succumbed to its virulence.

Of course the wild birds suffered as much as the people. Gangs of famished Rooks* swarmed on the roads, in the fields, or by the river's edge, searching for the food they could not find. Some, more lucky than the rest, had discovered a partially uncovered rubbish-heap. I drove them away, and picked up one of the "field-post" letter boxes used by the French regiments.†

---

* Some ladies in England reared a young Rook which was blown out of its nest. Instead of evincing its gratitude by quitting its benefactors when it grew up, this tractable bird built two nests of holly leaves; but ultimately it joined its sable companions, showing that its natural instinct was in the end stronger than anything else.

† I read a curious account of the wounded soldiers at Sedan beckoning for the field-postman before calling the ambulance, showing their extraordinary eagerness to communicate with their friends. Blank sheets were generally carried with each box for the men to write upon.

It is not necessary to describe all the villages we visited. It was the same sad spectacle of beggary, dirt, and disease, the same affecting complaints made by men in their earnest dialect at most of them; but now and then, in happy contrast, one came across some peaceful hamlet which was not in the "path of war."

January 6th, 1870. No place that I saw was more thoroughly given over to the flames and despoiled than the once well-to-do Peltre. I should say about three-fourths of this large village was blackened and roofless. The rights of the story will probably never be known, but the Prussians are accredited with having set fire to it when they evacuated it. Thus the poor inhabitants were forced to look on while their homes were flaming, if indeed their ruthless masters did not make them assist in firing them. It was pitiable to hear the "chers sœurs" (nuns) tell their tale of woe. They were turned out of their convent at an hour's notice, where they had been sedulously tending the wounded of both nations, with scarce time as they said "to put a clean collar on," their habitual love of neatness asserting itself at that dreadful moment. This building was very large for a country village, with a children's school and a substantial chapel at the back. The railway station was reduced to a heap of ashes; so was the church. The carved images had dropped from their pedestals, and the cross of the tower had fallen. The clock likewise had dropped in, leaving one hand still sticking on the wall, and a chaos of its wheels and works was lying on the ground. The wooden pews were burnt, the iron was bent, the lead melted, the windows fallen in, the altar rails broken. But the wasteful ruin had not stopped here. In the village all was havoc and confusion. Burning shutters had left their marks upon the houses, chimneys stood by themselves, cellars were exposed. Everything had stamped upon it in characters only too intelligible the progress of a devouring and implacable fire.

9th. Business connected with our Society took me to Phalsburg. It was three weeks and two days since this stronghold had fallen. Darkness set in ere we could climb the steep ascent, and it was night when we heard the challenge of the sentries summoning us to halt. The orders of the guards were to be very particular about admitting any persons after nightfall. After a short parley we were permitted to show our credentials, and when they had been examined and nothing treasonable found, we were marched off under military escort to the guard-house, where, after being detained for an hour like prisoners, we were permitted to go our way. The tight little city of Phalsburg underwent three assaults, and forty houses were destroyed irretrievably. However, it fared better than Thionville, for whole streets were untouched ; but the petroleum shells had set the church ablaze, and the stone of the tower had peeled off in great flakes. It does seem wonderful to me that these cities did not prefer surrendering at once, knowing that they must eventually capitulate, by which they might have saved an infinity of property. After an hour spent with the authorities, we set out for the villages under the guidance of a lad.

The Curé at the village of Mittlebrun appeared to be a more honourable man than some of his fraternity. He told us frankly that he did not consider his parishioners to be in want, indeed he said they were well off compared with the villages round Metz. The next place was the Protestant village of Zilling. Only about eighty inhabitants, few of whom could speak French. They said the principal trade of the place was the straw hat manufacture. Since the war broke out, trade had been depressed, and they had only been receiving two " sous " a hat, straw provided.

On our way home I went to see the earthworks of one of the Prussian batteries. The guns had been placed on the brow of a slope, facing away from the town, so that while able to pitch in their projectiles, they were themselves in a great measure protected. This was much more dexterous than putting them on the top of the slope. I believe there were not more than a dozen large guns at each battery.

At Nancy I saw a Missel Thrush, which I mention because M.M. Krœner and Fournel say it is a summer migrant. There is a Common Buzzard, pure white even to the claws, at the Museum. It was killed at St. Barthelemy marshes hard by. I saw another one quite as good and bought it for the Norwich Museum, at Metz. There are also at Nancy local specimens of the Hawk Owl and Tengmalm's Owl, and a brace of Ring Ouzels with pied heads. I saw similar Ring Ouzels in Alsace, particularly in the public Museum at Carlsruhe, and since my return home I have seen several (Zoologist, s.s. 2607, 2805). Both at Metz and Nancy I was shown Long-tailed Titmice, with the white head, and without it. Fournel clings to the exploded idea that the nest of the Long-tailed Titmouse has two openings. I call it exploded, but I am not at all sure that this observant naturalist may not be right, in spite of the weight of testimony against him. I can say, as others have said, that I never saw a nest with two holes, but negative evidence is not worth much. See "Land and Water" of May 11th, 1872.

The birdstuffer at Metz was M. Buchillot, and I have much pleasure in recommending him as a skilful taxidermist. Where all retail trade is at a low ebb, bird-stuffing is not likely to come to the fore. He quitted the town before the war was over and came to England, but I hear that he is now set up in business at Rheims. I saw a Greater spotted Woodpecker brought in to him, and a Grey-headed Woodpecker. I had never seen the latter in the flesh before. It is decidedly scarcer than the Green. I was informed that the Middle spotted Woodpecker was scarcer than the Greater spotted. One of the latter at M. Buchillot's was remarkable for having the throat and breast chesnut colour. It may have been only a stain. All varieties of Woodpeckers are curious. I have a cock, shot at Easton in Norfolk on the 18th of June, 1870, which is strongly tinged or stained with this chesnut colour on the occiput and scapulars.* If Malherbe, the author of the great work on Woodpeckers, had been alive, he could have settled the question. He lived at Metz, and I had the pleasure of being introduced to his widow. In the Transactions of the Imperial Academy of Metz for 1866, will be found a memoir of him, and a list of his works. Only the duplicates of his collection of Woodpeckers—in number about 200—are in the Museum; the rest were sold. At his death he left some 1,500 stuffed birds, and a collection of eggs, which were purchased by the Frères de Beauregard, of Thionville, at whose college I saw them. No localities marked upon the tickets. How much this diminishes the interest of any collection! If Naturalists would reflect that the particulars known only to them will infallibly be lost after their death, they would surely be more careful on this point. His Natural History library was also disposed of.

The titles of the books upon the "Ornis" of Lorraine are :—

1st.　A catalogue of Buchoz, 1771.

2nd.　Faune du department de la Moselle, Holandre, 1825.

3rd.　Supplement, 1835.

---

* My father also has or had a similar one, which was shot near Norwich. At a gentleman's house at Brandon I saw a curious young Greater spotted Woodpecker with the nape and lesser wing coverts chocolate brown. I have seen another very similar in a collection at Cambridge; also another—a cock—in the late Mr. Newcome's collection, with brown back and very brown wings ; and again another is recorded in the "Zoologist" having the scapulars and a portion of the back "an intensely rich brown colour" (p. 8199).

4th.   Faune de la Moselle, Fournel, 1836.

5th.   Zoologie, dans la Statistique du department de la Moselle, Malherbe, 1854.

6th.   Espèces d'oiseaux observées récemment.   Malherbe. 1855.   "Bulletin de la Société d'histoire naturelle de la Moselle."

7th.   Zoologie de la Moselle.   Malherbe.

8th.   Zoologie de la Lorraine.   Godron.   1863.

It will be seen from the above list, which I believe may be depended upon, though I have not seen all the works, that Lorraine is a " Norfolk " among the provinces, and that of patrons there have been plenty for our favourite study.

The fine collection of indigenous birds, formed by M. Hollandre, should have found its proper resting-place in the town Museum; but they are already so much cramped there, that there was no room for them, and they are at the Hotel de Ville at present.

I obtained of M. Buchillot a most beautiful variety of the Grey-headed Wagtail, without a speck upon it.   It is white, pervaded with the most delicate tint of canary yellow.   He was so good as to get down all the rarest birds in his shop to show me.   One which I would particularise was a Great crested Grebe, with all the underparts of a deep rufous colour, especially about the lower neck, which was almost chesnut.*   Another was a Crossbill with the upper mandible greatly prolonged, the lower not being prolonged at all, similar to a malformation mentioned by Mr. Stevenson in the "Birds of Norfolk," vol. I., p. 239.   A third was an old cock Merlin, which he said was rare in the adult state.   A fourth a Grey Plover in breeding plumage.   And a fifth, a cock Blue-throated Warbler without any pectoral spot— *Cyanecula Wolfi* (Brehm)—(Dresser B. of E., pl. 228).   He told me it was not the only spotless one he had seen.   The

---

* The colour did not extend beyond the tips of the feathers.

white spotted form generally occurred, the red spotted never (he added), which tallies with a statement of M. Marin, of Lille (formerly of Metz) to my father.

He told me the names of four species which were not included by Fournel (l. c.), but of which he had stuffed specimens. The Spoonbill (imature, killed at Forbach),. Purple Sandpiper,* Grey Phalarope, and Double Snipe (twice).

January 16*th*. At the market, Common Buzzard, Hazel Grouse, Reed Bunting, Yellow Hammer, Goldfinches, Green-finches, Linnets, and many Bramblings. I bought the Buzzard for two "sous." It had been killed at Sarbruck, and frozen as stiff as a board. After being thawed in a portable cooking-stove it made a good skin. It was very rufous on the under-parts. I did not think much of this market, but M. Buchillot told me he had obtained there the Meadow Bunting *(Emberiza cia)*, and other good birds occasionally.

20th. Called again on my friend the birdstuffer, and found him in the act of skinning a Whooper Swan,† one of a pair just sent in from Auboué. They were very plentiful about this time in England, *vide* Zoologist (ss., 2601).

21st. Two dead Barn Owls shown to me; identical with the English white-breasted kind. I have good reason for believing that the fulvous variety figured in Rowley's "Miscellany" occurs. Fournel says they eat bats (l. c., p. 102); so does Dr. Altum.

---

* I have shot the Purple Sandpiper at Blakeney, in Norfolk, with down adhering to the neck, but there was no reason to suppose it was bred there.

† Among the numbers of Whoopers which I have seen, for the most part hanging up in markets, I have very seldom seen a cygnet, and never a Bewick's cygnet. My father, however, has bought a Bewick's cygnet in the market at Norwich.

The following is a newspaper cutting. The species is not mentioned, but I have read of a Tawny Owl (*Strix stridula,* Lin.) giving a man who ventured to meddle with its young such a box on the ears that his face was lacerated, and it might have easily cost him an eye; but I cannot credit an Owl taking vengeance for her ravished offspring *four days after their abduction* :—

"The *Avranchin* states that in a Commune, near Avranches (in Normandie), an Owl has taken terrible vengeance for the loss of her young, which had been killed by a farmer's lad. For four days the Owl was on the watch, and on the fifth, upon the boy leaving the farm-house, the injured bird, which had been perched upon a tree, pounced down upon him, and with one stroke of its claws tore out his left eye, the sight of which is permanently destroyed."

On the 27th I drove by way of Thionville to Longwy with Mr. S. James Capper, who has given a lengthy but very graphic account of our ride and its results in his "Wanderings in Wartime." It was a long way. About two o'clock in the afternoon of the second day I caught sight of our destination, and joyfully exclaimed, "There is Longwy!" "No," said my companion, "it is a ruin." We were both right. Longwy it was, and as utter a ruin as modern artillery could make it. This celebrated fortress, built by the great Vauban, had capitulated two days before at 10 a.m., and was now the disastrous chaos which we saw. Sixty out of its 300 houses were computed to be entirely destroyed, and most of the rest were much battered. Of course the petroleum had set some on fire. A few of them were not yet extinguished: I even saw one in flames. All the public buildings—the cavalry barracks, the artillery caserne, the hospital, the church, etc., were more or less destroyed. The main thoroughfares were blocked with debris of stones, slates, laths, and rafters; and every street was besprinkled with hundreds of fragments of bombs of all shapes and sizes. We had come away from Metz directly we received the news of the surrender, and hence we viewed war's hideous desolation in all its recentness. However, they say you cannot be the first Englishman anywhere, and sure enough the "*Times*" correspondent was at Longwy before us.

A German artillery officer took us round the fortifications, and really it was wonderful to see the effect of modern missiles from large mortars. Nothing gave me a better idea of the force with which they came than the mangled trees* on the ramparts. They were most dangerous things to have there. I could quite believe that the Frenchmen dare not show themselves near them for the splinters. A jagged splinter wound is more intractable than a shot wound.

During the nine days' rain of bombshells, the inhabitants, to the number of 400, took refuge in the casemates. On visiting these, I found them to be low arched passages under the fortifications. Dreadful places, with scarcely any ventilation. I cannot think how so many people herded into them. Even here they were not safe, for in spite of being warranted bomb-proof, I saw one place where the massive roof had been broken. Hundreds of beds in rows, which the people had slept in, were still there, and some sick and wounded were not yet removed. For nine days they had endured this black hole, amid the noise and din of 30,000 bursting bomb shells. Yet such good care did the French soldiers take of themselves, that by all this extraordinary burning of powder, only a very few were killed of the 1,800 who formed the garrison of Longwy. On the German side the destruction of life was equally small; only nine men killed and twenty wounded. I should think there are very few instances on record of a fortified town being besieged and captured with so little loss. Before they began to bombard, the Germans generously allowed all the women

---

* At another place I saw some good-sized timbers cut clean in two.

and children to go out who wished, but no men. As to this they were very strict. About 2,000 took advantage of their license. Their conduct was certainly characterised by humanity all through the affair.

The French soldiers were marched off the first thing after the town was ceded, but some of the officers were still there. Whether they were on pârole I did not ascertain, or whether they were permitted the convenience of remaining to pack up after the common soldiery had gone.

We transacted our business with M. Offeld, the "juge de paix," whose father commanded the artillery of the National Guard in 1814, and who had seen Longwy bombarded three times; and then set our faces towards Longwy Bas, a village at the bottom of the hill, where we left our horse and cart, to have the extreme "satisfaction" of discovering that a rogue had stolen the harness. After three hours' worry we got some more; but our troubles were not over, for at Aumetz the gallant steed ran away while we were in the inn, and broke spring, trace, and dashboard!

We drove into Metz on the Sabbath morning. As we drew near, the distant reverberation of cannon was borne to us on the frosty air. Paris had capitulated, and flash after flash gleamed from the lofty heights of Phlappeville and St. Julien in celebration of her downfall. Two hours later, and we rattled up the streets crowded with men of both nations, who were hailing the good news of a three-weeks' armistice.

On this journey I saw a great many Buzzards (*Buteo vulgaris*, Leach). Some thought the dead horses attracted them, but I fancy that this kind of carrion was mostly underground before Christmas.* At any rate I saw enough

---

* The son of the castellan of Raglan Castle, near Monmouth, had a tame Buzzard when my father was at the castle in 1872, which he had obtained from an adjacent wood. He told him that he gave it twenty-

on that frosty morning's drive to know that war does not scare them away, as suggested in "The Field" of March 11th, 1871, and by Lord Clifton in the Zoologist, (pp. 2481, 2561). Again and again, as we rode along the crisp highway, I had to shout to make them get off the poplar trees; and often I longed for a gun to procure some of the singular varieties, for few birds vary more than the Common Buzzard. I also noticed a good many Kestrels asleep in the trees, and now and then a small covey of Partridges *(Perdix cinerea)*. The so-called French Partridge* is exceedingly rare in Lorraine, and not found at all in Alsace, according to Krœner (l. c.).

After my return to England, Count Cotlosquet had the goodness to have shot and to send me a very fine Kite, which had its nest in a wood near Metz.

---

eight dead rats at once, which was enough to nonplus most Hawks, but the undaunted Buzzard proceeded most methodically to split their heads open, and eat the brains of every rat in succession. I dare say they are still found in limited numbers in that part of Wales.

* A gunner of the name of Hornigold chanced to see eight birds alight in Lynn Wash—that is to say on the water. Wild fowl being his livelihood, he lost no time in "lying down" to them in his punt, but great was his surprise when instead of Ducks they proved to be a worn-out covey of Red-legged Partridges. They may have been a band of migrants, though I do not think it. More likely frightened and shot at on land, they flew they knew not whither, and losing their way in the fog, escaped Scylla to perish in Charybdis. Hornigold bagged them, and no doubt thought a covey of eight Red-legged Partridges was an unusual booty.

SIX MONTHS'

BIRD COLLECTING IN EGYPT.

CHAPTER I.

On the 7th of January, 1875, at the first streak of breaking day, the shores of the great land of the Pharaohs and the Pyramids became dimly visible to a small knot of expectant gazers standing on the after-deck of the good S.S. Hindostan, one of the finest boats, after the Australia, belonging to the P. and O. Steam and Navigation Co.

The Herring Gulls of the Mediterranean in their unsullied purity had been our constant companions. For four whole days a flock of them had followed in our wake, nor do I suppose it was because they were hard up. Theirs was no slender chance of daily bread, for in fact a great deal of broken victuals were constantly being thrown overboard; besides, with what unctuous rapture the grease from the engines of a steamer is gobbled up by your hungry Gull!

I had never been in Egypt, and as the day broke I could not enough admire the panorama stretched out before me. To the right lay the suburb of Ramleh, and the Viceroy's Summer Palace. To the left the lighthouse and a frowning fort, which seemed to keep the peace between the "old harbour," and a capital modern mole, three quarters of a mile long and sixty feet wide. In the foreground, the harbour, with all its varied flags of many nations. Behind, Great Pompey's Pillar, tall and meaningless; and to back all, a blue sky of such transcendent purity as no painter could depict. As we approached nearer I could perceive, with the help of my glasses, the swarthy sailors with their fantastic clothes and strange headgear, and then our good steamer snorted horribly and came to anchor, and the quarantine men leapt on board, and after that Achmed Abdallah, our Dragoman, all smiles and welcome.

Alexandria is utterly different from Cairo; as much so as St. Petersburgh is from Moscow. In each case the northern is the Europeanized representative of the southern. It is delightful in its way, but besides being far less rich in remains of antiquity, it is not so healthy as Cairo; and yet I think tourists are wrong in allowing their Dragomen to hurry them, unless, as was our case, their Diabeyha* be already engaged and waiting for them.

There is the celebrated Cleopatra's Needle, which it would never do to go away without seeing. It is about its sister obelisk (for obelisks are all in pairs), that there has been so much discussion lately. The facts of the case are that it belongs to us, but our government, deterred by the tremendous expense which our neighbours put themselves to in removing one of the Thebes obelisks to Paris, have not liked to take it; albeit, there have been sundry rumours that the Prince of Wales meant to bring it home, and suggestions that he should dig a channel up to it and put it on a raft, for it lies near the sea. It is also a question with right-feeling people whether all objects of antiquity are not best left *in situ*. The two "needles" stand in a stone-mason's yard, and about as much care is taken of them as of

---

* Nile boat.

most of the other Egyptian monuments, that is to say, none at all.

Our first sight ornithologically speaking, was perplexing, for we passed some men carrying Greek Partridges and Pheasants, where from I cannot say, but certainly not from Rosetta, the locality given me. It was unfortunate that the latter were soiled, for specimens of the true unmixed breed are not easy to get in England.

Let me here mention that there are two birdstuffers in Alexandria, M.M. Piacentini and Mayer; but the former had no stock, and appeared to have almost given up the business, (or the business to have given him up,) and the latter talked of moving to Cairo, where I should think he might meet with some custom from the numerous influential visitors who take up birds for pastime or for study.

It may also be serviceable to others to say that the gunmaker is Mr. W. Redding, behind St. Mark's Church; and the gunmaker at Cairo, M. Cassegrain. They supply fair powder at a price, and central-fire cartridges.

The railway journey from Alexandria to Cairo was the most interesting I ever made, for the line skirts Lake Mareotis, and every moment I kept seeing some new species of bird which I had never beheld in the live state before, so that we laid the commencement of that long list of species observed, which ultimately reached 223,—a number, I think I may safely say, never surpassed by any other observer in one tour in Egypt.

This line was constructed in 1851, and was the first railway ever made in Egypt. Now there are railways to Minieh, Damietta, Zagazig, and Suez; and the Khedive's engineers are even constructing one in Soudan. Formerly it was all praise to him for his enterprizing spirit, but now men begin to say that if he saps the public funds much more, he will permanently diminish the country's resources, and that he must be hard up to sell his shares in the Suez Canal.

Grand Cairo is truly an Eastern city, despite stucco houses and other inroads of modern innovation.   Its streets, dirty, narrow, and badly paved, are the worst thing about it ; yet even these are redeemed by the antique wood carving of the lattice windows.   The lofty tapering minarets, and the numerous Mosques, are unique in their way.   I went over the Mosques of the Citadel and Sultan Hassan.   From the ramparts of the former a noble view is obtained of the city, of the distant Pyramids, of Boulac, and the shipping, and of the silver river winding its course to Rhoda.*   Here the last of the betrayed Mamelucks, when his companions were fallen and dead, made his despairing plunge into the gulf below.

It is the Sultan Hassan Mosque that is partially built of the polished casing of the Great Pyramid.   It has been long falling into sad decay.   Most of the Mosques are banded in the most extraordinary way with red and white, not blocks of granite and alabaster as any one would naturally suppose from the paintings of Roberts and others ; but tawdry, vulgar paint.   This is very bad taste in embellishment, and it extends to the houses and coffee shops, many of which are bedaubed with most absurdly grotesque figures of ships, trees, lions, and all manner of nameless monsters.   Such is the art of painting among the modern Egyptians ; and to make it worse, they will often erect a hideous thing like a scaffold for tying coloured lamps to on fantasia days.   It was never my fortune to witness one of their illuminations, but they need be very splendid to compensate for the excessive ugliness of the scaffolding at all other times.

The shops and bazaars present a glittering appearance

---

* There are two islands called Rhoda, but this is "Nilometer" Rhoda.

with their swords, and carpets, and rich Stambouli shawls, and lamps, and turquoises (which are very cheap at Cairo), and grand amber mouthpieces, and red slippers, and attar of roses. The curious system of shopping is altogether the most inconvenient that ever was invented, and it shows itself, for instance, in buying pipes. If you want to purchase a *chibook*, you go to one shop for the stem, to another for the bowl, and to the bazaar for a mouthpiece, and you haggle over each purchase until you beat the price down one half, losing your temper and wasting your valuable time. If the article be a costly one, the arguing lasts proportionately longer ; coffee is sent for ; and passers-by mix in and freely give their opinion on the value of the goods. Time is no object in Egypt, as many a western traveller has discovered to his cost. There is no fixed price for anything, and you waste an hour over what could be bought in five minutes in London.

There are three kinds of pipes in general use—the *Chibook*, the *Nargeeleh*, and the *Gozeh*. I have smoked them all, and give the preference to the *Nargeeleh*, though that is said to be the most injurious from the effort of pulling, which causes the smoker to inhale the tobacco into his lungs like air. The *Chibook* is perhaps the one most commonly in use. It is a stick, some five feet long, of cherry or jasmine, with a Siout pottery bowl (brown or black), and a handsome amber mouthpiece. *Cerani* is the best tobacco for the *Chibook* ; *Tombak* for the *Nargeeleh*.

I wish I knew how to give an idea of gay Cairo, the ancient city of the Memlook Sultans, the capital of modern Egypt, and its busy throng. In the cramped and crowded Mosquee* all known trades would seem to flourish, and are represented by all known languages, which issue forth in a

---

 ° The principal street in Cairo.

strange Babel from the mouths of men clad, I may say, in all known hues of burnous, scarf, and turban.   Like Brewster's kaleidoscope are the ever-shifting tints of so great a multitude of many-coloured dresses beneath the vertical glare of an eastern sun.   The noiseless camel with heavy load bumps against the passer-by.   Black eunuchs attend the carriages of the ruler's hareem.*   Veiled women ride on white asses, nobly caparisoned.   Gaily-dressed runners precede the carriages, vociferating to the crowd to get out of the way,—and he who is run over after that, must blame himself.

The seller of tobacco sits cross-legged on his divan.   The money-changer counts up coins of many nations.   The vendor of sweet liquor clatters his brass cups as he walks about. There are men for every trade, and purchasers for every ware.   Pot-bellied boys, bareheaded derwishes, and bleareyed beggars jostle the subtle Greek with the embroidered scarf and the grave old Bey on his red-pomelled ass—jostle American tourists, English speculators, French engineers— jostle soldiers, muezzins, and artizans—all who come in their way, rich and poor, high and low, walkers, riders, drivers, in alleys so blind, in streets so crooked, in lanes so narrow, as only the mind of an eastern architect could have conceived.

The public garden is called the Ezbekeah.   It has been laid out at great expense by the present Viceroy.   Notwithstanding every difficulty, a beautiful lawn of grass has been obtained, such as I never thought to see in Egypt.   On the ornamental sheet of water are pinioned Tufted Ducks and Pochards.   Warblers resort to the trees, of which many

---

* Eastern etiquette requires that all people should turn their heads and look another way when the Hareem passes. He who does not comply with this custom may chance to receive a blow from the flat of the eunuch's sword.

foreign kinds have been introduced ; and even the Barn Owl finds a retreat there, and is to be seen at night fearlessly flying over the gas lamps. A few years ago, before the Viceroy took it in hand, this place was a swamp, and at high tide was a "*birket*" full of water.

CHAPTER II.

WE started from Cairo on the 12th of January, for
Damietta. The following are the names of the crew, as
taken down by one of my compaions :—

Reis Taha (Captain).
Reis Ismail (steersman).
Mohammed.
Hassan.
Ahmed.
Alli.
Alli el Safeêh.
Ahmed Dar.
Hassanin.
Faguir.
Mensoor.
Selim.
Machmoud (the companion of our walks, whom we
    afterwards took to the Faioum).
Abdalla.
Ahmed.

Dragoman.

Ahmed Abdalla (from Alexandria).

Waiters.

Stephano Rinaldini (a Swiss).
Mohammed Ali.

Cooks.

Abdou (from 2nd cat.)
Khaire (from 3rd cat.)

Dragoman's Boy.

Pharach.

The above may seem a large retinue, but it is impossible with the present system to do the Nile voyage with less, unless you are content to go up in a steamer ; but no one should think of that who has plenty of time to spare, and can afford a Diabeyha.

Little need be said of the voyage down the Damietta branch. There are no ruins, and it is only undertaken by those who go to shoot. At the Barrage we were detained several hours both in coming and going. Unless tourists agree otherwise in their contract, they will have to pay about seven pounds toll on the bridges, and the same on their return. We had a great deal of rain, and lightning several times, and our sailors, many of whom were Nubians, appeared to feel the cold very much.

I must now try to describe the night I passed on Lake Menzaleh. I dare say some persons have seen in English estuaries flocks of Ducks so large that they might be estimated by acres; but I am not exaggerating when I say that I saw there such droves as could not be distinguished from extensive islands. For over three miles the whole horizon sparkled with one vast unbroken horde, which, when they rose in countless myriads, seemed to darken the air. Pochards were the commonest species; next to them Shovellers, Pintails, and Widgeon, in about equal numbers. Nor was this amazing sight of Ducks all, for in the distance I could perceive an immense line of Flamingoes, whose reflected hues of white and roseate were flashed back from the water, while the helter-skelter of a mighty army of

Coots, as they rose, sounded like distant thunder. Alone by himself, a stately Pelican rode at anchor like a monarch of the waters; and the shrill cry of Gulls and Terns was heard as they passed us in the air.

The fishermen had an order to procure four Swans for the Viceroy, and one man had been on this special quest five days. Hasselquist (1751) mentions Swans on the coast at Damietta, and Mr. Macgregor says he saw some on Menzaleh, ("Rob Roy on the Jordan," p. 70,) but still it is someway south for such noble denizens of more northern regions, and the Viceroy is quite right to get them when he can. But in this instance the fishermen evidently thought his wishes could not be complied with, in which case the bastinado awaited the delinquents. An order sometimes comes (so they told us) for a thousand Ducks to be sent alive to the capital. Thereupon they have to bestir themselves, and the Sheik assigns about three hundred to each company of seven boats, with the alternative of twenty guineas' fine if they are not forthcoming by a certain date. They had now in a week only got 113, the order having arrived since the commencement of the moon, which had been full on the 21st. As we approached cautiously to the boats, three in number, I could see that they were slowly driving the Ducks to where the nets were set. Great care is necessary, for if they go too fast or tack too slanting, the Ducks are up directly, and all their trouble will have been for nothing. The nets are not unlike what were in use among the ancient Egyptians (see Rossilini, fig. clap-net). The men have a rope to pull; they are concealed on an island, and when they see the Ducks are in the right place, they all unite their strength, tug at the rope, and entrap them before they have any time to swim further. A couple of forked sticks are seen standing out of the water, and when the Ducks are between them, this indicates that they are in the right place. The net may be about twenty-five yards long; the rope is at least seventy. Too ponderous an affair for one man to manage. The haul was only one Widgeon—not much for many hours' labour, for I was told they had been driving since daybreak.

The thing was done on a smaller scale by our own boat-men, who placed a small clap-net at the end of the island where we anchored, and made a kind of *cache* in which one of them spent the night, and next morning he produced a drake Pintail which he had caught, and which we kept alive in a hutch for long after.

I must now describe how Coots are captured, for it was more particularly to see the mode of taking them that we had come out. As soon as night sets in, four or five "Coot-catchers" sally forth in a flat-bottomed boat, provided with a fireplace of baked mud, and a couple of punting poles, for the greater part of this immense lake is very shallow. Soon the distant "muttering" of the quarry is heard. The boat is propelled circumspectly, silence is enjoined, until from the increasing volume the men judge that they are within a few hundred yards of the place the sound comes from. Then one, more hardy than the rest, slips aside his pelisse of sheep-skin, stands erect for a moment, naked save a thin waistband and a tight-fitting black skullcap, winds a long casting net round his right arm and jumps into the water; and now the use of the skullcap is seen, for as he is immersed to his nostrils it is the only part which shows, and of course it resembles a Coot exactly.*

He makes a trial essay with his net, which he throws with consummate skill. I have seen men in England who thought they knew how to throw a casting net, but I never saw one who could equal in dexterity these Menzaleh fishermen. I should say he would be certain death to any

---

* Formerly a white *plaque* was added to represent the frontal shield, but this is now dispensed with.

Coot within twenty-five feet, though there is no cord attached to the net.   As soon as he has disappeared in the darkness we lie down again and wait the result ; nor have we long to wait.   On a sudden the rush of many wings is heard.   The affrighted Coots are up.   He has made his cast : there is no longer any need for silence.   His comrades in the boat make up the fire, and after throwing out a bundle of blazing reeds to show they have moved, pull rapidly towards the place the sound came from.   We strain our eyes in peering through the darkness until in a few minutes we perceive him returning dripping wet, with the Coots alive in the net, having been absent little more than a quarter of an hour,—long enough all the same to freeze him to the very bones.   They wrap the poor wretch in a "burnous," and then he stands over the fire and literally steams.

All night these sturdy fellows follow the working of the Coots with dogged perseverance if they go on feeding, but if the night is calm, Coots do not feed after twelve.   On a still night they sleep best, and then as many as 150 are sometimes caught.   They have an ingenious mode of securing them by tying the tips of the wings together under the body in front of the legs.   A fat Coot sells for a shilling, a thin one for a franc.   I saw basketfuls on sale in Damietta, but I imagine a good many are consumed on board the boats, for near Geut-El-Nosara* quantities of wings were to be seen floating on the water, which had once appertained to Coots.   I searched for the Crested Coot, but could not learn that such a bird was known.

Before leaving the lake, we anchored against a small island which had been once a Roman station, for there were any amount of urns of all shapes and sizes, (but none of them perfect,) and bricks in squares, and hundreds of little

---

* i.e. the Christians' country,—the port at the west end of the lake.

pieces of glass of brillant and varied colours. Besides these treasures we found a ring, a polished seal, and many coins of copper or bronze. Nor is this the only island that those ancient heroes dwelt on, for on one which we did not visit, so many valuables have turned up that it is commonly called the Island of Gold.

Our Diabeyha returned to Cairo on the 14th of February, and before starting for Upper Egypt it was resolved to devote a day to the Pyramids. They stand on a rock, and cultivation or *hagar* goes nearly up to them. The ascent of the big one is generally made at the north-east corner, where the pathway to the summit is well marked. Half way up several large stones have been removed, where the pilgrim can rest awhile, and one regrets to see that many are gone from the base at the corners. The Pyramid Arabs are an unmitigated nuisance. They have a nominal right to a tarif of two francs: of course they exact four shillings, and would be a cheap riddance at the price, but go they will not while one of the *Howadjas* is left. Between the second Pyramid and the Sphinx, fragments of mummies are lying about in various directions: these things ought to be put underground. I saw a great many at Massara, where the Viceroy has been making a tramway to the quarries. One of the skulls had some hair upon it of a reddish colour.

I will not inflict on my readers any long account of the Nile voyage, which has been worn threadbare. I will only say that I cannot imagine anything more delightful. Unfortunately it is very expensive, and is becoming more so; yet to the invalid and antiquarian it is money well spent. Master of a well appointed boat, he sees an ever-changing panorama pass by him of Pyramids, Temples, and Tombs, altogether unparalleled in the history of the world. He sees the creaking *Shadoof* and the *Sakia*-well, the pigeon village, the raft of pots, the swimming *Derwish*, the browzing camel, and the *Dourra* Palm, the women who draw water, and the naked children with potbellies and filthy flies clustering around their eyes, and marvels anew at each bend of the river.   As he smokes and lounges on the quarter-deck, he hearkens with amusement to the shrieks for *backshish* with which an infant population rend the air, in the insane hope that the Diabeyha will stop for the express purpose of giving them a present.   *Backshish* is the potent word of Egypt, and it is probably the first they learn to utter.   It assails the traveller almost before he can set foot upon the quay, it follows him out shooting, it goes with him to the temples, it becomes obstreperous at the Pyramids, and the night after his visit there, *backshish* will mingle with his dreams of those mighty relics of the past.

The principal stopping place is generally made at Thebes, which is only a small place, but the unrivalled ruins— grander than any others in the whole known world—are naturally a great attraction.   The magnate of the place is Her Majesty's Consul, Mustapha Basha.   To him we lent "Moss Gathered," or a "Guide Book to Thebes," by R. S. Ferguson, which must have tickled the old gentleman, who had never seen it, and who there found his peculiarities and the minutiæ of his daily life set down at full length!

I do not like to pass by Thebes without describing the glories of the great hall of Karnac, but I feel that I can say nothing which has not been better said by others before me. With regard to the superb tombs of the kings, I shall not forget what a broiling walk I had to them, how deliciously cool they were after it, and how richly the sight of the paintings, fresher far than anything I saw in any other part of Egypt, rewarded me.   That day is fixed in my mind for another reason, for, coming back from the rocky gorge, I encountered five new species of birds (Lesser Kestrel, Rock Thrush, Nightingale, Collared Flycatcher, and Glossy Ibis,) and shot four of them.

At Thebes, in accordance with the custom, we illuminated

our boat, and very pretty she looked with about 100 lanterns, each reflected in the water.

Minieh, Siout, and Keneh, are good-sized towns, which merit a visit. Keneh is celebrated for its dates, which are too much flavoured with musk for my taste. At Siout there is a manufactory of pottery very much patronised by English tourists. The principal things turned out are red and black pots trays, gooleh jars, pipe bowls (some of them on wheels), coffee cups, and "Crocodile foot scrapers," which are bought for a mere nothing and packed in crates by the vendors.

CHAPTER III.

THERE were three rifles on board, but they were not
suited for crocodiles, nor were they of much use for birds.
The fact is, it is extremely difficult to hit even a very large
bird at 150 yards from a Diabeyha, and a couple of Storks
was all our rifles killed. The banks are too populous—
particularly in the Delta—to use a long-range weapon with
safety.

The following is a list of some of the birds we shot which
have more interest to the sportsman than to the naturalist.
We arrived too late for good Duck shooting; indeed, anyone wishing to visit Egypt for the winter sport ought to go
in November.

Snipe	136	Garganey Ducks	7
Jack Snipe	46	Teal „	6
Painted Snipe	29	Marbled „	6
Egyptian Geese	10	Sandgrouse	35
White-fronted Geese	2	Senegal Sandgrouse	12
Pintail Ducks	18	Pelicans	3
Pochard Ducks	4	Crane	1
Nyroca „	3	Storks	7
Tufted „	2	Spoonbills	16
Wild „	1	Eagles	7
Widgeon	1	Avocets	12
Ruddy Shelduck	1	·Quails	307
Shoveller Ducks	8		

Small birds can be conveniently preserved with carbolic
acid by those who have not leisure to skin them. We car-
bolized 200, and lost ten per cent., chiefly from keeping

them too long before they were done, but they are more susceptible to the attacks of insects than skins. The *modus operandi* is as follows. First break in the keel of the breastbone. Then cut with your long-handled, sharp-pointed scissors from the posterior margin to the vent, and after applying plaster of paris freely, squeeze out the entrails by pressing on the back with the thumb. Then remove lungs and heart, and stop up the cavity with acid and wool. Half a teaspoonful is enough for a Dunlin, which is as large a bird as you can safely do. It then only remains to put a quarter of a teaspoonful down the mouth, and the bird is done.

The crystallized carbolic is best, as that is undiluted. It must not be exposed to heat or light, or it will become liquid and lose a portion of its strength.

Great care is necessary not to drop any on the fingers. It hardens the flesh and takes away the sense of touch, or it may produce an ulcer. The antidote is to wash it off immediately, and steep the part in oil. The "Collector's Vade Mecum," by Mr. Hume, gives a still graver caution. "Remember," says the author, "that the smallest drop of the acid in the eye permanently destroys the eyesight." This useful *brochure* gives full instructions for preparing birds by carbolic acid and other means. I ought to say that though birds preserved with it can be skinned afterwards, they are a great deal of trouble, and never look well.

BEASTS.

There is no large game on the Nile, except Crocodiles and a few Gazelle. A small herd of the latter inhabit the desert at Gow, where we saw them in the up voyage, and again in the down voyage. Hyenas are said to exist, and at the Memnonium I saw a beast one night which I was told was a Wolf. Jackals cannot be very common, as I never observed any. Going along the edge of a field one day in the Delta, I met three large Ichneumons following one another up a rut, their backs appearing and disappearing as the waving corn—then about six inches high—was bent down by the wind. On several occasions we came upon these creatures—always unexpectedly, which was probably why we never shot one. At Assouan I bought a Monkey's skin, probably brought from Soudan. At the Faioum a Hedgehog was offered to us.

BATS. " Woofwat."

Egypt with its rock-cut tombs and temples, is a great country for Bats. As I did not know their names, I could only distinguish them by size. There was one very small species, smaller than our Pipistrelle ; another somewhat larger went in flocks. Perhaps this is the species which attacks the Palms ; I was told at Damietta that they suffered greatly, and that men were employed to search out the Bats systematically and kill them. In a tomb at Siout I saw about 200 of the largest size, and shot a male and female ; the former, which was the larger, measured twenty-two inches from tip to tip. I also saw hundreds of Long-tailed Bats go down a hole at Beni Hassen.

In the square, one afternoon in June, at Alexandria, there were many which had come out before their usual hour, and they were flying so low that the coachmen were hitting at them with their whips.

FISH.

The fish of the Nile are poor and unpalatable, though they grow to a large size. I saw one enormous creature dead at Girgeh ; it must have weighed 100 pounds. Two Griffons were watching its decomposition with an appearance of interest. They are mostly taken with hooks. Macgregor mentions small fish jumping into his canoe at Menzaleh. This occasionally happened to us in our punt.

REPTILES.

A "woiran" or Monitor Lizard was shot at Gebel-Abou-Fœder, fifty-six inches long. It was clinging to the base of the cliff. This was the largest of the tribe we saw, but Egypt is full of Lizards and Snakes. I believe no Crocodiles are found below Abou-Fœder. We saw a small one there, and several larger ones higher up.

INSECTS.

No sooner had we arrived on board our Diabeyha than we became aware of fleas in large numbers, which marked us out as their legitimate quarry. Whenever in Upper Egypt, owing to a head wind or for the sake of sport, we stopped, we became a prey to a malignant host of devastating flies, who were not to be banished by the infusion of quassia, or by a nightly slaughter among their serried ranks.

At the Faioum an alarming incursion of insects took place into our tents almost every evening, generally about eight o'clock, chiefly flying beetles of strange contour and vast proportions: while at Shepphard's Hotel, night was rendered hideous by pertinaceous mosquitoes, which no amount of smoking would keep off.

PALM TREES.

The common tree of Egypt is the Date Palm. Every Palm pays a tax to the Viceroy—not much inducement to the fellaheen to plant more. There is frequently so little soil on their roots, that it seems as if the first puff of wind must bring them down; but they have rather a tenacious grasp of the ground. I consider them very bad trees for birds. The wood is not of much use. The inhabitants of ancient Syene take a six-foot log of it, and on that venture to come down the cataract of El Bab. We purchased logs of them, and after a good deal of practising, one of my companions attained some proficiency in this art of paddling. Some time ago a young Englishman was so excessively foolhardy as to attempt the cataract, which no one but a native can·safely do: his rashness cost him his life.

In Upper Egypt the Date Palm gives place to the Dhom, the tree from which vegetable ivory is obtained. The fruit grows in clusters, and is about the size of a large apple. Those I examined were hard and brown. Having with considerable difficulty cut one open, I found the vegetable ivory to be the core. There is also a third species of Palm called the Dourra, which is hardier and more generally distributed than the Dhom.

CHAPTER IV.

LET me try to sketch an ornithological walk, any bright Spring morning, in the land of Egypt. The rising sun is bursting through a cluster of stately Palm trees, but it sheds its light on no birds there, for the Palms, contrary to what has been said by some, are not good trees for birds save and except the moping Night Heron, who is now so sleepy as to be indifferent to the presence of the arch-enemy, man; but in the line of Sont trees on the other side, a sparkling flock of Beeeaters are celebrating their arrival by flashing backwards and forwards in its rays, unmindful of the herds-man and his flocks. In the midst of the grove stands the village with its 150 inhabitants, who dwell in squalid houses built of mud. They are the heavily-taxed and oppressed *fellaheen*, the agricultural population of the country. Some of them are smoking the long *chibook;* others squat on their hams and do nothing, or idly watch the laden women returning home with *Goolehs* of water on their heads. That invariable accompaniment of every Egyptian village, a pond, is now nearly dry, but a dainty Stilt Plover thinks there is enough water to wade in, and I may here remark that I never saw this bird avail itself of its unusual length of limb for deep wading, preferring rather the shallows, for which one would not imagine from its contour that it was so well adapted. The yellow Pariah dogs, which have been eyeing the strangers with a national hatred, no longer kept back by their masters, rush furiously out, and their barking quickly frightens the Stilt away. At the same time a

Green and a Common Sandpiper, which had been feeding unnoticed on the mud, fly up, but settle again at the end of the pond; while a flock of Temminck's Stints, too accustomed to the noise of a village to be disturbed, only stop feeding for a minute, and then resume again, running about and feeding as if their very lives depended upon getting through a peck of marsh worms by sundown.

The villages are generally about a mile apart, and at every village there is a Palm grove. They are seldom far from the banks of the Nile, which at this time of the year is low, uncovering many a tempting sandbank, where flocks of Herons preen themselves, and the Egret—the loveliest of all known birds—performs its solitary ballet dance. A word must be given to the sandbanks. Here the Ziczac Plover, that most characteristic of Egyptian birds, flies at the intruder, and with a winnowing motion of its armed wings endeavours to intimidate him, and reiterating its harsh cry, drives the crocodile, which had come out to bask, to his lair at the bottom of the river. Here too the gay "Pluvian" flies low over the surface of the water, and here six Garganeys, the last left of all the Duck tribe which swarmed a few weeks ago, disport themselves in a backwater such as one sees in many a tidal harbour.

The most careful steering will not prevent Diabeyhas from running on to sandbanks, and sticking hard and fast there. When this happens there is nothing for it but to tug and strain and heave and bellow until they are got off again, and this is sometimes a work of many hours, even occasionally of days. Meanwhile the mortified passenger sees the *cangia* and the lighter *merkeb* pass him by with impunity. But this delay is an opportunity for striking inland to where the desert and cultivation meet, a limit defined for miles and miles, which the shifting sands may modify but can never obliterate.

The last field is soon reached, and there is no animal

life beyond that, according to my experience, save perchance at its very fringe a few Chats, and the Crested Lark which is omnipresent; but nothing, I am convinced, to repay a long and weary trudge into the Sahara. It is not the desert, it is the ripening barley and the strips of lentils which will tempt the sportsman and beguile him to keep the Diabeyha waiting with a favourable wind, for these teem with Quails so fat, so tender, and so luscious, as to more than merit the high praise which has been bestowed on them. It would give an English yeoman a fit to see the *Howadjas* walking through the standing crops, but not a word does the farmer of Egypt say. He looks on with perfect indifference: no complaint escapes him. Even a smile lights up his stolid face, and he appears to be inwardly applauding when his tame Pigeons go by, and a successful shot brings them down. Different races have different ways. Truly *de gustibus*, etc. But he really cannot stand it when the *Howadja* walks among his water-melons for a paltry Rufous Warbler, and he does feel called upon to object to his trampling down such valuable plants for such insignificant game. Accordingly it is only due to him that his wrath should be appeased with a *backshish* of powder, a present more acceptable than the copper alloy coins, of which every dragoman thinks it necessary to bring a sackful.

All this time there has not been a cloud overhead, and only a close scrutiny into the clear blue sky will reveal the Griffon Vultures which circle far up, like dots, in the vault of heaven; yet nothing escapes them from their dizzy height. If there be a carcass or any putrid matter about a village, the Neophrons are the first to find it out, by their eyes and not by their nostrils. "Pharaoh's Hens" are a marked feature in the zoology of Egypt, and valued for their sanitary qualities, for they are the birds which preserve the public health by clearing away the filth and festering offal, of which the very stench alone is enough to breed a pestilence. Scavengers they are, at once the most loathsome and the most useful of winged animals on the face of the earth. You may see them distended with dung, their beaks reeking with gore, yet still tearing at the meal with which they are already overgorged. You may see them again at sunset congregating to roost; and you see them again next day still ravenous as ever to partake of that which it is their office to remove.

Second only to these harpies of the air are the Yellow-billed Kites, in their usefulness in removing tainted matter, and the Board of Health of Egypt, or in default of such an institution, public opinion, has decreed to both protection. They are as bold and audacious as birds would be which are dependant on man for their living.

The hovering Kestrel stands out in bold relief against the sky, but the Sparrowhawk prefers to keep among the trees, where he waits his opportunity to make prey of the White Wagtail, which was so abundant a short time ago. The Harriers also do not object to perch on trees, though it is not their general rule. They like beating the fields better, which they may be seen doing any day in April in a workmanlike manner. The Marsh Harrier is commonest, Swainson's second, then the Hen Harrier, and lastly Montague's, which perhaps is accidental or only found on migration.

I have been led into somewhat lengthy remarks on the *Accipitres;* of all families it is the one best represented in Egypt; so much so, that the most unobservant person cannot fail to be struck with it.

While my attendant is rolling a cigarette, I pause a moment to wonder what goal all the thousands of pale Egyptian Swifts which are careering by can have. They pass by, but there is no check; others take their place. Can they who press on with such steady purpose stop short of

Europe? Their heads are all to the north; they are flying low, like birds with a settled object. Less numerous, but still innumerable, and with the same aim, and flying in the same direction, I see a cloud of Sand Martins. At the rate they are now going they will soon be decimating insect life at Cairo, and hawking over the pools of El Fostat, in conjunction with the Rufous-breasted Swallow and its distinct English congener. But all Egyptian birds are not migrants. There are the stay-at-homes, and one of these is the Hooded Crow, which sits in the Sycamore-fig, announcing with loud caws, to all who may be interested in the fact, that she has laid her eggs; and another is the parasitic Greater spotted Cuckoo, which chuckles at the thought of having added one to the number. These belong to a class which is divisible into flats and sharpers; birds who "do" others, or are themselves "done."

In the long grass the Fantail builds her gem of a nest, and the *Drymœca gracilis*, another minute Warbler, chirrups to her young ones, "branchers" already with little bodies and no tails.

Small rodents spring into the ditches: lizards scuttle up the walls of the houses; the moving snake eyes the fledgling; and the sly fox trots away among the tobacco plants. So great is the overflow of animal life, that no one can fail to be struck by it. Only those can appreciate the scene in its zoological aspect who are capable of discriminating between the many species, though all can and must, listen with unmixed feelings of pleasure to the chanting of the choristers, and the hum of many insects, and all must feel the balmy air and fragrant luxuriance of foliage and blossom, and derive enjoyment from the view before them, the rock-cut tombs, the tents, the camels, the Bedouins with their long guns, the latteen sails upon the river, and the mountains in the hazy distance.

I shall be pardoned if I next submit a brief companion

picture of the prominent species to be met with in June at such a lake as the Faioum (Birket-El-Korn).   First the little long-tailed African Cormorant goes by with straight undeviating flight, like one who knows what place he wants to go to and is going there, leaving behind him the wanton Terns, who have no object in life but lightly to sport over the water as they watch for their finny prey, assured that the warm sun will take care to incubate their eggs.   In noisy conclave the Buff-backed Herons trim their nests, and the shyer Squacco is uneasy at any disturbance the meaning of which he does not understand, while the cautious Egret takes his stick away again, wisely jealous of revealing the whereabouts of his yet unfinished edifice.   The Dalmatian Pelican swims away with all sail set, or flaps and glides, and flaps and glides over the water, his huge form mirrored on the surface, startling the basking fish, which hurry from the presence of their enemy.   Marbled Ducks in pairs rise from among the sedges: agile Grebes put their trust in diving: the tall reeds quiver as the Green-backed Porphyrio seeks their friendly shelter: the Reed Warbler sounds a loud alarum.   All fly to the nearest cover, and in those thick beds they find a secure haven.

CHAPTER V.

I HAVE often thought it would be convenient if collectors
would give a short summary of the results of their expedi-
tions. The only absolutely new bird to Egypt which I can
claim to have got was the Lesser White-fronted Goose,
bought of M. Filliponi; for the Norwich Museum contained
a specimen of the Desert Buzzard* from Rosetta; the
English Swift was admitted to inhabit Egypt, though it had
never been obtained there; and the Marbled Duck was
once got by Canon Tristram, albeit the fact was not made
public; but these three species now appear as Egyptian for
the first time on positive information. The confirmation of
Captain Shelley's suppositions concerning the first two is of
great interest. With regard to the Green-backed Porphyrio
and African Cormorant which we got at the Faioum, though
they had escaped the observation of the English, they had
been noticed by some of the continental authors; and here
again the corroboration which we are now able to give to
the latter was very desirable.

Several of the birds collected by us differed in a marked
manner from British specimens, but while giving the points
of difference under their respective heads (see the Stonechat and Sand Martin), I have felt that it would be too
great a risk† to describe any of them as specifically distinct.

---

* Also see the Huddersfield Naturalist, Vol. II., p. 304.

† It would appear that quite seven-tenths of the names which have
been bestowed on "new birds" within the last few years, have already
sunk into synonyms, and the advance of science has thereby been im-
peded.

Of species previously supposed to be winter visitors, we got the Sanderling and some others in May, and the Avocet, Little Stint, Pigmy Curlew, and Lesser Tern in June ; and I may add the Little Bittern in the same month, about which nothing certain was known.

The range of the Olivaceous Warbler and the Scissorbill was extended north, and that of the Caspian Tern, White-winged Tern, Linnet, and one or two other species, south.

The right of admission was also confirmed to sundry doubtful birds, and I regard this as one of the best results of our researches, such as Baillon's Crake and Montague's Harrier, which were only admitted into his work by Captain Shelley on sufferance.

All the birds which we got and he did not get I have marked in my list with a star (*). For convenience sake I will here give a list of them :* Sociable Vulture, Bonelli's Eagle, Honey Buzzard, Montague's Harrier, Grey Wagtail, Black Redstart, Rock Swallow (?), Orphean Warbler, English Swift, Reed Warbler, Great Sedge Warbler, Baillon's Crake, Dunlin, Sanderling, Marbled Duck, Eared Grebe, White-winged Tern, Lesser Tern, Lesser Pelican, African Cormorant, and twenty-second and last, the rare Lesser White-fronted Goose.

Eighteen hundred and seventy-five was reckoned a cold spring, and a backward summer. There was no *Khamseen* (the hot south wind). In spite of this I noticed some very early migratory arrivals ; for instance the Egyptian Swift (*Cypselus pallidus*) was seen on February 14th ;† others, on the other hand, came later than the time given for them in the "Birds of Egypt," as, for example, *Turtur isabellina*,

---

* All but three are *included* in the "Birds of Egypt."

† Mr. E. C. Taylor tells me that he does not consider that *Cypselus pallidus* is a migrant.

which we had been looking out for full three weeks before we saw it on the 26th of March.

The following parallel columns of dates are intended to show the difference in the time of arrival between Egypt and England, but they are not the same individual birds which pass from the one country to the other, at least we may fairly surmise that they are not. The dates for Egypt are from my notebook, those for England being the mean of twelve years' observations of earliest arrivals made by my father, or abstracted by him from the various periodicals.

	EGYPT.	ENGLAND.
Sand Martin	February 21st	March 18th
Wheatear	March 8th	,, 10th
Swallow -	,, 14th	,, 26th
Reed Warbler	,, 31st	April 25th
Redstart	,, ,,	,, 23rd
Turtle Dove	April 2nd	May 8th
House Martin	,, 3rd	April 2nd
Sedge Warbler	,, 5th	March 28th
Cuckoo -	,, 7th	,, 18th
Nightingale	,, 13th	,, 26th
Lesser Whitethroat	,, ,,	April 28th
Greater ,,	,, 14th	,, 21st
Spotted Flycatcher -	,, 22nd	May 6th
Whinchat - -	,, 23rd	April 15th
Tree Pipit	,, ,,	,, 14th
Golden Oriole	May 1st	May 6th

I will now draw a further comparison between Egypt and Algeria, and it may be as well to remember that Algeria is upwards of 600 miles, or more than ten degrees further north than the tropic of Cancer, which bounds Egypt to the south; yet there is very little difference in the time of the arrival of its migrants.

	EGYPT.	ALGERIA.
House Martin	April 3rd	February 17th
Swallow	March 14th	,, 19th

	EGYPT.		ALGERIA.
Tree Pipit -	April 23rd		March 18th
Sand Martin -	February 21st	-	„ 22nd
Sedge Warbler -	April 5th		„ 24th
Redstart - -	March 31st		„ 27th
Nightingale -	April 13th		„ 31st
Greater Whitethroat	„ 14th	-	April 1st
Turtle Dove	„ 2nd	-	„ 11th
Spotted Flycatcher	„ 22nd		„ 24th
Roller -	„ 9th		„ 25th

It is in April that the great tide of birds press northwards,
and ours, which happened to be by many weeks the last
Diabeyha up the river, just hit off the feathered pilgrims,
as I had calculated it would do. A mighty army they
were, bound many of them for the Delta, many of them for
the more northern shores of Europe. By the 29th the main
troop had passed: the rush was over. The Tree Pipit and
the Golden Oriole, the last of the migrants, had arrived.
When these stragglers had passed we saw no more birds, except the residents and a few Turtle Doves, Rufous Warblers,
etc., which had found their journey's end sooner than the
main body, and were already commencing the duties of
incubation, not to migrate any more until the returning
wave in autumn should impel them south again.

I am not one of those who think that migration in Egypt
is very dependent on the overflow of the Nile. I know
that the early writers attributed it to that, but they seem to
have ignored the fact that the vernal and autumnal movements take place just as much in any other country, though
I can well believe that it is nowhere more observable or
more patent to everybody's eye. I am of course aware that
the Nile at Christmas offers a splendid resort to all water-
birds, and countless throngs avail themselves of it, but
these very birds show that they are not wholly governed
by the subsidence of the waters by not quitting before
March, a period when the river is comparatively low, and

when Ducks and Geese are equally quitting England and other countries in Europe. Again, I do not believe that they come to Egypt before November or late in October, though I cannot speak from my own observation. The river Nile begins to rise at the end of May, so that it must be nearly "high Nile" before they arrive.

No doubt thousands of Spring birds which come to Egypt have wintered not further south than Abyssinia ; but many probably come from a region beyond the equator, where winter is turned into summer, having already bred once. These bring their offspring with them, which, being in the puzzling plumage of immaturity, lead closet-naturalists to set them down as being two years in arriving at maturity.* Others may breed on the great lakes which are the sources of the Nile. In that class I should put the Grey-headed Wagtail, of which I saw large flocks at the end of April, composed almost entirely of young birds, yet fully grown. I think this is the only way to account for the young of Insessorial birds turning up in Europe in April, at which time, in the ordinary course of things, they ought to be in full dress. Instances of their occasionally doing so must have come under the notice of every ornithologist in England.

I do not think the sum of the birds of Egypt can be put at more than 316, which may be roughly divided into 138 residents, 70 accidental stragglers, 48 winter visitors, 33 spring and autumn visitors, and 27 summer visitors. Further researches would probably extend the last item. What is wanted is to work the country between June and October, for the collections which have come to England and America—and they have been numerous, though for the most part made by unscientific persons—have been

---

* In Zambesi, says Dr. Kirk, birds pair in October and breed in December. (Ibis, 1864, p. 313.)

formed almost without exception in the winter and spring.

The most likely place for a future investigator to get new facts is Lake Bourlos (as yet unvisited by any English ornithologist), which lies between Alexandria and Damietta. It is forbidden to shoot on Menzaleh, and Mareotis and the Faioum have been pretty well worked.   Indeed the Faioum has been visited by at least four collectors.   Going however as late as we did, I was sanguine that we should drop on something new, and if I had not been unwell I have no doubt I should have done a good deal there; as it was, we saw enough to repay us for our journey.   Let me recommend no one to go the Faioum without a filter, as the water is disgustingly dirty.   For getting about the lake a "Una" boat* would be the best thing to bring, as punts, canoes, and indiarubber boats are too small.

---

* Mr. Broadway of Cairo has two, but he objects to letting them out except for the Nile trip.

CHAPTER VI.

I SHOULD now like to say something about a bird on which
a special interest centres in connection with Egypt, because
in old days the pagan dwellers in that land worshipped it,—
the Ibis *(Ibis æthiopica,* Lath., *I. religiosa,* auct.)   What
they saw in this fowl to make it one of the objects of their
veneration is a vexed question.   Some content themselves
with saying that it was so; some jump to the conclusion
that it was a deadly foe to noxious reptiles; some quote
the plausible Plutarch, who gives three highly recondite
reasons, viz., that its black and white plumage resembled
the moon's gibbosity, that the space between its legs formed
an equilateral triangle, and that it was supposed to make a
medicinal use of its beak !

Alas! alas! the Sacred Ibis is no longer found in Egypt.
What would the shaven priests say if they could live
over again?   My humble opinion is that they would
say that in their wild state they never were anything but
rarities, and confirm the theory of Dr. Adams (Ibis, 1864,
p. 32,) that they were imported from the south.   I look
upon them as an imported exotic, for I cannot conjecture
what natural cause can have operated upon them to produce
their extinction, if they ever were natives.   They were
domesticated, in time they became totally dependent on
man, Egypt was conquered by another nation, the hand of
protection was withdrawn, and the breed died out.*   But it

---

* The great men who wrote so many reams of paper about its my-
thological history, never seem to have known that it was extinct or
moribund.

will be fair to place before my readers all that is to be said in favour of their having been natives, a view hitherto adopted by the majority of naturalists.

First.   We have a representation in Rosselini of young Ibises in a nest of water-plants (Monumenti Civili., Vol. II., plate XIV.) The body of a nestling in the British Museum is white, the head and neck are black and covered with down. This does not tally very well with the plate; my father suggests that they may be young Glossy Ibises.*

Secondly.   Herodotus says they are common and often seen, an expression more likely perhaps to be used of wild birds than tame ones.

Thirdly.   I have found a second species figured in Rosselini's " Monuments," supposed to be *Geronticus comatus* (Ehr.), which, though never sacred, may, for ought we know, have been once common in Egypt, and now retired further south. If that was so, what happened to the *Geronticus* may have happened to the Ibis.

The Sacred Ibis then is, from past association, an illustrious fowl, and so accommodating is it to the gentry and nobility of England, that like Cook's placards, all who go to Egypt see them; but to the ornithological portion of the community *it never reveals itself !* The downright nonsense which has been written about the " Sacred bird of Thoth " would fill a book. The hundred and one authors who have raved about Egypt, vie with each other as to who can say the most improbable things about it. Each chronicles the never-to-be-forgotten moment when at last he saw the venerable Ibis of antiquity. One of the fraternity, at a loss for an epithet, dubs it " the pink-eyed Ibis ;" another, with a fine power of imagination, avows that it came nothing short of " a winged star, dazzling in the sunshine." Yet

---

* It appears however that the young of that bird is the same colour as the young Sacred Ibis (cf. Zoologist, ss. 15.)

probably none of these people have ever seen the real bird. They are the dupes of dragomen; and indignant as they would be if they were told it, the Buff-backed Heron has been passed off upon them as the *rara avis*, its unsuspicious character rather assisting than otherwise in keeping up the deception. This has been the real object of their aspirations, or some other white bird of the Heron tribe.

The fact is that the only modern author who has fallen in with the genuine article, as far as my reading has carried me, is Savigny, and as the account which he gives of its habits seems to have been overlooked, I will quote him. He writes :—

"Vers la fin du mois de fructidor de l'an 8, [September, 1800] comme je descendois le Nil pour me rendre á Rosette, j'apperçus les premiers Ibis blancs, neanmoins, je ne pus les suivre m'en procurer et les examiner attentivement que plus de trois mois aprés, pendant un sejour que je fis dans les environs de Damiette et de Menzalé. On voyoit encore, à cette époque, quantité d'Ibis noirs, mais deja les blancs commencaient à devenir rares; je ne les retrouvai même en certain nombre que pres de Kafr-Abou-Said sur la rive gauche du Nil, à 3,000 metres de ce fleuve et à 20,000 de Damiette dans de grandes inondations qui s'etendent jusqu'au lac Bourlos."

At p. 50 he says that during autumn Ibises of both species are found in the markets of Lower Egypt, particularly Damietta, with their heads cut off; and that the Glossy Ibis has been often brought him alive, and once the Sacred Ibis; and then at p. 52 he adds :—

"Il paroit que l'espèce séjourne en Egypte environ sept mois, au moins encore quelques individus à Kafr-Abou-Said, le 24 nivôse (14 janvier)."

Its extinction therefore must be of comparatively recent date. Fortunately it has not been extirpated altogether, like the Great Auk and the *Nestor productus*. It is still common in more southern regions, though driven from its stronghold in Egypt.

A statement has been made that it is still a regular migrant in small numbers to Lake Menzaleh, but for this I could find no foundation. If it occurs, it is only as a straggler, and the most unlooked-for rarity. The only reliable instance that I could hear of its being seen of recent date was by Captain Arkwright, who being familiar with it in Abyssinia, may be supposed to know the bird well. He saw one at the Faïoum. There are also two said to be Egyptian, but I attach very little credence to them, in the mixed collection at the Kair-El-Aiainy at Cairo, and two or three more in our British Museum with "Egypt" on their stands, but I should not dream of placing the slightest reliance on these after my experience of wrong localities placed upon British Birds in the national collection.

A few years ago I saw an Ibis in a garden at Eastbourne in Sussex, the property of Mr. Hurst. It had been shot in the neighbouring parish of Bulverhithe, and being only winged, and that slightly, was purchased and kept alive by a huckster. From him it passed to the keeper of a public house, and from him to Mr. Hurst. It was generally supposed that it had escaped from a ship, as vessels come rather near to that portion of the coast, but there is no proof that it was not a voluntary migrant. As it was in good condition and not shy, I was able to make a careful examination and compare it with a specimen of *Ibis æthiopica*. There was a difference, and the conclusion I came to was that it was the Indian *Ibis melanocephalus*.*

Other birds were venerated in Egypt besides the Ibis, though it is as hard to understand what guided the ancient

---

* In Gerbe's edition of "Degland" (II. p. 327), it is stated that the Prince Bonaparte turned the *Ibis æthiopica* of Egypt out of the European list, and admitted *I. melanocephalus* of India in lieu thereof.

people in their choice, as it is to comprehend why the wisdom of parliament should enact that the Chiff-chaff be protected and not the Willow Wren (35 and 36 Victoria, chap. 78).

Captain Shelley thinks the Kestrel was made sacred because it destroyed that great pest of Africa, the locust; but then did it not destroy also the much-loved *scarabæus*, the most sacred of all the emblems of palmy Egypt? I believe, *if it was sacred*, that it was chosen out of many for affecting the haunts of men, building its nest as it yearly does in the walls of the houses. Did we in England deify a bird as sacred to home and hearth, the Martin would be selected, or the Swallow, which always court the society of man. But the Kestrel was not the sacred emblem of Horus. That bird was probably the Lanner Falcon (*Falco aroeris* of Wilkinson, vide "The Ancient Egyptians," V., p. 210), pourtrayed on the monuments with a dark moustache. Dr. Adams, it is true, treats of the bird of Horus as the Kestrel, but I am of opinion that all his remarks really apply to the Lanner (cf. Ibis, 1864, p. 11).

With regard to the identification of the numberless birds on the monuments, it is a subject which has been never fully investigated. Before going through the few memoranda which I made respecting it, I would draw attention to the statement in Murray's guide book that the names are written under some of the animals, which ought to assist considerably in elucidating their species.

In the Museum of Mariette Bey at Boulak, there is an undoubted portrait of two Red-breasted Geese, a species not given in Shelley's "Birds of Egypt."* They are half

---

* The Red-breasted Goose has another and a far more recent claim to be called an Egyptian bird. The late Mr. Allen, while resident in Alexandria, obtained a specimen (not adult) which is now in Mr. Crichton's possession. It is figured in Gould's "Birds of Great Britain."

the size of life, and are painted, together with four White-fronted Geese, upon a slab which was found by the gentleman who has amassed this unrivalled collection, at Meydoun. They are supposed to be older than the Pyramids themselves. They are the best executed, and by far the most life-like of any bird-pictures that I saw in Egypt.   The White-fronted Geese are not adult, having but little or no black barring on the under surface ; and curiously it was the same with those which we got, which looks as if the species was longer in arriving at maturity than in England.

The only other bird in the museum which calls for remark, though there are many other things of the highest interest, is an exquisite Sacred Ibis, very fresh and very faithful, which has been drawn, not from the conventional pattern of the tombs, but from nature.   In the temple at Edfoo there is a delineation (uncoloured of course) most wonderfully like a Bustard, a species included by Wilkinson with a query ; and in the last tomb but one at Beni Hassan it is easy to make out the Spoonbill, the Barn Owl, the Masked Shrike, and sundry others.   No one, naturalist or not, ought to go. by this grotto without visiting the two end tombs, though the pictures have been shamefully defaced.   The unrivalled cartoons in the tombs of the kings, the beautiful temple of Philæ, and many other tombs and temples have been almost spoilt by the selfish cupidity and crass ignorance of a class of visitors who are an unmitigated disgrace to whatever nation they belong to.   The Viceroy sees and knows that this is going on, and yet he provides no custodian for any of these places except Dendera.

To return to the birds which occur in the sculptures.   Sir Gardner Wilkinson gives a list, with a facsimile of outlines, in his "Manners and Customs of the Ancient Egyptians," among which one can recognise the Lesser Ring Dotterel, Spurwinged Plover (a very characteristic Egyptian bird),

Avocet, Common and Demoiselle Cranes; and in the second volume of Rossellini's "Monumenti Civili," there are some capital plates which cannot fail to interest. My father and I think they may be identified as follows :—

Plate　V.　Night Heron.
　„　VII.　Pintail Duck.　Ruddy Shelduck.
　　　　　　Mallard.　Teal.
　„　VIII.　Red-backed Shrike.　Hoopoe.
　„　X.　Avocet.
　„　XI.　Dove.
　„　XIII.　White-fronted Goose.　Sacred Ibis.
　„　XIV.　Pelican.　Ostrich.　Young Ibises in
　　　　　　nest (see antea).

In Vol. I. a *Geronticus*, probably *G. comatus*, Ehr., will be found at plates XXXI. and CLV. There is also a figure in Wilkinson's plate LXXV., which I refer with very little doubt to *Leptoptilus crumenifer*, Cuv.*

I have mentioned elsewhere that the Red-breasted Goose is to be considered a bird of Egypt. I will conclude this chapter by enumerating a few others · which put in a claim.

First. Captain Shelley originally admitted the Eleonora Falcon ("Ibis," 1871, p. 42), and I think it should be reinstated, as my father considers that the figure of a young male *Falco gracilis* (A. and L. Brehm) killed near Cairo in September, 1851, (Archiv fur die Ornithologie, 1856, p. 194,) is undoubtedly nothing else.

Second. There is in the Norwich Museum an adult *Accipiter sphenurus* marked "Egypt," but I greatly doubt the correctness of this locality. It was obtained from a dealer named Warwick.

---

* A Marabou Stork, probably this species, is believed to have occurred at Ajmokra in Eastern Algeria. (Zoologist, 2591.)

Third.   There is in the same institution an example of the small race of the Spotted Eagle (*Aquila maculata*) from Nubia.

Fourth.   Messrs. Dresser and Blandford mention an Abyssinian Roller (*Coracias abyssinica*, Bodd) from Egypt, (the "Ibis," 1874, p. 337,) which is a species which is said to have occurred in Britain (Bree "Birds of Europe," I., p. 157).

Fifth.   When Macgregor speaks of a large Indian King-fisher arrayed in red and blue, on the Zrier river near Man-sourah, in "The Rob Roy on the Jordan," he probably alludes to *Halcyon smyrnensis*.

Sixth.   At p. 278 of the "Histoire Naturelle d'Egypte," Audouin and Savigny include the Grasshopper Warbler, and in their thirteenth folio plate they give a figure of it. The species, however, treated of by these authors are some of them Syrian.

Seventh.   The Striped Bunting (*Emberiza striolata*, Licht.) is stated in Temminck's "Manuel" (3rd part, p. 641) to have been brought from Egypt by Ehrenberg and Rüppell, but there is probably a mistake here. I find no mention of Ehrenberg's specimen in the "Symbolæ Physicæ," and Rüppell's, if correctly named, were probably brought from southern Nubia.   Here let me enter my protest against the loose fashion in which the term Egypt is made use of.   Egypt proper ends at Assouan (the first cataract), though Captain Shelley, for the convenience of Nile tourists, has very properly extended his work as far south as Wady-Halfeh.

Eighth.   *Saxicola erythræa*, Ehr, *S. libanotica*, Trist., *S. finschii*, Heugl., are three names referring to one species, which, though not included by Captain Shelley, is stated to have occurred by Mr. Dresser on Von Heuglin's authority, and by Canon Tristram, who mentions having obtained it from Egypt ("Ibis," 1870, p. 495).

Ninth. The author of the "Birds of Europe," in his article on *Fuligula rufina*, says, "Schlegel speaks of *Fuligula rufina* as occurring in Egypt, (Mus. Pay Bas, anseres, p. 25,) and Von Heuglin records it from Lower Egypt in winter," which adds another to the list of Ducks.

CHAPTER VII.

In arranging my notes on the Birds of Egypt, I have consulted all the works I knew of likely to give me assistance, except the German works of Heuglin, Rüppell, and others, which for lack of a knowledge of German I have been unable to use as I could have wished. In particular I have made free use of Dresser's "Birds of Europe," and of all the papers in the "Ibis" which have any reference to Egyptian Ornithology. Of Shelley's "Birds of Egypt" I needly hardly say that it was of the greatest service to me. No one should think of going to shoot birds in Egypt without it. I can bear testimony to the accuracy of his field notes. I was surprised not to find it on sale at Robertson's, the English bookseller, either at Cairo or Alexandria, but perhaps the edition is exhausted. The general manual of ornithology for the British tourist is Smith's "Attractions of the Nile," and a very good book it is, but it is not sufficient without the more scientific work of Captain Shelley; and those who wish to make a good use of their opportunities should provide themselves with *both works before leaving England.*

It does not seem necessary to enumerate the titles of all the publications which have treated of Egyptian birds, but there are three on which I should like to offer a few remarks, Hasselquist, Savigny, and Sonini. The title of Frederic Hasselquist's work is, "*Iter Palestinum*, eller Resa til helige Landet," etc. Stockh, 1757. It was translated into German in 1762; into English in 1766; and into French in

1769. My references are to the English edition, which has a different pagination from the original. Nearly half the book is about the Natural History of Egypt, and thirty-five birds are enumerated with remarks. His letters (reprinted from the Literary News of Stockholm,) extend from the spring of 1750 to the spring of 1751, during all which time it is believed he was either at Alexandria or Cairo. They are full of references to Natural History. He died at Smyrna on the 9th of February, 1752, and to Linnæus the Queen of Sweden committed the task of arranging and publishing his notes.

The title of Savigny's work is "Explication Sommaire des Planches dont les dessins ont été fournis par I. C. Savigny pour l'histoire naturelle de l'ouvrage—Oiseaux de' l'Egypte et de la Syrie—par Victor Audouin." I learn from the preface that some of the drawings are by M. Prêtre, the rest by M. Savigny, and that the letterpress is by M. Audouin, assisted by M. Payrandeau (cf., p. 286). It appears that M. Savigny was unable—owing to illness—to complete his work, but as Government required its publication, the Minister of the Interior assigned the office of editor to M. Audouin, Savigny's former pupil.

Sonini's "Travels in Upper and Lower Egypt," 1799, can hardly be called an ornithological book, though a great many notes on birds are scattered through his three volumes. The accuracy of some of his remarks, as that on the flight of the Pelican, I can fully confirm; at the same time I think he is mistaken in the names of several birds; for instance, he mentions both the Titmouse and the Woodpecker, two genera which have never professed even to come to Egypt. He informs us that the quantity of Quails at Alexandria (on their migration) is really past belief. Four were to be had at the market for three farthings. "The crews of merchant ships were fed upon them; and there existed at the consul's office at Alexandria several complaints preferred by mariners against their captains, for giving them nothing but Quails to eat" (III., p. 321). Extraordinary as this may appear, I can quite believe it from what I have seen and heard.*

He gives a lengthy account of the habits of the Egyptian Dove, and mentions two instances of nests on window-sills where he was lodging. In more than one place also he mentions the abundance of the White Wagtail. At p. 202 of Vol. II. he remarks—"There is no kind of bird more plentiful in Egypt. *   *   * Some of them came into the vessel's cabin during our voyage upon the Nile, and would feed close by our sides with engaging security." At p. 136 of Vol. II., he has rather an interesting note on the Ostrich. I could not hear that these birds are ever to be found in Egypt now, though I believe that fresh eggs are to be sometimes bought at Assouan. Their plumes are often brought there, together with native spears, ebony clubs, and monkey skins, from the Soudan.

It only remains for me to acknowledge the special civility of M. Eugene Filliponi of Damietta, who has enriched this volume by a list of all the Arab names of birds he has been able to collect in that neighbourhood. I beg to acknowledge myself greatly indebted to him for his courtesy in furnishing this very valuable contribution. Mr. T. B. Hughes had collected twenty-four such names, and I had also collected a few, but I have determined to give the preference to M. Filliponi's names in every case. I have added a few which he omitted, viz., the Nightingale, English Turtle Dove, Kingfisher, (and Bat) on Mr. Hughes' authority ; and the Neophron Vulture, Little Owl, Egyptian Turtle

---

* At p. 510 of Sir T. F. Buxton's Memoirs I find the following :—
"Sir Thomas Cullum told me that on the 2nd of May, two or three years ago, he found upon enquiry that duty had been paid on 80,000 Quails. Pretty well for one day." This was in Italy, about the year 1837.

Dove, Sandgrouse, and Wild Goose, on my own; and in a few cases where our names differed considerably from his, I have thought well to give both. Any discrepancy is easily accounted for by the difference in dialect between Upper Egypt and the Delta.

Let me say also that my best thanks are due to Mr. T. B. Hughes for the loan of his large collection, and also to the Hon. E. Russell and Mr. S. C. Buxton for their assistance. I have also to thank Captain Shelley for kindly giving me access to his Egyptian skins, and Mr. E. C. Taylor for a like civility.

*1. SOCIABLE VULTURE, *Vultur nubicus.*

On the 21st of April, one of the largest Vultures I ever saw was killed in the act of flying from a carcass on the river near Bellianeh. This immense brute measured 109 inches from tip to tip, and looked, when hung up on the boom to dry, larger even than a Griffon. It was 39 inches long; the wing from carpus 30; the tarsus $5\frac{1}{4}$; weight $14\frac{1}{2}$ lbs. The head was bare, and of a purplish flesh colour. The skin of the crown white; round the ear a few feathers; the chin coated with black bristles pointing backwards; mouth purple; eye hazel; legs and cere bluish. No feathers on the sides and thighs; these parts were entirely covered with down. It is possible that this species may be much commoner than is supposed in Egypt.

2. CINEREOUS VULTURE, *Vultur monachus* (Linn.).

We saw this species not unfrequently; at least some of the Vultures were so very dark that I set them down as this species. I believe Von Heuglin found it rarer than the Sociable Vulture *(Vultur nubicus)*, from which it is not easily distinguishable at a distance.

3. GRIFFON VULTURE, *Gyps fulvus* (Gmel.).

This again is another splendid Vulture, which is considered to be resident; a common bird, and generally distributed, barring the Delta, where we did not see any. Those who are only acquainted with northern Europe can form no conception of how big Vultures look when their wings are spread, or what a grand spectacle a score or so present sailing on motionless pinions in the neighbourhood of their eyrie, which is generally on some steep mountain side. There was a place of the kind opposite Minieh, where some two score had located themselves on the ledges of the steep cliff on the east bank. They were too far for our guns, and they knew it, though I could have got them if I had used a poisoned sheep. I never had the luck to catch one gorged—an event which surely cannot be so common as some authors would have us believe; but at Girgeh a brace of them were inspecting the carcase of the very largest fish I ever saw, and I fancy they meant to have a good "tuck in" when we were gone. I never myself met with any recognition of the name *Nissr*, by which this species is known among the Arabs in some countries.

4. EGYPTIAN VULTURE, *Neophron percnopterus* (Linn.).
(Hasselquist, 14) ; "Rackham."*

These are unsavoury birds, but useful as scavengers. That is their foul office, and where there is any offal there they congregate. The lists I have consulted do not say they are less common in Lower Egypt than in Upper, yet we only saw one or two north of Cairo. In that city of picturesque dirt and eastern filthiness they were common enough, and it was the only place where old and young

---

* The Arabic names are given in inverted commas.

seemed to be in equal numbers. In Upper Egypt the former greatly preponderated. Hasselquist notices their part in Nature's scheme as follows :—

"The inhabitants of Egypt cannot be enough thankful to Providence for this bird. All the places round Cairo are filled with the dead bodies of asses and camels; and thousands of these birds fly about and devour the carcases before they putrefy, and fill the air with noxious exhalations" (l.c.).

That the celerity with which Vultures find dead animals is marvellous, is true; but I am of opinion that in nearly every case they are guided by their acute vision.

I never could understand how they managed to soil their backs, for that part never was pure white, which I presume it ought to be naturally.

5. SHORT-TOED EAGLE, *Circaetus gallicus* (Gm.).

I had long had a keen wish to get this large Eagle, and as I was returning from Quail shooting, on the 20th of March, at Erment, I was lucky enough to make a very long shot at one with a wire cartridge. Perhaps it was the same which had waited over us in the lentils, so high up that it looked like a Goshawk, with every bar perceptible in that clear atmosphere. I have no doubt it had killed the four snakes which we found lying together in a field close by. For what reason it brought them together, or whether it left them to watch us, I cannot divine. It seemed to take a great interest in our Quail-shooting, but I never saw it attempt to catch one. It proved to be a female, as I expected from its large size, for it measured twenty-six inches in length, and five feet seven inches in expanse. Its stomach only contained a frog. Legs, stone-colour; weight, 3¾ lbs.; eye, light yellow, but very bright; pupil small; head disproportionately large.

The Short-toed Eagle is not uncommon nor very shy, and I rather wonder that we never succeeded in killing another. Shots were obtained at Gou-El-Kebeer and Edfou, but were not so successful as they ought to have been ; but I would particularise these as good places for them. According to Von Heuglin it is mainly a spring and autumn migrant ; but I imagine it would be more correct to speak of it as a resident, whose numbers are increased at those seasons. I am quite confident that I saw some at the Faioum* in June, and if I did not observe it in winter, others have done so.

✳6. BONELLIS' EAGLE, *Nisaetus fasciatus* (Vieill.).

A fine female was shot on the 22nd of April at Bellianah. It had been chasing pigeons, and was resting on a sand bank. Weight 4½ lbs. Length 28 inches; expanse 60 inches. Eye, light hazel ; legs and cere, yellow ; beak, horn-blue. It was the only specimen which we met with in our travels. Canon Tristram has a specimen which was killed somewhere above Cairo by Mr. Meddlycott.

7. BOOTED EAGLE, *Aquila pennata* (Gm.).

On the 22nd of April—the same day we got Bonellis' Eagle—two Booted Eagles were shot out of palm trees, where they were apparently taking a nap after a meal upon rats. On the 19th of May another was shot, and several seen near Benisuef. Weight of a male 1½ lbs. Length 18 inches; expanse 13 inches. This is a small insignificant bird for an Eagle.

---

* The Faioum and Birket El Kairoun are the same place ; a lake near Cairo in the fertile province of Faioum.

8. GREATER SPOTTED EAGLE, *Aquila clanga* (Pallas);
Aquila vittata (Hodgson); *A. nævia*, part.

We did not see on an average more than one or two a
week, and none that I remember after April.   Most writers
agree that it is only a winter visitant.   A pair frequented the
lake at Rackaba, in company with numerous Marsh Harriers.
On the 29th of January, Monsieur Filliponi and I were poled,
about among the reeds which fringe that lake, and he made
a very long shot at one of them and brought it down.   It was
only winged, and we tried killing it with *eau-de-luce*, but I
do not recommend either this or ammonia, though prussic
acid might do.   I believe simple pressure on the breast with
the thumbs, or with the knee in case of large specimens, is
the speediest way of killing wounded birds.   Mr. S. Bligh
says a good plan is to tightly press the thumb on the
trachea just by the roots of the tongue.   (See, Ceylon Branch
of R. A. Soc., trans.)   It had a beautiful gloss, which I have
noticed upon the plumage of other specimens: also on the
Osprey shot at Mershoom, which was a freshly-moulted
female.   This Eagle was in the immature spotted plumage.

9. IMPERIAL EAGLE, *Aquila mogilnik* (Gmel.).

In the Institute at Alexandria there is a dust-covered
and most dilapidated Eagle, which I believe is of this species.
That some of the Eagles we saw in the Delta were also the
Imperial I have no doubt; but they are not much addicted
to the society of man, and we did not get a chance of forming a near acquaintance with any of them.

10. OSPREY, *Pandion haliæetus* (Linn.).
"Mansouri" i.e. Conqueror.

We frequently saw Ospreys on the sand banks—single
birds, often in the vicinity of Herons or Gulls.   Rifle shots

were occasionally tried at them, but the Delta is too populous to admit of much rifle practice.   However, a fine specimen was shot with the gun at Mershoom.   Going up the Nile we saw eighteen in two days, but very few in coming down again.   At Gebel-Abou-Fœder a pair seemed to have a nest in the cliffs.   My father has shown me that, according to Dr. Bree's translations from Von Heuglin, it nests in the Gulf of Suez in February and April.   It may be, therefore, that some remain the summer on the Nile, but I did not see any, to identify them, after the 1st of April.

The head of this species and the Spotted Eagle are very hard to pass in skinning.

11.   LANNER FALCON, *Falco lanarius*, Linn. ;
F. feldeggii, Schleg.

I cannot say for certain if the Lanner was seen by us below Cairo, but I identified it to my satisfaction at the Pyramids.   By the second of those mighty memorials of a bygone age, my guide sprung a Quail, and an unmistakable Lanner instantly dashed off in pursuit of it.   The quarry settled and the Falcon "waited on," but when I went up to flush it again for her, she flew on to the face of the Great Pyramid, but I had seen her light head, and albeit Peregrines were at that time (February 16th) still plentiful, I was satisfied.

No doubt in Egypt, as in other countries, the Arab sheiks have trained their Lanners to the noble sport of falconry, and their high courage has enabled them to be used for larger game than their natural instincts would lead them to attack.   I imagine that their usual natural food is the Quail when it arrives.   I have sometimes, when shooting them, had a Lanner dash past me like a flash of lightning, which I had myself seen an instant before a mere speck in the sky.   Yet from that great height he had seen that one of the Quails

was wounded, and had come down like a rocket on the
spent quarry, which only just escapes by dropping into the
lentils.

They are not a vindictive bird, though they occasionally
get wrathful with a trespasser near their nest. I once saw
a pair go at an *Elanus* and buffet him, in a wide open plain
where there was no apparent excuse for such conduct.

In the rocky gorge which leads to the tombs of the kings,
the only birds we saw were a pair of Lanners, hermits in
that unutterable solitude.   When those renowned sepulchres
held the monarchs for whom they were made and painted,
to kill a Lanner was a crime which could only be atoned
for by death; but although on the present occasion
Mr. T. B. Hughes and I had no compunction, the birds
evidently remembered their sacred character and refused to
come within range.

On an island in Birket-El-Kairoun I found the only nest
which was accessible on a projecting rock. Never having
had much experience in Falcons' nests, I was not a little
amused at the collection of rags and bones. It only wanted
a few ropes and bottles to be a regular marine store-shop.
Clearly the prosperous couple had decided, when the duties
of incubation were over, to convert it into a *salon à manger*.
Not to mention the various rags, bones, and remains of
aquatic birds, there were about two score fish, which, before
they were picked, weighed I should say in the aggregate
25 lbs., of the same species I believe as I had seen basking
on the water.   I had no idea before that they were piscivor-
ous.   There was no mistake about the ownership of the
nest, for I shot one of the Falcons, nor was this an act of
cruelty, for they only had one egg, and that was empty and
broken.   It seemed to agree fairly with the figure in the
"Ibis" (1864, p. 183, fig. 1).   I see from my note-book that
in Upper Egypt I also shot four.   I cannot detail the circumstances attending the capture of each, but I have a

remark to offer about the plumage of an immature female, killed on the 22nd of April at Bellianeh.   In colour it was a dark brown above; and below was marked with broad longitudinal streaks of the same, moreover had none of the luteous crown, except one or two very small feathers. It was remarkably small for a hen bird, measuring only 16⅜ inches long, tarsus 2, wing 12½. We all hoped it might turn out to be a Barbary Falcon, but my father has carefully examined and identified it. There is a match for it in the Norwich Museum; and I saw another, only rather larger, but in similar dark plumage, in the great hall at Karnak; so for the present it stands as a Lanner.

The adult Lanners found in Egypt sometimes vary considerably from the ordinary type, by presenting a deeper tone of coloration especially on the upper parts, thus approaching the darker race which is found in Nubia and Abyssinia, and which by some naturalists has been treated as specifically distinct, under the name of *F. tanypterus.* In the case of an adult pair, shot by my companion and myself whilst flying together from the same tree, on the 12th of April, in the neighbourhood of Esné, the female was of the ordinary type of coloration, whilst the male was much darker on all the upper surface except the tail; the head, nape, and upper interscapulary feathers, being even quite as deeply coloured as in the adult of *F. tanypterus.*

Saker Falcon, *Falco saker*, Schlegel.

I believe this Falcon was also seen, but as no specimen was shot, I could not identify it with certainty. My father thinks that Von Heuglin may have confounded *Falco babylonicus,* Gurney, which he calls "tolerably common," with the rufous phase of *F. barbarus.*

12.   PEREGRINE FALCON, *Falco peregrinus*, Gmel.

Our first Peregrine caused great excitement on board.   It was a gorged bird, sleeping off a meal of Wild Duck on the sands.   My companions were quite sure it was a Greek Partridge, a species we had seen a day or two before in Alexandria, and really it was not easy at a distance to say what it was.   The Diabeyha was stopped, and "my noble, generous Falcon" circumvented and slain, when she proved to have inside her not only the Duck, but also some grain. Duck and green peas would have been more proper, but Ducks and grain were her fare on this occasion ; and the explanation probably was, that the former had eaten the latter before being herself eaten by the bird of prey.*   It was not so curious as finding a Partridge's egg in a Peregrine's nest, or a rat's head in a Woodpigeon's.

Our next one was shot in the act of carrying off a Pewit, and the next had been making a heavy repast on locusts, which did not surprise me, for I believe it is ordained that almost all animals should help in keeping down the numbers of this destructive pest, which in times of a great visitation (fortunately rare) will come to a district in such appalling clouds as to threaten absolute ruin to the poor *fellaheen.* This Falcon would seem to be commoner than the Lanner in winter.   Old "Tiercels" are said to be rare.

13.   HOBBY, *Falco subbuteo*, Linn.

I was shown an adult at M. Filliponi's, killed near Damietta last September, which was the only one we came across.

---

* In the autumn of 1871, I was shown a Peregrine at the birdstuffer's at Lydd which had overgorged itself, and been stoned. What its last heavy repast may have been was not known, but a hare was found near the spot with one of its eyes gouged out.

14 WESTERN RED-LEGGED FALCON, *Falco vespertinus*
Linn.

I purchased an immature one at Damietta.

15. MERLIN, *Falco æsalon*, Tunstal.

Middle Egypt appears to be the habitat of the Merlin, but I did not find it so abundant as some have done. All that we saw were, I believe, cocks, which agrees with former observations.

16. KESTREL, *Tinnunculus alaudarius* (G. R. Gray);
"Sakre ahmar balad."

In a family so largely represented as the *Accipitres*, the familiar English Kestrel was by far the commonest, and so tame were they, in the Delta especially, that I have often seen stones thrown at them before they would fly away. They were less common and decidedly shyer in Upper Egypt, probably because they are more exposed there to the incursions of the gun-carrying tourist.

I think that in North Africa Hawks go to nest earlier than with us. Already in January the Kestrels were paired, and some of them nesting, for the most part choosing crude brick walls and palm trees. One of my companions saw one feeding its young on the 13th of January at the Barrage, that beautiful bridge which spans the Nile at its bifurcation. They are plucky birds, these Egyptian Kestrels. Once I winged a Senegal Dove, and almost before it touched the earth, a hovering and hungry Kestrel bound to it, nor did he at once give up possession to the lad who went for it. A Sparrow-Hawk served me the same trick one day, but it is more remarkable with a Kestrel.

It is said that Egyptian Kestrels are smaller than English ;

at any rate I think they are bolder. I have seen one swoop
at a Booted Eagle, and I have also seen one feather a
Hooded Crow which ventured too near its nest.

16B. LESSER KESTREL, *Falco cenchris* (Cuv.)

On the 13th of April, as we were riding across the wide
treeless plain of the Memnonium, we saw a great many
Kestrels. They were almost too scattered to term a flock :
the game they were after was large insects. On shooting
a pair I found to my delight that they were the Lesser
Kestrel, which I had been long looking out for. They
really had not seemed any smaller than the Common
Kestrel, which in appearance and flight they exactly resemble. This flock consisted of both sexes ; one I shot
was a hen (cf. Ibis, 1864, p. 236), the other was a cock,
which still retained immature plumage on the wings.

17. SPARROW HAWK, *Accipiter nisus* (Linn.).

Very common, and I am surprised that it has not an
Arab name, but the natives of the land of Ham are "lum-
pers," not "splitters." I need not recapitulate the habits of
so well known a bird. There are many stories extant of
its audacity, to which the following is now to be added. I
was sitting on the deck of our Nile boat, or Diabeyha as it
is called, with my friends, discussing the fragrant *Cerani*,
when a terror-stricken Sparrow flew under the divan almost
between my legs, and behind him came the pursuer in the
shape of a mettlesome little cock Sparrow-Hawk. He was
baffled of his prey this time, and before we could rise from
our seats he had made good his escape, and the Sparrow,
perceiving that the coast was clear, flew away also, but still
in evident trepidation. I expected to see the chase re-
newed, but the Hawk had clearly had a fright, and the

Sparrow had had quite enough of it. A few days afterwards a pair had the impudence to settle on the sails.*

I examined every specimen which was shot for the Short-toed Sparrow-Hawk, but we did not detect one.

18. BLACK-WINGED KITE, *Elanus cæruleus* (Desfontaines);
"Sakre Abiad," i.e. White Hawk.

These are very pretty Hawks, and fairly common. I have seen them hovering over a field just like a Kestrel, but a garden with good large trees is their favourite resort. They are generally to be seen in pairs. They were certainly commonest in Middle Egypt; none were seen, that I know of, south of Keneh. One shot on the 11th of May contained the remains of a small bird.

19. YELLOW-BILLED KITE, *Milvus parasiticus* (Daudin);
"Hiddayer."

No village in Egypt would be complete without its *Hiddayer*. I think this Arabic name, which is in universal use there, is as strong evidence as you could well have that the Hebrew words *dââh*, *dayyâh*, and *ayyâh*, in the Old Testament, should be translated Kite. In this hot and sultry country, Kites perform the part of scavengers, and most useful are they in clearing away the carcass and the offal which the natives are too lazy to bury, and the putrid stench of which would be quite sufficient to breed a pestilence in hot weather. When the Diabeyha has been at anchor, and we have been skinning, I have seen them pass and repass within a few feet, attracted by the tempting

---

* In Durham the Sparrow-Hawk is still common, and holds its own in spite of gamekeepers. At the mouth of the River Tees, at the fall of the year, I have seen many cock Sparrowhawks skimming over the fields, but it was a very rare thing to observe a hen.

body of some bird which had been flayed and thrown out of the window. The audacity of the Kites of India is pro-verbial; they are as bold in Egypt, and I do not doubt many stories might easily be collected about them, such as their snatching meat out of the poor people's hands. One actually brushed the cheek of Mr. Russell in swooping at a large *Woiran** which the steersman had been skin-ning; but I cannot say I ever heard of their molesting young Pigeons, as described by Dr. Adams (Ibis, 1864, p. 10). The Lanner will do so, and, indeed, goes by the name of Pigeon-Hawk in some parts. When our boom was lowered to go down stream, we found a lizard sticking to the top, which some Kite had left half-eaten. The top of a mast is rather a favourite perch, and was so in old times probably, for Wilkinson represents a boat with fish hanging out to dry, and on the mast a Kite (No. 333). He remarks that the manner in which it shrieks while wait-ing for the entrails of the fish is very characteristically shown in the original. I do not doubt that fishes, dead or alive, fresh or stale, would be acceptable to any Egyptian Kite; but in the mountains, where I always noticed that they were cleaner, they certainly prey largely on reptiles. I have occasionally seen them flying about with such things as snakes and lizards in their talons.

I have observed them two or three times, whilst flying, to deliver some food from the foot to the mouth. My father was well aware of this habit, which he says is common to all the Kites, and has been noticed in the Lammergeyer of the Himalayas. I once saw a common Rook apparently do it.

I was never tired of watching the graceful flight of the *Hiddayer;* unclean as one knows it to be, there is something beautiful about its slow-sailing flight, with wide-spread tail,

---

* *Monitor niloticus.*

and pinions which seem to be almost without motion.   It is the rudderlike tail which enables it to turn with such consummate ease.

During the winter they were shy, and many a cartridge was expended on them in vain; but as spring drew on and tourists went, they forgot their shyness and thought about making a nest.   Indeed a few misguided birds take the trouble to nest twice or thrice, for the noise of their young being fed in the nest was heard in the Ezbekeeah Gardens* in January.   Their nests, which by April are nearly as common as Crow's nests, are untidy fabrics, the chief part being sticks and rags, put together anything but neatly. They are generally in trees, sometimes in cliffs or on houses. One of the most accessible I saw was on the tombs of the Caliphs.   Mr. E. C. Taylor took several on the second Pyramid.   I never saw any very young birds: there were two in Shepheard's Hotel garden when we returned in May, which had left the nest and could fly.

I must say, to give them credit for one cleanly habit, that I have seen them standing in the water and washing themselves.   They are often on the sand banks, whether for fish or to digest their last meal, I do not know: I never saw one gorged, though I have seen their crops distended with offal.   It is not very usual to see a great many together.   I remember noticing a big flock in a high wind at Minieh, and a still larger one of perhaps seventy on a sandbank at Siout: what they were doing unless digesting I cannot guess; they were not near together as if they had found carrion, but were sitting apart at intervals, lazy and quiet.   But the largest congregation of all was at a place just outside Cairo, not far from the citadel; here on the 18th of February, just after we had shot the bridge and Rhoda was opening into view, I beheld a surprising flock of Kites, and

---

* The public gardens in Cairo. (See ante.)

about a hundred Egyptian Vultures, in graceful soaring circles, wheeling far up in the blue vault of heaven. I suspect this may be "the square called Rohneli, below the castle, which is the place for executing capital offenders," mentioned by Hasselquist in his " *Travels in the Levant,* 1749—52," where he says these birds assemble with Egyptian Vultures every morning and evening to receive the alms of fresh meat, left them by the legacies of wealthy great men, or at any rate that the two places are near one another.

A bird of this species has lived twenty years in my father's possession, and is now (Christmas day, 1875) in good health. It was sent from Sierra Leone.

20. BLACK KITE, *Milvus migrans* (Bodd.).

I cannot have much doubt that we saw this bird, perhaps very often, yet I do not feel sure. There is much conflicting evidence about it, but at any rate I can say positively, that the Yellow-billed Kite is much the commoner of the two species.

21. COMMON BUZZARD, *Buteo vulgaris,* Leach.

A very dusty specimen in a birdstuffer's at Alexandria, which I have not much hesitation in referring to this species. I am the more disposed to think so, as my father has lately obtained a specimen from M. Boucard, which was killed at Zagazig.

22. DESERT BUZZARD, *Buteo desertorum* (Daudin).

In "The Ibis" for 1871, Captain Shelley hazarded a guess that this Hawk would be found in Egypt. I am now able to report two authentic cases. The first was shot by

me on the 15th of May at Massara, and dug its claws into
my hand in a way I shall not forget.   The second was killed
three days afterwards at Bibbeh.   Several others were seen.
My father has examined the birds, and has compared one
of them with the series of *Buteo ferox* in the Norwich
Museum.   He thinks it can always be distinguished from
that species by its smaller size.   The one I shot was 18
inches long; the wing 14; the tarsus 2.7.   The iris was dull
yellow.   In the other specimen it was, according to a note
by Mr. Hughes, bluish black.   On this point see some remarks by my father in Bree's "Birds of Europe" (I., p. 99).
The first bird was much the more rufous of the two; the
thighs in particular were very red.   The middle tail feathers
were so abraded that little was left but the shaft.   There
was already in the Norwich Museum a specimen from
Rosetta, received from M. Panzudaki of Paris.*

23.   LONG-LEGGED BUZZARD, *Buteo ferox* (S. G. Gmelin);
        "Garrah," i.e. one that wounds.

The year 1875 was not favourable for the observation of
this species.   We certainly did not see many, and shot
none.   It is said that they are sometimes common.

✳24.   HONEY BUZZARD, *Pernis apivorus* (Linn.).

A fine adult male was shot by Mr. Russell in a grove at
Bibbeh, where it may have been nesting, May 20th.   Length
22 inches; expanse 43.   I believe this is the first authentic
instance of its occurrence in Egypt.

---

* Some time ago Mr. Gould lent me a specimen killed at Everley in
Wiltshire in 1864. From a comparison with nine skins sent up from
the Norwich Museum, my father was quite satisfied of its being correctly
named.

25. MARSH-HARRIER, *Circus æruginosus* (Linn.)

The Marsh-Harrier was the most numerous Hawk near Damietta, the Kestrel always excepted. On the plain of Gebel Silsilis they were still commoner, and we shot old and young in about equal proportions. They are not at all shy, but require large shot to bring them down. They fly at no great altitude, and often alight on the ground, but not on trees I believe. Some monstrous ticks had fastened on the face of one which was shot. I have several times observed them on sand banks. None of the females had the grey on the wings and tail peculiar to the adult male.

26. HEN-HARRIER, *Circus cyaneus* (Linn.)

I cannot say anything about the distribution of this Hawk; at the same time I have not the least doubt but that we saw it.*

27. SWAINSON'S HARRIER, *Circus macrurus* (S. G. Gmelin).

I seldom went out without seeing a Swainson's Harrier or two beating low over the fields, yet we only shot three. Females were commoner than adult males, but not very much so. In England Harriers are not considered to perch upon trees,† but I have seen this species do so several times in Egypt.

---

* I have seen Hen-Harriers in Durham, and also the Marsh-Harrier, quartering the meadows at Teesmouth like a well-trained dog, but both are decidedly rare there.

† In Hunt's "British Ornithology" there is mention of a Marsh Harrier's *nest upon a tree*, on the authority of Archdeacon Glover of Southrepps, and it would appear that this is not unique. (cf. Yarrell, B.B., fourth edition, I., 130.)

✳28. MONTAGU'S HARRIER, *Circus cineraceus* (Mont.).

Captain Shelley mentions at p. 324 of his work, being "very sceptical of *Circus cineraceus* having ever been met with in Egypt." It is satisfactory to have now set this point at rest, for whatever difference of opinion there may be about the young birds, there can be no mistake about the adult male, and we shot two fine old cocks at Gebel Silsilis on the 3rd of May.

**29. EGYPTIAN EAGLE-OWL, *Bubo ascalaphus*, Sav.;
"Buma hamra bi urun."**

Although I visited Great Karnac by the pale moonlight, and lay in ambush in the mountains behind the Memnonium, I never got a sight of this fine Owl at Thebes; but about half way up the second Pyramid I was shown a well white-washed eyrie. After a great deal of poking we ejected the Owl, and he flew swiftly out and round to the other side. I sent a man after him who flushed him again, and he flew to the Great Pyramid, but I could not get him. No doubt it was from one or other of the Pyramids that two pairs of young birds which I saw at Cairo came. In one pair there was a conspicuous difference in size, which I have noticed to be the case in the young of the Barn Owl. The same thing has been recorded of the Bittern and the Yellow-billed Cuckoo (vide Audubon). It holds good also of Montagu's Harrier, the Kestrel, and other birds of prey. One pair belonged to M. Marco, taxidermist and dragoman, who also had an old one. He had been in the Soudan. In Upper Egypt or Nubia he told me he had come across an Owl larger and darker than *Bubo ascalaphus*. Possibly he referred to *Huhua cinereus*, of which there is a Nubian example in the Museum at Norwich, though that is decidedly not larger, but on the contrary smaller. It may however

L

have been the larger species, *Huhua lacteus*.   A fine Eagle-Owl was shot while we were in Egypt by the Duke of Connaught's party.

30.   SHORT-EARED OWL, *Asio accipitrinus* (Pall.) ; *Otus brachyotus* (Forster).

I saw skins to sell at Alexandria and Damietta.   Mr. Allen says it comes in April (Ibis, 1864, p. 236).   Can this be a misprint ?

31.   BARN OWL, *Strix flammea*, Linn., (Hasselquist, 196) ; " Buma Beda."

During the day they generally repose in the crown of a palm, or in the recesses of cliffs.   Once north, and repeatedly south of Cairo, we met with this Owl.   I found one in the sanctuary, or adytum of Edfou, and all my efforts could not dislodge him ; but the place where we saw most of them was in the lofty cliffs of Gebel-Abou-Fœder.   Here I counted as many as three pairs in an afternoon's row.   They had all chosen lower holes than the Egyptian Geese which were nesting in the same locality, seeming, like the numerous Pigeons, not to go above high water-mark.   On the 27th May I saw one in the Ezbekeiah garden at Cairo.*

32.   SOUTHERN LITTLE OWL or ATHENIAN OWL, *Carine glaux* (Savigny) ; " Booma."

This is a comical little bird, and very common in every village.   In some parts there is not a clump of Palm tree

---

* From Mr. Combin, the keeper of the Cromer lighthouse, I learn that Barn Owls are attracted by the moths which come in large numbers to the lantern.   He has seen them catch them.   I believe this fine light, visible at twenty-seven miles' distance, has been the death of many a rarity,

that does not hold its pair, and the Nabuk, the Cypress, and all the other trees which afford shade and shelter, are acceptable to them. Again, they are equally at home on the flat roofs of the mud hovels, or down the inside of the "shadoofs;" or if there are any dismantled mills or caverns, there you will see the "Booma" bobbing to his own music and turning his head round to get a look at you. They certainly pair early, and are more diurnal than most Owls for I have seen them about and on the feed at noonday. I have marked one rise into the air some thirty feet, catch an insect—apparently a locust—and return to his perch on a Sont tree.

33. ROLLER, *Coracias garrula*, Linn. ; "Zeturney."

No one who has not seen a Roller can form an idea of its exceeding beauty. Fortunately for them, they do not arrive in Egypt until long after the majority of the travellers have left. The first was seen on the 9th of April, though it was half a field off us its colours showed out brilliantly; and it was not until the 22nd that we saw a second. They never became at all common. Indeed I must consider them much rarer than the Golden Oriole. Food, small frogs, etc.

34. BLUE-CHEEKED BEEEATER, *Merops ægyptius*, Forsk; *M. superciliosus* (Ibis, 1871, p. 75).

This handsome species was seen on the 29th of March. Flocks of a score or so were going north, and we often heard their clear note before we could see them. A week later and the Common ·Beeeater began to come in great numbers, when the Blue-cheeked totally disappeared; but in May we again found a few pairs settled apparently for the summer. At the Faioum there were a good many along the Bar-El-Wady, doubtless nesting in its steep mould banks.

A hen bird, shot on the 10th of May, was of a very remarkable blue tint. If it had not been paired with a cock of the ordinary colour, I should have set it down as a distinct species. It is probably this variety of hue which has gained the Blue-cheeked Beeeater and the Little Green Beeeater so many cognomens.

35. BEEEATER, *Merops apiaster*, Linn.

First seen on the 19th of April, and soon became very common to the exclusion of its Blue-cheeked cousin. The last week of the month in particular, flocks were to be heard all day at a great height migrating. Their call resembles that of the Sandgrouse, and like those birds they are oftener heard than seen. Towards evening they fly lower, and at sunset they are one of the first birds to go to roost in large troops upon the Sont trees.

The roof of the mouth is semi-transparent, as is the case with some other birds of large gape. The tongue is split into two or three points, and the beak is very sticky. The thighs are bare. They are very easy birds to skin, and we preserved a large number of the three sorts of Beeeaters. First arrivals were not so bright as some which were obtained later. Captain Shelley says the greater number do not remain to breed, and I only saw one in June. In some examples the centre tail feathers taper more than in others. A short time ago a consignment of a thousand arrived in England to make plumes !*

---

* The first known British specimens of the Beeeater were shot in Norfolk in 1794. One of them was given by Mr. Thomas Talbot of Wymondham to Sir J. E. Smith, who after lending it to Mr. Lewin to take its portrait (B.B., 11, p. 28) and exhibiting it to the Linnean Society, gave it—according to the late Mr. Lombe's MS.—to Lord Stanley, and I suppose it is now in the Museum at Liverpool.

36. LITTLE GREEN BEEEATER, *Merops viridis*, Linn.
(Hasselquist, 20, *Corvus ægyptius*) ;* " Huader."

Two days after leaving Cairo we fell in with this exquisite
bird, the most tropical form we had seen ; and it continued
very common as far as Assouan. The central tail feathers
in the best one I brought home extend three inches beyond
the others.

37. BLACK AND WHITE KINGFISHER, *Ceryle rudis* (Linn.).
(Hasselquist, 22) ; " Tayr betaa es sàmak."

I should say this well-marked resident was infinitely
commoner below Cairo than above it, though others may
not have found it so, but it was commonest of all at the
Faioum. There were several pairs always to be seen within
a few hundred yards of our camp, and I spent hours watching them. It is not necessary to re-describe the process of
fishing, but I may mention that they were much more
successful there than I ever saw them on the Nile. At
Benhouk a Hooded Crow was seen to knock one into the
river more than once. Nobody would think their feet
adapted for a wire, but they sometimes use those of the
telegraph as a perch. I have also seen one perch upon a
tree. On the 13th of April, Mr. Russell observed one chase
a bat, probably in play.

38. KINGFISHER, *Alcedo ispida*, Linn.

The English Kingfisher was often to be seen in the Delta
in January and February, but I doubt if it remains there
during the summer. Sometimes one would be perched on

---

* Hemprich and Ehrenberg refer *Corvus ægyptius* to the Common
Kingfisher.

some root, overhanging perhaps a ditch, from which eleva-
tion it would dart off with a straight steady flight, its little
back gleaming the while like an emerald. One day one
of a pair was shot at and wounded. It fell into the water,
and immediately its mate—undeterred by the presence of
three people—attacked it in the most savage manner, and
struck it furiously a number of times with its beak. It
seems to be a law of nature that the strong should kill the
weak, sickly, and wounded, among animals.

My specimens have much whiter throats than British
ones.*

39. HOOPOE, *Upupa epops*, Linn. ;   *U. major*, Brehm. ;
"Hidhid."

Familiar denizen of the villages, the Hoopoe stalks about
on every dung-hill, perches on the mud-walled houses, pries
into the sakias,† and is seen on the fertile banks of the
river. In the Delta, where they are everywhere common,
I could have sometimes killed three at a shot; but like the
Ziczac and many others, they become scarcer up the Nile.
The gape in the young bird is quite as yellow as Gould
makes it in the "Birds of Great Britain." In Upper Egypt
the Arab name is *Hud Hud*; in the Delta, and in the
province of Faioum it is *Hid Hid.* In Algeria I found this
bird to be a migrant, but in Egypt which is several hundred
miles further south, it is a resident.

---

* In the north of England a friend was fishing one day on the
Cocker stream, when a Kingfisher settled on his rod. He was amazed
and delighted at the mistake the bird had made, but of course it did
not stay many seconds. The incident, though curious, is not unique. I
have read of parallel cases two or three times.

† Sakias are wells, and a description of them may be found in every
book on Egypt.

·40. GREATER SPOTTED CUCKOO, *Coccystes glandarius* (Linn.)

This fine bird is common in Middle Egypt, and we had no difficulty in shooting as many specimens as we wanted. Old birds and young of the previous Spring were in about equal quantities. It was generally to be found singly on the Sont trees *(Acacia nilotica)*, but I have also seen it perch on the Palm and the Cypress. Other writers say it is generally to be found in pairs. In these minor points observations of different naturalists must often differ. I have seen as many as five in the course of a short walk, yet they were barely near enough together to be called a flock. I have frequently heard it give a loud harsh chattering cry, and I suppose it utters "cuckoo," as a native boy applied that name to one I shot (cf. Ibis, 1862, p. 357).

Underneath the feathers there are a number of large hairs. The testes are small as in the Common Cuckoo. Small birds will sometimes mob it, but I never saw it meddled with by Hooded Crows, though I have seen it most suspiciously near their nests.

41. COMMON CUCKOO, *Cuculus canorus*, Linn.

April 7th, I shot one at Gebel Silsilis. May the 10th several were seen in a garden belonging to the Viceroy at Minieh, and a female, still in the brown plumage, but with blue rump, was shot. It struck me that they were quite mute: they were evidently migrating.

42. ISABELLINE GOATSUCKER, *Caprimulgus ægyptius*, Licht.; "Bakkak."

With the other spring migrants came Goatsuckers. I always saw them flitting over the water or very near to it, but though we tried two or three times to shoot them from the Diabeyha, we never got a specimen ; and I am undecided whether to set them all down as the Isabelline Goatsucker or not. I was inclined at the time to think that some of them were the English one, which is larger.

✳43. COMMON SWIFT, *Cyselus apus*, (Linn.).

As it was a great point to establish this as Egyptian, I kept a sharp look-out among the thousands of pale Swifts. Near Gebel Silsilis, on the 29th of March, I had the great good fortune to see one and obtain it, but it was the only one we ever fell in with.

44. PALE EGYPTIAN SWIFT, *Cypselus pallidus*, Shelley.

First seen near the Barrage on the 14th of February. On the 26th, I shot one on the top of a mountain at the Massara stone quarries, but it was not until April that we really saw them in great numbers. It seems incredible that a portion of the hundreds of great flocks which were then pressing north should not go beyond Egypt. The mouth of one shot at Esné was crammed with small insects.*

45. ORIENTAL SWALLOW, *Hirundo savignii* (Steph.) ; *H. riocourii* Audouin.
"Hasfur El Genneh," i.e., The Bird of Paradise.

Is one of the most abundant native birds in the north of Egypt. Numbers of them any day may be seen skimming

---

* The White-rumped or Galilean Swift is not an unlikely species to be found in Egypt. It is the *Cypselus affinis* of Gray. Mr. Dresser states that it is non-migratory and very local. It has a white rump, and at first sight might be mistaken for a House Martin.

noiselessly, low over the pools in search of insects.   Yet it is not common in Upper Egypt; and when we were returning north from Assouan, we did not see many compared with the Chimney Swallow, which was then becoming very plentiful.   In the beginning of May I noticed a great many very light-breasted ones on the telegraph wires at Minieh. They were no doubt all young Oriental Swallows, but the tone of colour was not darker than is sometimes seen in the Chimney Swallow.

46.   CHIMNEY SWALLOW, *Hirundo rustica*, Linn.

The first one shot was on the 4th of March, but these harbingers of spring did not become plentiful until some time after.   I think the first large flight I saw was on the 20th of April.   As there were still a good many when I left in June, I surmise that this species breeds in the country. The specimen shot on the 14th of March was a short-tailed bird with a brown head, like the one Captain Shelley shot on the 25th of February, which I have seen.   But it is evidently a mistake to call either of them young birds, as the Swallows, when they leave England for the sunny south, have already blue heads.   Messrs. Sharpe and Dresser have shown that the head becomes brown again while they are wintering in Africa.   (P. Z. S., 1870, p. 244.)   My specimen agrees with No. 4 of their series.

47.   HOUSE MARTIN, *Chelidon urbica* (Linn.)

On the 3rd of April a few were seen at Silsilis, and one shot.   I also saw it at least once in May, and once at the Faioum in June.

48. SAND MARTIN, *Cotyle riparia* (Linn.) ;
C. littoralis (Hemp. and Ehr.)

The first of the spring migrants.   On the 21st of February
they appeared in large flocks ; after that they became very
common, and were daily to be seen by hundreds skimming
over the water.   On the 6th of March they had commenced
nesting operations at Siout, but Canon Tristram seems to
have found them breeding in February (Ibis, 1859, p. 27).
Long after the 6th of March I saw large flocks which were
restlessly pressing northwards, having evidently no fixed
abode in Egypt.

The three specimens which I brought home are lighter
than English ones, and the pectoral band is much less
strongly marked, besides which there is nearly half an inch
difference in the wing, which is longer than in the English
bird.   I suspect this is the bird referred to by Von Heuglin,
but I cannot reconcile it with the description of *Cotyle
minor* (Cab.) given by Mr. Sharpe (P. Z. S., 1870, p. 303).

49.   PALE CRAG SWALLOW, *Cotyle obsoleta* (Cab.)

Is probably a partial migrant.   During April I sometimes
observed them skimming over the crops as if they had just
come from the south, whereas, when we first saw them, it
was only in the mountains.   They nest in comparatively
accessible places, beneath the overhanging ledges of a cliff,
in the Tombs of the Kings, in the Temple at Philœ, etc.

*50.   CRAG SWALLOW, *Cotyle rupestris* (Scop.).

Mr. C. B. Cory showed me a Crag Swallow which he obtained at Girgeh on the 18th of January, which from its
large size and dark coloration was I think *Cot. rupestris*.
It had a much darker back than the specimens of *C. obsoleta*

in his collection, and rather darker under tail-coverts. At the same time some individuals of *C. obsoleta* are much darker than others, as remarked by Dr. Adams, and the pink tinge noticed by Mr. Smith ("Attractions of the Nile," II, p. 247) varies much in Egyptian specimens.

51. PALLID SHRIKE, *Lanius lathora*, Sykes; "Deknasch surreti."

I saw some, birds of the year, on the desert side of the Faioum, upon the tamarisk bushes; and just before leaving England, I was shown four or five at Mr. Cutter's shop, which had been sent to him from the Delta, but it certainly cannot be common.

52. RED-BACKED SHRIKE, *Lanius collurio*, Linn.

I bought a female of M. Piacentini, killed at Ramleh near Alexandria.

53. WOODCHAT, *Lanius auriculatus*, Müller; *L. niloticus;* "Deknasch."

First shot March 26th, and soon became common. Its actions are not sprightly. It is often seen alone on the top of a plant. Does not as a rule fly far, or perch high.

54. MASKED SHRIKE, *Lanius nubicus*, Lichtenstein.

The Masked Shrike arrived at Minieh on the 1st of March, and soon became extremely common. It varied much in intensity of colour, some of the earlier specimens being much blacker than later ones. I suppose these were more advanced in summer plumage. The sexual difference was certainly not sufficient to account for it. The Woodchat varies in the same way (cf. Yarrell, B. B., fourth edition, p. 219.)

55. SPOTTED FLYCATCHER, *Muscicapa grisola*, Linn.

A scarce bird in Egypt. I got it first on the 22nd of April, and from time to time I saw single birds up to the second week in June.'

56. WHITE-COLLARED FLYCATCHER, *Muscicapa collaris*
Bechst.

I shot a hen at the Memnonium on the 13th of April, which I refer to this species.

57. WHITE-VENTED BULBUL, *Pycnonotus arsinoe* (Licht.)

Five seen at the Faioum, of which I shot two. The natives called them *Bilbil*, and said they ate apricots. There was an apricot tree close to where I shot them. One was seen near Medinet on a tall palm, singing. Hemprich and Ehrenberg obtained their first specimens in this province, therefore I cannot say we have extended its range, but the bird is really a Nubian species. I compared one of my specimens with one of their types in Captain Shelley's collection, marked "Dongola:" it was somewhat larger and rather whiter on the under parts than mine.

58. FIELDFARE, *Turdus pilaris*, Linn.

I saw one at Mayer's shop at Alexandria, no doubt the same seen by Captain Shelley.

59. SONG-THRUSH, *Turdus musicus*, Linn.;
T. planiceps, Hemp. & Ehr.; "Chahrur."

Two were shot in the Delta.

60. BLACKBIRD, *Turdus merula*, Linn.

I insert this with some doubt: it was seen by a friend on the 23rd of January. I also saw a couple in cages. Captain Shelley says it comes to Egypt.*

61. GOLDEN ORIOLE, *Oriolus galbula*, Linn. ; "Sufri."

This is about the last of the migratory *Passeres* to arrive. The first seen were old males; then several young males and females. They prefer the thicker foliaged trees, as has been observed, and in spite of their bright colours are not very easy to see when sitting. Only once did I hear the flute-like note of the Oriole, and it appears to me that many of the spring visitors, which pass through Egypt in April, are not near enough to the time of their nesting to be in much song. The Cuckoos, for instance, were mute, but in England the first announcement of their advent is their familiar note. I believe very many birds pair *en route*, but I believe also that they reserve their song of exultation until they reach the scene of their labours for the summer.

62. BLUE THRUSH, *Monticola cyana* (Linn.) ;
 ? "Hamamet-Um Aby."

If not got when first seen, it is of little use following the crafty Blue Thrush, for it will keep on ahead taking short flights, alluring one on, but always taking care to be just out of gunshot. We shot one in the great hall at Karnac, and saw another at Medinet-Haboo. It is not at all un-

---

* In April, 1838, a pair of Blackbirds were put into my father's aviary, and *mirabile dictu*, these little monsters, in about forty-eight hours, killed twenty-six small birds which were confined there with them.

common. I see my first specimen is marked the 26th of February; I take it this is a resident speçies, but that its numbers are increased in spring and autumn.

63. ROCK THRUSH, *Monticola saxatilis* (Linn.)

A spring and autumn visitor. I met with it on migration, and shot two cocks as we were going down the Nile; the first in the Memnonium, the second at the village of Radam. Is said to be partial to graveyards; but though I went to many, I never happened to meet with it there. In fact it is much scarcer than the Blue Thrush, of which I have seen as many as four in a day. We never met with an adult male of either.

64. BLACK-THROATED CHAT, *Saxicola melanoleuca* (Güld.)

The above seems to be the correct specific name, and *S. eurymelœna*, H. and E.; and *S. zanthomelœna*, H. and E., synonyms. The species is common in Upper Egypt. The first I shot was on March 17th, a very bright clear bird with black throat and wings. Then afterwards I shot four more without black throats (that part being of the same colour as the breast and belly,) which I set down as being the same, but Messrs. Dresser and E. C. Taylor have examined them, and decide that they are the young of the next species, *S. stapazina* (L.); but as I am not satisfied about it, I shall keep them under the present heading. Probably they were birds bred during the winter season further south.

65. EASTERN BLACK-EARED CHAT, *Saxicola stapazina* (Linn.); *S. amphileuca*, Ehr.

First seen on the 10th of April; not so common as the Black-throated Chat.

66. MENETRIES' WHEATEAR, *Saxicola isabellina* (Rupp.);
S. saltatrix, Menetr.

Their flight and appearance is so far different from
S. œnanthe (the Common Wheatear) that one soon learns to
distinguish them at a distance. From the Pyramids southwards Menetries' Wheatear is common, but neither this nor
any other Chat was seen by us in the Delta.

67. COMMON WHEATEAR, *Saxicola œnanthe* (Linn.).

I think this is about the commonest of the Chats. A
cock, shot on the 8th of March, had nearly completed its
summer plumage on the back and wings.

68. DESERT CHAT, *Saxicola deserti* (Rupp.).

Rather common after Girgeh. Several hens were seen,
S. homochroa, Tristram. These Chats can hardly be
termed gregarious, as they are frequently seen alone, or with
S. œnanthc and *S. melanoleuca*. A little bush, high enough
to raise them a few feet above the plain, is always a favourite
perch, or the banks of a field, or the mud walls of a garden,
or in default of these a stone. They occasionally fly high,
but seldom go far without alighting.

On placing my series of five skins in a row with five
which I shot in Algeria, I take note that the latter are
several shades more rufous on the back, a point which
appears to have escaped Mr. Dresser.

69. MOURNING CHAT, *Saxicola leucomela* (Pall.).

First seen at the Pyramids, and next at Massara.
Probably to be found along the east bank as far as Minieh;
but we did not generally go on that side, as there were so

many islands, and so little water for the Diabeyha. Higher up we did not see any. Among other things I believe they eat locusts, as one was seen to catch a locust by a friend (cf. Dresser, B. of E., part XXVII.) Audouin and Savigny say that locusts are the principal food of *S. leucopyga*.

In a large series collected by Mr. Cory between Cairo and Thebes, I did not see any of the white-vented species (*S. morio*, Ehr.; *S. leucomela*, Jerdon). See Dresser, B. of E., part XXVII.

70. WHITE-RUMPED CHAT, *Saxicola leucopyga*, Brehm.

The granite rocks between Assouan and Philœ are a sure find for this species. It is true I did see some further north, and Mr. E. C. Taylor has obtained it at Cairo (Ibis, 1867, p. 59). I found white-headed ones (*Saxicola lucomela*, Brehm.) rarer than black-headed, but mottled specimens were frequent. The perch they like is the top of the biggest granite rock they can find ; and though they have an objection to fields, they have none whatever to houses, on which I have seen them.

71. STONECHAT, *Saxicola rubicola* (Linn.).

We found the Stonechat common enough in the Delta, and I shot one as far south as Gebel Silsilis, but I never detected Hemprich's Stonechat. Captain Shelley gives as its distinguishing mark, "basal half of the tail white." This is not very apparent in a female in his collection shot at Esné. My Silsilis specimen is such a very light bird that I think it may possibly not be *S. rubicola*. Through the kindness of Mr. Sharpe I compared it with a large series at the British Museum, but I was unable to determine it satisfactorily.

72. WHINCHAT, *Saxicola rubetra* (Linn.).

I had expected to meet with this species during the winter in the Delta, but I only saw a few, males, towards the end of April in returning down the Nile.

73. WHITE-SPOTTED BLUETHROAT, *Ruticilla leucocyana*
(Brehm.).

I shot one, which I have no doubt is a female, at Silsilis, on the 3rd of April, with an entirely white throat ; also a male at Samanhoud with only a little red.   The red-spotted are decidedly much the commoner.

74. RED-SPOTTED BLUETHROAT, *Ruticilla suecica* (Linn.).

This proved to be not near so common above Cairo as in the Delta, where I should say it is one of the commonest small birds in winter.   In May and June I did not shoot one: it may be therefore that it leaves in summer.   It is a bird that is almost always on the ground, and you may recognise them immediately by their tails, yet it is exceedingly difficult to get a sight of the breast spot, as they invariably turn their backs upon you.

75. REDSTART, *Ruticilla phœnicurus* (Linn.).

This bird appears to be resident in small numbers. Captain Shelley hints as much, and Dr. Adams, whose notes refer to November and the two following months, says— "Not uncommon in Lower Egypt, and seen at Thebes" (Ibis, 1864, p. 18).   Mr. Allen, however, who was a very correct observer, says it is *not* seen during the winter.   This is a point for further investigation.   We did not shoot one until the 31st of March, after which it was rather common.

M

In this species, and in the case of most of the spring migrants, the males came first. The specimen I brought home is still in winter plumage as to the throat.

✳76. BLACK REDSTART, *Ruticilla titys* (Scop.).

This is a common bird in Europe, but it is scarce in Egypt. We however saw six, viz., four (upon trees) in the Delta and two at the Pyramids, and shot five of them. One of the males had no white on the wing. I have a Plymouth specimen without it—one of those alluded to by Mr. Gatcombe in Part V. of the fourth edition of Yarrell's " British Birds." With regard to the spelling of the word *titys*, see the Ann. of N. H. for 1872, p. 227.

77. NIGHTINGALE, *Daulias luscinia* (Linn.);
Philomela luscinia; " Bulbul."

We encountered some Nightingales at Thebes on the 13th of April, and shot two, midway between the Tombs of the Kings and the river. I think there were five in all, evidently a migratory party on their way to Europe. We were not regaled with their delightful notes.

✳78. GREAT SEDGE WARBLER, *Acrocephalus arundinaceus*
(Linn.).

I bought one at Alexandria, which I was informed had been got at Ramleh.

79. CLAMOROUS SEDGE WARBLER, *Acrocephalus
stentoreus* (Ehr.).

This is doubtless resident, as we got one at Damietta on the 23rd of January. I believe it had not been got before in the winter.   On the 29th I went out on purpose to shoot some, but though three were seen, their skulking habits rendered it impossible to get them.   I have nothing to add to the admirable account given by·Captain Shelley, beyond confirming the accuracy of his observations.

✳80.   REED WARBLER, *Acrocephalus streperus* (Vieillot);
Salicaria arundinacea.

On the 31st of March I shot two in a barley field at Silsilis, and the following week I saw a few more.   We found it again in June among the reeds at Lake Faioum.

81.   SAVI'S WARBLER, *Acrocephalus luscinoides* (Savi).

Single ones were seen between Siout and Girgeh in the luxuriant corn fields, but none were got.   Captain Shelley's account of their habits agrees exactly with my observations. He only brought home one specimen (Ibis, 1871, p. 132).

82.   SEDGE WARBLER, *Acrocephalus schœnobœnus* (Linn.);
Salicaria phragmitis (Bech.).

A few seen in the barley fields at Silsilis the first week in April, and others in ditches at Minieh the beginning of May.   I did not shoot any there, but I brought home one example from Damietta.   It is decidedly greyer than British ones, but this may be owing to winter plumage.

83.   MOUSTACHED WARBLER, *Acrocephalus melanopogon*
(Tem.).

I shot two or three at Damietta in the winter.   It was met with nowhere else.

84. RUFOUS WARBLER, *Aedon galactodes* (Tem.).

Was got first on the 24th of March, and shortly afterwards it had become common in the tobacco fields, etc. It is very fond of the lower branches of the Sont tree. I have seen *one* perch as high up as twenty feet, but that is exceptional. It is generally to be seen upon the ground, strutting about with its tail cocked up. I found this species at the Faioum. In Dr. Bree's translation of Heuglin, it is stated that Dr. Hartman observed one at the end of November in Lower Egypt, but I cannot help suspecting that there may have been a mistake as to the species seen by him.

✳85. ORPHEAN WARBLER, *Sylvia orphea* (Tem.).

I shot this in a low tree near Benisouef, February 24th. It appeared to be alone : I did not see another one, and indeed I should not expect it to be mated so early.

86. BLACK-HEADED WARBLER, *Sylvia melanocephala* (Gm.).

I hardly know if I am justified in including it, but every other writer seems to have found it common. Mr. E. C. Taylor even goes so far as to say that it is perhaps the most abundant Warbler in March (Ibis for 1867, p. 62). I believe that I saw it once or twice ; and as the probabilities are thus strongly in its favour, perhaps I should be least justified in omitting it.

87. LESSER WHITETHROAT, *Sylvia curruca* (Linn.).

Probably this is a migrant which winters in Egypt further south than the Chiff-Chaff, and yet not so far as the majority of the Warblers.   Whether any stop north of Thebes during the winter I cannot say.   We first met with them on the 1st of March at Minieh, and as we progressed further south they seemed to get commoner every day, until at Assouan they literally swarmed.   I shot one in which the feathers of the crown were stained by something it had been feeding upon, bright purple.*

88.   GREATER WHITETHROAT, *Sylvia rufa* (Bodd).

I shot one on the 14th of April near Karnac.   It is very much rarer than the Lesser Whitethroat, the above being the only specimen we obtained.

89.   LONG-TAILED DRYMŒCA, *Drymœca gracilis* (Rupp).

I think this minute species is commonest at the Faioum, where I obtained the egg, but it is not nearly so common on the Nile as the Fantail.   I saw some on a little island on lake Menzaleh, which must have made a long flight to get there.   It is very comical to see the young birds which have no tails.

90.   FANTAIL WARBLER, *Cisticola schœnicola* (Bp.).

Resident and common in every field.   When frightened it rises angrily into the air, going straight up with its jerking flight, and uttering a loud note for so small a bird.   I

---

* The Lesser Whitethroat is decidedly common near London.   In the beginning of September I have seen nearly fifty alive in a single shop, all of which had been caught in the vicinity of the metropolis. Further north it is rarer.   In Durham, for instance, though some may be met with at Darlington, it is so uncommon at Teesmouth that I never shot but one there.

was never lucky enough to find a new nest: indeed, broods
of young flyers were to be seen by the end of March.   I
saw the first that could fly on the 15th.

91.   OLIVACEOUS WARBLER, *Hypolais pallida* (Ehr.);
Sylvia elœica, auct.

Found apparently over the whole country in summer.   I
shot one as we were coming down, at Minieh, about the 1st
of March, and at the Faioum it was tolerably common.   But
it was most abundant at Assouan where there was hardly
a camelthorn which was not swarming with these birds.
Strange to say, Messrs. Adams, Taylor, and Smith appear
not to have met with it.

92.   WILLOW WARBLER, *Phylloscopus trochilus* (Linn.).

I am not sure whether this bird or the Chiff-Chaff is the
commoner in the Delta, as I confess I did not accurately
distinguish between them.   There, I never could find any
other sort of Warblers.   As spring advanced it became
rapidly scarcer, but two were shot and others seen, as late
as the 27th of March at Philœ.

93.   CHIFF-CHAFF, *Phylloscopus collybita* (Vieill.);
Sylvia rufa, auct.

In the Delta in winter the Chiff-Chaff frequents every
bush, and is seldom seen singly.   The smaller Warblers are
all classed under the name of *Abu Fisai*.   As I have already stated, I owe most of the Arab names to the courtesy
of M. Filliponi.   It must be borne in mind that they were
collected at Damietta, for I noticed that some of the common ones were pronounced differently in Upper Egypt.

94. BONELLI'S WARBLER, *Phylloscopus bonellii* (Vieill).

Naturally Dr. Adams failed to meet with this in the winter. It is a spring migrant. We first got it at the most southern point of our journey, Philœ, on the 27th of March. It may be best distinguished from the Willow Warbler by the underparts being white from the vent to the beak very faintly shaded, and by the lower part of the back being yellow. My specimens are rather lighter in the back than two Spanish ones in my collection, marked Vittoria and Gibraltar.

OBS. SUBALPINE WARBLER, *Sylvia subalpina*, Bon.

I thought I saw this once in April, but may easily have been mistaken.

95. TREE PIPIT, *Anthus trivialis* (Linn.);
A. arboreus (Bech).

Captain Shelley says this bird arrives about March, but the first I shot was on the 23rd of April, after which I saw it plentifully in the groves. On being flushed from the ground, it would generally fly into an upper branch of the nearest tree.

96. RED-THROATED PIPIT, *Anthus cervinus* (Pall.);
A. cecilii, Aud. (Desc. de l'Egypt, p. 281, 1825); *A. coutellii*,
Aud., ? l.c.

This was extremely common, more particularly in the Delta, where you could hardly cross a field without seeing numbers of them. I shot some without the least red on the throat in January and February, others with only a little.   Some naturalists consider that *A. cervinus* and *A. pratensis* are not to be distinguished in winter, but there is an appreciable difference in the colour of the back.   I am not aware that I saw any Pipits at the Faioum.

97.   WATER PIPIT, *Anthus spipoletta* (Linn.).

I shot one at Mientanosara, near Ziftey, February 6th, and bought another in the market at Cairo.

98.   TAWNY PIPIT, *Anthus campestris* (Linn.).

Is rather common.   Specimens shot out of a flock on March 12th were in winter plumage, while some shot before were in breeding plumage.   I never saw it perch on trees, which the *Anthus cervinus* sometimes does.

99.   WHITE-WINGED WAGTAIL, *Motacilla vidua*, Sund.

A specimen was obtained at the First Cataract, where everybody meets with it: but it appears that it is not very common even at this, its northern limit, or we should have shot more than one.

100.   WHITE WAGTAIL, *Motacilla alba*, Linn.;
"Abu fasada."

This is by far the commonest bird in the Delta in the winter.   And really they rather pall on you after a time, for one sees White Wagtails at every step, in every field, on every pathway, and frequently in company with Sand-pipers on the sand-banks—singly, in pairs, in family parties, in flocks of hundreds;   and sometimes they came upon the Diabeyha.   A large flock will generally have some Red-throated Pipits with it. But as spring draws on and one goes further south, both these birds become scarcer : indeed I do not remember seeing any White Wagtails in June. The last great flock I saw was on the 12th of March,—a countless stream migrating northwards. The next day there was not one. Wilkinson says that *Abou fasada* means " Father of corruption." An explanation of this name more probable than that which he and Dr. Adams favour, has been given to me, viz., that the Wagtail seeks its food (small flies) among the droppings of the cattle.

✱101. GREY WAGTAIL, *Motacilla sulphurea* (Bech).

I got this the first day we went out. During January and the early part of February I saw at least six, all alone. I observed one pecking about and flirting its tail in a boat in the town of Mansourah, and more than a fortnight afterwards, when we were coming back, I saw it again in the same place.

102. *Budytes flava* (Linn.), *M. neglecta*, Gould.

103. *Budytes viridis* (Gmel.).

In Egypt, at any rate, these two "species" cannot be kept apart ; but as the latest authorities still sunder them, of course I cannot do better than follow suit. They are very generally distributed, but specimens without the eye stripe are commoner than those with. At the end of April I saw large flocks of young birds of the year. They are very different in colour from the old ones, having on either side the throat a marked black band, and no yellow at all. They were like Mr. Dresser's figure of the young *B. flava* (*loc. cit*).

104. BLACK-HEADED YELLOW WAGTAIL, *Budytes melanocephala*, Savi.

Of this trio of Wagtails the Black-headed was the commonest in Upper Egypt, but we never saw it in the Delta. Some of the old males were magnificent. I have found it to consort with *B. flava* (with the eye stripe). I have seen both sorts running in and out among the goats, and picking up the insects behind them, and have killed them both at one shot. They are very fond of cattle, particularly on a field of grass, which is rather a rare thing in Egypt. Splendid old cocks were sometimes to be seen by melon fields, poppy fields, and corn fields, the contrast of black and yellow glistening as they ran about among the herbage, but without wagging their tails so much as English Wagtails would have done ; or feeding in a wet ploughed field where it is amazing how they can be a minute without getting muddy. Where the river's edge was sand or mud I seldom saw them, and I never detected one perching in a tree. When we came upon a flock I considered that they were migrating. If there were forty or fifty birds, the number of males would not exceed ten.

105. CHAFFINCH, *Fringilla cœlebs*, Linn.

Three or four times I met with small flocks on the trees, in the Delta, clad in the same suit which we know them in at home.

106. COMMON SPARROW, *Passer domesticus* (L.) ; "Asfur dururi."

Egyptian Sparrows are certainly less obtrusive than English ones, but they show the same dependance on man, and

are as much at home among the mud-built hovels of an
Arab village as in the streets of Belgravia; and their plumage is brighter and cleaner.   The roofs of the fellahin's huts,
built of mud and straw, are a favourite resort for a flock to
cluster upon, or small road-side bushes of the long-thorned
tribe.   About the middle of March they betake themselves
to the fields of ripening corn, and I sometimes roused very
large flocks indeed.   Compared with English Sparrows, the
crown of the head is decidedly greyer.*

107.   SPANISH SPARROW, *Passer salicicola*, Vieillot.

As to the relative abundance of this species, my observations lead me to agree with Captain Shelley (Ibis, 1871,
p. 141), but certainly not with his predecessors.   I only met
with it in the Delta, and there it was far less numerous than
the Common Sparrow (*P. domesticus*, Linn.)†

108.   TRUMPETER BULLFINCH, *Erythrospiza githaginea*
(Licht.); *Pyrrhula payraudæi*, Audouin.

First seen at Minieh, after which hardly a day passed but
the clear tinkling note of the Trumpeter Bullfinch was heard,
and on some occasions, as at Gebel Silsilis, very large flocks
of them were seen.   It was an old Algerian acquaintance,

---

* I have more than once met with a variety of the (cock) Sparrow in
England, having the throat and chest, which normally should be black,
a rather bright chocolate brown.

† Mr. Hazel states in "Naturalist" for 1853, p. 20., that a *Fringilla
Hispaniolensis* was shot in some woods near Portsmouth, and afterwards placed in the Museum of the Philosophical Society.   From
enquiries I have made I believe that museum is now broken up, but
the specimen may be at Haslar Hospital Museum.

there considered rather rare. It is almost always on the ground in the fields and not in the desert.*

109. LINNET, *Linota cannabina* (Linn.).

Flocks were sometimes seen in the Delta, and specimens shot. I had noted down " Cairo, February 18th," as the last appearance of this Finch ; but to my surprise, on the 21st of April I saw three near Girgeh, but unluckily failed to get one. The cock which I brought home, marked the 13th of February, has the red breast which in England characterises the breeding plumage.

OBS. BUNTINGS.

We saw no Buntings at all. This seems singular. Canon Tristram obtained seven species in Palestine.

110. BIFASCIATED LARK, *Certhilauda alaudipes* (Desfontaines) ; *C. salvini*, Tristr.

I am rather surprised that Captain Shelley did not find this bird commoner. I saw it twice in the market at Cairo, and twice in our shooting excursions, viz., at Gow and Gebel Silsilis. At the latter place a flock of about a dozen appeared to have taken up their quarters on a little sandy waste about two miles from the river. Shooting a portion of them did not frighten the rest away, as I saw them every

---

* Collectors naturally think that if they go a couple of miles inland beyond the beaten track of tourists they will find birds plentiful ; but in reality there is nothing beyond the limits of vegetation, a limit which varied greatly, but never in the largest plain we came to, extended beyond a few miles from the banks of the Nile.

time I went, running swiftly over the sand. Their legs are white, and their bleached appearance is most typical of the true desert. They varied somewhat in plumage. One was evidently a bird of the year—though so early—April 3rd, with crescent markings on the upper plumage like a young *Cursorius gallicus*, and no chest spots; but what struck me most was the extraordinary difference in length of beak, and in size. The smallest measured $7\frac{7}{8}$ in. ; the largest 9 inches. The bill of the smallest was broken, but the culmen of the next measured $\frac{7}{8}$, while the largest was $1\frac{1}{8}$ in. My two smallest specimens I attribute to *C. salvini* (Tristram), but as Mr. Dresser has united that with *C. desertorum, (loc. cit.)* I do the same.

111. SKYLARK, *Alauda arvensis*, Linn. ;
A. intermedia, Swinhoe.

Rather common in the Delta, where I shot one on the 13th of January. The last I saw was in the market at Cairo on the 17th of February.

112. CRESTED LARK, *Alauda cristata*, Linn. ;
"Umbar" or "Kunbarah."

There is little to be said of this very common resident. They pair early, and I often found their eggs. On the 2nd of March I saw a young one already able to fly. By the time they can fly a little the crest is well developed: it differs from the crest of the adult in being tipped with white.

I have seen Crested Larks panting with the heat when the thermometer stood at about 85°, and again when it was nearly 100°. Sonnini mentions having noticed them "in the middle of the day with their bills half open, and the muscles of their breasts agitated, breathing with difficulty, as if they panted for respiration" (*o. c.*, III., p. 199). I have had my attention drawn to the same thing in other and larger birds.

113. SHORT-TOED LARK, *Calandrella brachydactyla* (Leisler).

First met with on the 3rd of March, and for the next ten days it was very common in flocks, no doubt migrating northwards. After that there was a decided lull. Captain Shelley thinks it does not stay to breed (Ibis, 1871, p. 140.) I certainly saw none in June, and I do not think I saw any in May. It is very terrestrial and very gregarious, preferring the plains, where its light-coloured plumage, assimilating to the colour of the surrounding ground, is a protection. None of my specimens have the crown at all rufous.

114. TRISTRAM'S DESERT LARK, *Ammomanes fraterculus,* Tristr.

Mr. Dresser unites this with *A. deserti* (Licht.), but looking to my series of seven specimens, I think there surely is enough difference in colouring between them and *A. deserti* to earn them specific rank. I found them very common from Thebes to Assouan, generally in pairs. In one of my specimens the culmen is 0.6; in another 0.45.

115. DESERT LARK, *Ammomanes deserti* (Licht.); *A. isabellina* (Tem.).

I shot one at Feshn on the 25th of February on the east bank, where a few pairs were singing blithely upon the stony barren hills.

116. STARLING, *Sturnus vulgaris*, Linn. (Hasselquist 47) ;
" Zarzur."

Small flocks seen not unfrequently in the Delta and Middle Egypt.*

117. BROWN-NECKED RAVEN, *Corvus umbrinus*,
Hedenborg.

A Raven was only once distinctly recognized in the Delta. Up the river they were generally seen in pairs, or gathered together in a flock—sometimes as many as forty together—near some carcase; and yet I have sometimes seen a large number of them where there was apparently nothing to attract them. They were not particularly hard to shoot, and we had soon got enough. I only once found a nest; it was on a solitary palm tree. The hen sat close.

Only one of those we shot could strictly be called brown-necked : it was a fine old bird. Some of the others were entirely black, so that it was an excusable error in certain former observers to mistake them for our English Raven. The immature ones are entirely black also. I believe that the variation in size, which I dare say has been noticed by others besides myself, is sexual. One specimen had the nasal feathers a dull yellow.

Yarrell, in his 1st edition (B. B. II., 65), accredits the English Raven with being found in Egypt. He says that

---

* In Norfolk, Starlings pair as early as the 2nd of February. As spring advances the habits of these birds undergo a change. Perched upon an ash tree or the gable of a barn, they raise their neck hackles to one another, and seek rather than avoid the proximity of man. One is surprised at the noise which they now make, and there is no doubt that they imitate other birds, such as Hens, Crows, Jackdaws, Ducks, etc. I never listen to them without feeling convinced that this is what they are really doing, but it all ceases by the 1st of May.

it is not molested, its services in removing offal or putrid flesh being considered useful. This is hardly correct even of the Brown-necked species, which I never saw flying in or over an Egyptian town.

118. ABYSSINIAN RAVEN, *Corvus affinis*, Rüpp.

This scarce bird is found in Egypt, but to my great regret I did not get a specimen. Soon after we anchored at Thebes I saw a pair on the sand, and tried to get near them both by land and water. On another occasion, having observed a quantity of Ravens congregated at a certain spot, one of my friends tried the experiment of lying down. The Ravens soon lost their shyness, and after he had lain still for some time, one of the rare "Abyssinians" came within shot, but just as he pulled the trigger a common one got in the line and received the charge. Altogether I saw four pairs, of which three pairs were with flocks of the Brown-necked Raven. I suppose the bird has been frequently overlooked, but the shape of its wings and tail are so different from the common one, that it ought to be distinguished instantly. At p. 71 of the "Ibis" for 1866, the distinctions are given in detail with a woodcut.

119. HOODED CROW, *Corvus cornix*, Linn.
(Hasselquist 85); "Gurab awar," i.e. The One-eyed Crow.

The "Hoodey" is the commonest of the larger birds in the Delta, and the tamest, but further south they are scarcer. One was seen at Boulac (Cairo) with a white patch on its breast, and another pied one was seen lower down the river. I have once or twice observed them perch on the Buffaloes' backs.

120. THE ROOK, *Corvus frugilegus*, Linn.

This was long ago ascertained to be Egyptian by Hemprich and Ehrenberg. I frequently saw flocks of them in the Delta—once a very large flock. On the 13th of February, as I was standing on the deck of the Diabeyha, I saw a lot of them crossing over the river, and shot two from where I stood. One was a glossy old bird, his visage was as shaven as any Rook's I ever saw; the other was a younger one which had kept its nasal bristles. There is nothing to call for remark in this. It is well known that in every Rookery a few keep the facial bristles until long after Christmas. I have shot a fine old glossy bird with them on the 1st of March in England.

121. WRYNECK, *Jynx torquilla*, Linn.

I shot two in Upper Egypt in April, but the bird is not common.

122. SCHIMPERS' PIGEON, *Columba schimperi*, Bp.

123. ROCK DOVE, *Columba livia*, Linn.; "Hamam agrak."

I bracket these two together, as I could not draw any line between them. At the same time it must not be supposed that they are equally common, for Schimper's quite outnumbers the other. Indeed I am not sure that I saw any Rock Doves which were quite like British ones.

The pigeon villages on the Nile are indeed a sight. The largest is at Bellianeh, near Girgeh. These pigeons' habitations differ very much in construction and shape. Sometimes they are funny little towers of brick and mortar, but more often they are the upper stories of the houses of the

N

fellaheen, who bear the mess and the fleas therein engendered with Oriental stolidity. The cote consists of numerous pots, a foot or so in diameter, which are let in, one above the other, with little round apertures for the pigeons to go in at. Branches are stuck into the masonry all round for the pigeons to perch upon. In Upper Egypt the pigeon houses are square and not generally domed. In Lower Egypt they are quite different, some of them being like ant-hills with the tops of the cone shaved off; but see Mr. Fairholt's remarks in "Up the Nile," pp. 112—120.

Rock Pigeons have been so brought under domestication in many countries that it is hard to say which are really wild ones, and nowhere more so than in Egypt. Even when we saw them in cliffs away from houses, at Abou-fœder and Gebel-El-Thayr, there were dark birds of domestic origin among them. At Abou-fœder, on the 3rd of May, there may have been thirty pairs scattered along the base of the cliff, of which I should think at least ten pairs consisted of one mottled bird, and one Rock or Schimper's. There was even one pale fawn-coloured bird paired with a Schimper's. The way in which they settle on the water to drink— like Gulls—has been remarked.* They seem to drink far more than other birds. All day, from every village, streams of them are passing to and returning from the nearest sandbank. They go to roost early. The young are capital, done spatch-cock fashion, and the old make good soup. I never heard any objection made to shooting them except in the Delta—where they are much less numerous—at a time when they had young.

---

* A writer in the "Field" newspaper (June 26th, 1875) narrates an instance of a Wood-Pigeon settling to drink, but it alighted on the water with outspread wings, which I never saw any of the Egyptian Pigeons do.

124.   TURTLE DOVE, *Turtur auritus* (Linn.)
"Yamâmeh."

First seen on the 2nd of April.   By the end of the month only a portion were paired.   They are much wilder than the other Doves.   Owing to their far lighter colouring, they are generally easy to be told from *Turtur isabellinus* at a considerable distance: indeed, they are lighter than any English examples I ever saw.   We certainly did not find the difference in time of arrival between the two nearly so great as Captain Shelley did.   I have notes of seeing two large flocks in May—100 or 200 in each—one at the Khedive's nursery garden at Minieh, the other on a bank at Fechn feeding upon the seeds of a species of thistle.

124B.   *Turtur isabellinus*, Bp., *T. sharpii*, Shelley.

Captain Shelley says this bird arrives in the beginning of February, but though a sharp look-out was kept by us, we did not get any before the 26th of March, when five were shot on Elephantine Island.   For the next ten days it was very common, and I saw some large flocks evidently migrating. Then it grew scarcer, and I began to think we had reached its northern limits; but I found it again at the Faioum. Here it probably nidifies among the tamarisk bushes, though I often saw it out on the lake.   The specimens we shot at the Faioum were not so sandy-coloured, nor near so bright as those we killed before.   One shot on the 27th of March contained a perfect egg ready for exclusion.

I am informed by Captain Shelley and Mr. E. C. Taylor that this species is *T. isabellinus*, though I should never have supposed it from Bonaparte's figure, but the type has been examined, and that settles the question.

125. PALM DOVE, *Turtur senegalensis* (Linn.); "Gumri."

It is hard to say where the Palm Dove is not found, so universally is it spread through the length and breadth of Egypt. It will probably be the first bird which the observer meets with when he sets foot on the quay of Alexandria, perhaps cooing on some stucco cornice, perhaps fluttering among the boats in the harbour. The only part where we did not find it was the northern portion of the Damietta branch, and there for more than three weeks it certainly was conspicuous for its absence. These Doves frequent the Palm, Acacia, Nabuk, and every other kind of tree that is known to grow in Egypt, and practise their love-arts in the green foliage. By night they roost in hundreds in some Orange trees at a village near Benisouef, and a grove of dwarf Palms is often a favourite place. In towns and villages there are always a good many ; whether consisting of the rickety tenements of the natives, or the modern innovation of lath and plaster, is all the same to the confiding Palm Dove. I saw some flying about the inside of a large sugar manufactory, where they appeared quite at home. I have often heard of their coming into rooms, and on one occasion one came into the cabin of our Diabeyha, and another day a pair settled on the awning; but it must be understood that they are not in any sense domesticated. Of their own free will they affect the society of man, and he protects them.

The immature Palm Dove is brown, and so unlike its parents that it might be taken for a different species. There is also an extraordinary amount of variation in the adults, a circumstance to which my attention was particularly drawn by shooting a very light yellowish female on the 12th of March. The differences lie especially in the tints.

of the head and neck. I could not reconcile them, and I suspect that the recent subdivision of *Turtur auritus* may before long be followed by a subdivision of *T. senegalensis*.

126. SINGED SAND-GROUSE, *Pterocles exustus*, Tem. ; "Gutta."

This species, which rejoices in the name of the Singed Sand-Grouse, is better known to the English as the "Desert Partridge." As a fine sporting bird and very fair eating, it finds favour with the sportsman in a country where there is so little game as Egypt. Unfortunately it is not very common, and so local that it is quite a lucky chance to meet with it; yet by dint of working for them I succeeded in shooting a good many at different places, notably at Beni-souef, (close to the town) Gow-El-Kebir, Manfalout, and Biba, and did not find them difficult to bring down if one could get near them ; but besides being local, they have the additional bad quality of being very shy, so that one is first made aware of their presence by their oft repeated "*gŭttă gŭttă*," as they are scudding away far out of shot. I believe this cry is never uttered on the ground. The specific name of one of the Algerian Sandgrouse (much more beautiful than either of the Egyptian) *P. alchata*, is derived from the native name which expresses the note. In the middle of April I noticed that they had become much more silent. Doubtless they had to think of the important duty of incubation. I apprehend that they continue to be gregarious when nesting, as they were seen in flocks at the Faioum in June. They are restless birds ; seldom still, and seldom silent. We generally saw them in coveys of about fifteen, flying very high and very straight, to or from the water in the early morning.

It is said that regularly at break of day they go to drink. Afterwards they spend the noon, some in the desert, and some in the plains of *Halfa* grass, and if there be a bare place of an acre or two near to tents, it is a likely haunt for them. At a place of that kind at Gow I saw a flock of these Sandgrouse and two tame Pigeons, apparently fraternising together very amicably.* It surprised me though I knew their affinity.

The belly of a hen I shot on the 9th of March was entirely black. I do not think it was the breeding plumage.

127. SENEGAL SAND-GROUSE, *Pterocles senegallus* (Linn.)
Symbolœ Physicœ, pl. XV. "Gutta."

The Sand-Grouse at Gebel Silsilis were, I believe, all of this species, but they were so shy that we only obtained two. At Radamr near Keneh I shot five, and we obtained a few more when we returned to Gow, where we had not observed this species in coming up. The furthest north that we saw them on the river was at Benisouef, but they come down to the Faioum, where I was at no loss to recognise one fine flock by their yellow colour. The note is also different: they generally say "*wheep gutta,*" and the Singed Sand-Grouse I believe only say "*gutta.*" One generally saw them early in the morning, flying high up and very wild. They are said to pass the day in the desert, going down to the river to drink in the early morning and in the evening. No doubt they do drink a great deal: some we killed at Gow had as much as a table-spoonful of water in their crops. I think it probable that they are gregarious all the year round, though I am ignorant of their habits after the hatching season.

---

* I possess a Ruff which was shot in Shetland while feeding with some tame Pigeons. The Turnstone has been shot in England in the same companionship (cf. Zoologist, 2652).

128. QUAIL, *Coturnix communis*, Bonnat (Hasselquist, 44) ;
"Semman."

A few winter in Egypt, but not very many : 1875 was
evidently a late season for them. Though most writers
speak of having found them in February, we found no
quantity until March. On March 2nd eight were flushed,
and previously only pairs or single birds were seen.* By
the 14th they had begun to arrive in large quantities. Then
one could realize the scene in the Israelitish camp, when
"the people stood up all that day, and all that night, and
all the next day, and they gathered the Quails ; he that
gathered least gathered ten homers" (*Numb.* xi., 31, 32).
Out of a patch of lentils twenty feet square I have seen, I
may safely say, fifty brace rise.

Although they are gregarious in the strictest sense of the
word, they never fly as a flock, but each, regardless of its
neighbour, goes its own course, straight and quick, about a
yard from the ground. They almost invariably get up at
your feet, and seldom fly more than 400 yards. I never
saw any on passage by day, and it is said that unlike the
Storks they only migrate by night.† As Captain Shelley
remarks, they are very unwilling to rise during the heat of
the day. Morning and evening are the best times to shoot
them ; and ripe barley, or strips of lentils *(ads.)* just ready
to cut, the best places in which to look for them. It is wiser
not to go into barley fields, etc., where the business of har-
vest has commenced, for the following reason, the national
laziness shows itself in the Arab husbandman, who prefers
reaping as he sits, Quails fly low, and his head, hardly

---

* On one day in February as many as seven were seen, of course not
together.

† Possibly it is because Storks are voiceless that they migrate by
day and sleep by night.

visible above the crop, is in danger of receiving the sportsman's charge. I never attempted to make any great bag, but I have frequently shot ten brace. The biggest bag I heard of was eighty brace to one gun, or rather to one sportsman with two guns, at Cairo. The neighbourhood of Cairo is very good; indeed it would be hard to particularise any place which is not good at the right time, but on the whole we nowhere got better shooting than in the plain of Thebes, right up to the very Colossi. Without a dog you must expect to lose a third unless your native is very expert in marking them. By the middle of April the migration was all past. On the 12th we killed thirteen brace: that was the last day we made a bag. After that they became just as scarce as they had been in the Delta in January.

That some stay the summer to breed is certain, and it would appear that a few nest in the winter or early spring, for on the 22nd of March I flushed an early "squeaker" able to fly, which must have been hatched some weeks. I never saw any others. I conclude the natives occasionally catch them for their own consumption, as I was now and then brought a snared one. In Hasselquist's time they netted them in Lower Egypt.

129. CORNCRAKE, *Ortygometra crex* (Linn.)

The only one I saw was a stuffed one at Mr. Mayer's, killed at or near Alexandria.

130. SPOTTED CRAKE, *Porzana maruetta*, Leach.

Was met with at Damietta and Benha in January. Captain Shelley may be right in thinking it a resident, but we did not find any at the Faioum.

✱131. BAILLON'S CRAKE, *Porzana pygmœa* (Naum).

Captain Shelley says he has "no other authority than that of Rüppell" for it, and he appears to consider Rüppell's authority worth very little, but at p. 327 he admits that *P. pygmœa* is a likely bird to be met with.   I shot it in the reeds of a pond at Benha, February 11th.   There were a quantity of *Rallidæ* there—for the size of the place, but I believe they were Spotted Crakes, and perhaps a few Waterhens.   I was attracted to it by its loud note, and after looking steadily for some minutes I saw it moving in the reeds.   I had visited the pond before, on the 15th January, but only saw a few Snipes and Dabchicks.   On one other occasion I saw an example, viz., on the 26th of January, on an island on Lake Menzaleh.   I flushed it twice, but could not rise it a third time; for though there was not a bush on the island, there was a good deal of scrubby stuff like heather, as high as a man's knee.

132. WATER-RAIL, *Rallus aquaticus*, Linn.

I saw one in the market at Alexandria on the 8th of January.

**133. WATER-HEN, *Gallinula chloropus* (Linn.)
" Misticavi."**

Markets at Alexandria and Cairo.   I am not sure if I ever saw it alive, but the species must be pretty common in the Delta to have an Arabic name.*

---

* The Water-Hen is but a blind flyer at times.   In February, 1838, my father's spaniel flushed one, which flew against a rail with such violence that it knocked itself completely over.

134. GREEN-BACKED PORPHYRIO,
Porphyrio smaragdonotus, Tem.; *P. ægyptiacus*, Heugl.;
P. hyacinthinus, Brehm, jun, nec Temm.;
P. chloronotus, Brehm.
(Poule de Ris, Hasselquist); "Dick sultani."

We made the acquaintance of this fine bird at the Faïoum, where it was frequently to be seen stalking about among the reeds at the mouth of the Bar-El-Wady canal. M. Filliponi informs me that they were once common at Damietta, but now are rare. He writes :—"Vers le 1856, chaque chasseur Arabe pourrait en tuer jusqu'à 30 par jour" *(in. litt.).*

They appear to have been common there in Hasselquist's time (1751), under the name of *Poule de Ris.** He says :—

" This is of the Hen tribe.   *   *   *   *   They come in May and the following months, taking up their quarters in the rice fields " (Engl. Trans., p. 211).

Von Heuglin says very much the same of his *P. ægyptiacus*, which Finsch and Hartlaub and Schlegel unite with *P. smaragdonotus* :—

" Common the whole summer in Lower Egypt, especially in the lake of Elku, Damietta, in the rice fields. If I rightly remember it is not there in winter " (Syst. Uebers, p. 65).

I doubt however its being exclusively a summer migrant.

Dr. R. Hartmann met with it at Mareotis (J. f. O., 1863, p. 231).

Chaptain Shelley describes his specimen under the name of *P. hyacinthinus* as having the back and scapulars green like mine. It remains to be seen whether the true *P. hya-*

---

* Sonini has an interesting note on this bird, ("Travels in Egypt," II , p. 57) and mentions that it is called the *Poule de Ris.*

cinthinus, Temm., is really found in Egypt. I have no doubt as to what my birds are, but they are not quite so green as three which I have alive.

Mr. Burton, the taxidermist in Soho, showed me a specimen which was obtained in Egypt some years ago by Mr. Baird.

I must devote a word or two to my tame ones. I have had them some years now, and they could not look better than they do. They are out of doors all the twelve months, but in the winter their cage is covered up at night with matting. I attribute their good health to its being a movable cage, which enables us to give them fresh ground as often as we like. If given fish, they only eat the head. They like a little grass, but their staple diet is sopped bread. For a long time they were dumb, but now not a day passes but they give utterance to the shrill note which carries me back to the swamps of Egypt.

134B. COOT, *Fulica atra*, Linn. (Hasselquist, 34).

I never saw any Coots on the river or at Birket-El-Kairoun, but at Lake Menzaleh I saw such multitudes as I should not have believed possible. See page 93 for an account of the method of taking them with a casting net.*

135. SOLITARY SNIPE, *Gallinago major* (Gmel.).

One at M. Filliponi's killed at Damietta. I have a very good female obtained on the 9th of May, 1863, by Mr. Allen at Damietta ; but it is not a common bird.

---

* Very few authors have noticed that the Coot at a certain age— just at that period when it begins to exchange down for feathers, has all the breast, foreneck, and chin, pure white. By the 17th of August these parts have generally turned grey.

136. SNIPE, *Gallinago media*, Leach ; " Kennes."

Very few Snipes were seen by us between Cairo and Damietta. Between the 13th January and the 20th we only shot 4½ couple. It was not until we came to El-Badalki on January 20th that we found them in great numbers, on the east bank, about four miles south of Damietta. I suppose it is the place alluded to by Captain Shelley at p. 25 *(o. c.)*. We shot over twenty couple that afternoon. Afterwards we were shown several marshes on the edge of Lake Menzaleh, and within easy donkey ride of Damietta, where very good bags might be easily made. They were inferior eating to English Snipes.

We did not expect to find any in our voyage up the Nile. Indeed there are no marshes suitable for them, but ten or twelve were shot, chiefly single specimens, on the sandbanks and backwaters. I am rather surprised that we met with so many. The last was on the 21st of April, and I think I remember flushing another or two about the 1st of May. I suppose however that there must be some place near Cairo where they are plentiful, as I heard of one gun getting forty couple on the 11th of January in that neighbourhood.

The majority had the outer tail feathers slightly elongated, though not quite so much as one I got at Moscow on the 20th of September, 1869 *(vide ante)*. This variety has received the name of *S. brehmi*.

137. JACK SNIPE, *Gallinago gallinula* (Linn.)

Very plentiful in the marshes at Damietta; its numbers in proportion to the Common Snipe being slightly more than would be the case in England ; for instance, a third of the bag would probably be Jacks. We did not see many anywhere else, and none above Cairo that I remember.

OBS. WOODCOCK. *Scolopax rusticola*, Linn.

It is possible that the Woodcock may come to
Egypt in very small numbers every winter, for
I conversed with three or four people at Cairo
who had met with it or heard from others of its
occurrence. Von Heuglin speaks of it as found
in March; and as it is a pure migrant and goes
to Algeria, I do not see why it should not be
found in northern Egypt; but I can hold out
no hope of cock-shooting to the adventurous
traveller such as he may get in Greece, or nearer
home, in Ireland.

138. MARSH SANDPIPER, *Totanus stagnatilis*, Bechst.

This was met with at El-Badalki, and other marshes near
Damietta, in January, sometimes in flocks; but what few
we saw in Upper Egypt in April were single birds. I do
not think it breeds at the Faioum. The tail-bars are much
narrower than in the Green Sandpiper, with which only a
casual observer would confound it.

139. GREEN SANDPIPER, *Totanus ochropus* (Linn.).

I did not find it nearly so common in Upper as in Lower
Egypt, where it was one of the commonest birds. It was
not seen at the Faioum. Probably it is scarce in summer.

140. WOOD SANDPIPER, *Totanus glareola* (Linn.).

I found the Wood Sandpiper frequenting the same localities as the Green, but it was by no means so abundant.
Some remain as late as May.

141. COMMON SANDPIPER, *Totanus hypoleucus* (Linn.).

This and Temminck's Stint were the commonest Sand-pipers in the Delta, but there is one marked difference in their habits; the latter goes in flocks, the former is almost invariably single. The Common Sandpiper is also nearly as abundant in the upper part of Egypt, and I saw a few at the Faioum.

The agility with which they dive is well known, as is their characteristic flight. With drooping wings they skim so low over the water that the points almost touch it, uttering "*wheet, wheet*" as they fly. The bird describes a semi-circle and settles again at no great distance; or if a a flock of Green Sandpipers or "Pluvians" are passing, he makes a dash at them and goes up stream in the capacity of "plover's page" to their rear-guard.

In general I believe the very small water insects are their food, but I once saw a very ambitious one with what I feel sure was a frog. He was walking about as if he did not know what to do with it; and truly it was a large morsel for such a mouth. Those who have used carbolic acid for preserving birds must have remarked what very small mouths the Sandpiper tribe have.

Some time ago there was a discussion in the "Zoologist" about the diving powers of the Common Sandpiper. I have seen it in England dive on three or four occasions when wounded, and I once caught one at Dungeness with my hand, in the act of diving, but I never saw it dive for pleasure. A gentleman who knows the bird well, told me that on one occasion he saw one dive to escape a Merlin, which Merlin he immediately afterwards struck into the water with his fishing rod.

142. LITTLE STINT, *Tringa minuta*, Leisl.

The Little Stint though very abundant in the Delta, and mixing with Temminck's Stint, was decidedly the least abundant of the two in 1875. A few which may have come from south of the equator, passed through Egypt late in spring. Specimens were shot on the 27th and 28th of April, and on the 7th of May; and in June I found it again at the Faioum, where it was rather common, and where I did not see any Temminck's Stints.

143. TEMMINCK'S STINT, *Tringa temminckii*, Leisl.

I found this plentiful in the Delta, and often in flocks. I shot two on the 21st of April, which were still in winter plumage; and I do not think I saw many after that. Captain Shelley does not state whether he considers this species to be resident, but I should not be much surprised if it was. In the winter plumage, this is as different on the back from the Little Stint as it is in spring and autumn. The Little Stint is mottled; the Temminck's is uniform.

✻144. DUNLIN, *Tringa cinclus*, Linn.

January 8th, two in the market at Alexandria. February 6th, one in the market at Cairo.

145. PIGMY CURLEW, *Tringa subarquata*, Güld.

I shot two in May, near Gebel-Abou-Fœder, and again in June I met with some at the Faioum. One shot by me on the 7th was in beautiful summer plumage.

Mr. E. C. Taylor informs me, that since the publication of his last list he has obtained this species at Port Said.*

✳146. SANDERLING, *Calidris arenaria* (Linn.).

I was much pleased at seeing some flocks on the 6th and 8th of May near Beni-Hassan, and getting three good specimens which were beginning to assume their breeding dress.†

147. PAINTED SNIPE, *Becassine doré* of the French ; *Rhynchœa capensis* (Linn.).

As the Painted Snipe is a bird which is a good deal sought after by the sportsmen who visit Egypt, it may be advisable to mention all the places where we met with it. At Chek Megahet—a pond in some fields belonging to Mr. Serrur—which lies between Damietta and lake Menzaleh, ten were found and seven killed. Chek Megahet—I give the spelling as near as I can—is half a mile short of the Snipe-marsh called Rogar. At Mientanosara, between Samanhoud and Zifteh, ten were shot as we were going south ; and the next day (February 8th) eight at Kafr-El-Arma, four miles north of Zifteh on the east bank ; and about a mile further on, four more the following morning on the same bank ; making twenty-nine specimens in all, besides four skins which were given us at Damietta. They are very tame birds, and when you think you have thoroughly beaten a place, you had better beat it again, as

---

* In the "Field" of October 9th, 1875, is an interesting letter on the migratory birds of Port Said.

† I have seen a Sanderling in Leadenhall market, London, in full winter plumage as early as the 19th of September, which is a case of very early assumption.

there will probably be some which have not got up.   As they fly a very short distance and go very slowly, it follows that when a colony of ten or twelve are found they are generally nearly all killed.   The only thing which saves them is the propinquity of their reedy haunts to the villages, and the native population who come out to witness the "battue," and are very much in the way.   One colony was established in the village cesspool—a small tussocky place, less than a quarter of a acre—within forty yards of the houses.   The rushes chiefly frequented by this species seemed to be the common flowering sort, with a triangular stem.   Painted Snipes should not be sought for in the Snipe-marsh, or the inundated rice fields: they prefer small reedy ponds, with tussocks such as I describe.   Sometimes we found these places inland, but in general they were only separated from the river by the tow-path.   Here they run about almost like rats, and might often be shot before they get up.   One took refuge in a brick-kiln, and two, strange to relate, were seen to perch on houses!   When only winged, I have seen one hiss with fright at the person who picked it up.   Their edible qualities are not remarkable.   After leaving the Delta we supposed that we had done with them, but a single specimen—the first solitary one we had seen—was shot at Benisouef.   We flushed it from a piece of ground where two of us had been looking twenty minutes for a dead Sandgrouse ; so reluctant are they to rise.   At the Faioum we saw some beautiful specimens, and shot one which had an egg inside it.   They were mostly in moist spots among the tamarisks, but I saw one squat down in the canal at the edge.   It was done to escape detection, and really it looked exactly like a lump of mud in the water.

I do not know whether it has been observed that in June the neck is bulged out in a curious way, and the skin of that part very much stretched.

At Alexandria I saw two unblown eggs with the old

birds from Buhoma.   They were stated to have been taken about the 2nd of June.

Eleven out of the sixteen skins brought home by us were females.   They are gayer. than the males, but the males have a more handsomely mottled wing.   In Savigny's book there is a good picture of a male with its wings spread to show the spotting.

148.   RUFF, *Machetes pugnax* (Linn.).

We did not get the Ruff in the Delta; indeed it was not until we got to Siout that one was shot, out of a small flock, on the Bar-Joseph.   In April, when we were higher up the Nile, some very large flocks were seen upon migration—in particular one flock upon the sand-banks at Erment.   Several times also these birds were seen in fields.   Some of the males which we shot were changing colour, but I never could distinguish any with a symptom of a ruff even in the largest flock.   They evidently throw it out with great rapidity.   According to Montagu it is scarcely completed in May (Ornith. Dict. Suppl.).   At the Faioum in June I saw some flocks of Reeves, but whether they breed in Egypt is not at present ascertained.

149.   CURLEW, *Numenius arquatus* (Linn.).

None were shot, though they were frequently seen.   The birdstuffer at Alexandria, however, had a specimen.

150.   SLENDER-BILLED CURLEW, *Numenius tenuirostris,* Vieill.

I include this with some hesitation, as no specimen was shot, though I believe some were seen both in the Delta and in Upper Egypt.

151.   BLACK-TAILED GODWIT, *Limosa ægocephala* (Linn.);
? " Bigueka Sultani."

At the Faioum we got one out of a small flock: it was still in winter plumage.   I saw this flock about at the mouth of the canal as late as June 11th.   This was the only one we shot; and I have some doubt whether Filliponi really intended the above name for this species.   I suspect one was never got so late before in Egypt.

152.   REDSHANK, *Totanus calidris* (Linn).

Rather common in the Delta.

153.   GREENSHANK, *Totanus canescens* (Gmel.)

We did not shoot more than two or three, yet it is far from uncommon, and probably resident.   It was seen at the Faioum on the 2nd of June.*

154.   GOLDEN PLOVER, *Charadrius pluvialis*, Linn.

Plentiful on the 20th of January at El Badalki, near Damietta.   One flock must have numbered three or four hundred birds; but we did not shoot any, and never fell in with them again.

---

* A painstaking naturalist tells me that Greenshanks are so tame in the breeding season in Scotland, that he has twice stroked the dam upon her eggs, which in one case were eight in number.   A Redshank's "nest" has been taken at Hickling in Norfolk with eight eggs, and it was surmised by the finder that two birds had laid together.   Another was taken at Wells with seven.

155. MIDDLE RING PLOVER, *Ægialitis intermedius*
(Ménétr.).

Is not uncommon in the Delta, associating with the
smaller species, but we did not get any south of Cairo.

156. LITTLE RING PLOVER, *Ægialitis fluviatilis*
(Bechst.).

A resident, universally distributed and very common. I
imagine they generally breed by the river; but at Gebel
Silsilis, a small flock had located themselves at the brink of
the desert a mile inland, at a place resembling Thetford
Warren in Norfolk (where *Æ. hiaticula* breeds inland).

How interesting it is to watch these Little Plovers running
nimbly over the sand, or gazing at the shipping on the
river, or with quick movements picking up the minute sub-
stances which constitute their food!

157. KENTISH PLOVER, *Ægialitis cantiana* (Lath.),
(Hasselquist 30).

The Kentish Plover must have been rarer than usual, as
I only shot one at Gow lake (with some *Æ. varius*), and
saw another in the market at Alexandria. Captain Shelley's
remark is that it is a very abundant Plover both in Egypt
and Nubia.

158. AFRICAN SAND PLOVER, *Ægialitis varius* (Vieill.);
Æ. longipes, Heug.;
Fig., Ibis, 1873, p. 262.

I did not find this species consorting with the Little Ring
Plover. It may be that it prefers lakes to the river. I

only met with it twice on the Nile, viz., at Gow lake, where there were some good flocks, and at a much smaller lake, or rather pond, at Samalout; but it was breeding at the Faioum in some numbers. The following is a description of a nestling. Feathers of the head and back edged with rufous; chest and over the eye buff; belly white; wing feathers black; secondaries and greater coverts tipped with white.

159.   LAPWING, *Vanellus vulgaris*, Bechst.; "Tuktak chamy."

Often seen, and occasionally shot. I also remarked its muteness during the winter, noticed by Dr Adams. Of this species, Hasselquist says :—

"Comes in great numbers in the beginning of October, and remains all the winter. I saw it about Cairo the 15th of December, 1750, where it is esteemed good eating" *(l. c.)*.

Captain Shelley says a few remain to breed, but Von Heuglin doubts it, and further corroboration is wanted.

160.   SPUR-WINGED PLOVER, *Hoplopterus spinosus* (Linn.), (Hasselquist 33); "Taktak balad."

Most conspicuous of Nile birds are the Ziczacs or Spur-winged Plovers, and very tame were they in the Delta, where I killed six at a shot as they stood in an irregular line by the edge of a field. Yet it is an unusual thing to see a large flock; more often they are in twos and threes. As far as their gastronomic qualities go they are not worth a cartridge, and we very soon left off shooting at them. They quite pervade Egypt. At the village pool, on every sandbank, in every flooded rice field—go at any season you like, you cannot fail to find them.   Similarly in the young wheat crops and in the clover fields they are quite at home. Sometimes when I have been scanning a clover field, my eye has been arrested by a white patch about the size of a florin, looking for all the world like an Oxeye Daisy ; but though a second glance serves to show that it is not a flower, it will remain still for several seconds, and you may imagine that you see resentment gleaming out of a red eye.   During this time the bird's head is straight towards you, as I have observed a bird's in a bush generally is, and he is working himself into a passion.   His next performance, when he cannot stand being stared out of countenance any longer, is to jerk his body as if someone was pulling at him with a string, to dart up into the air, menacing you with his armed wings, and to give utterance to the loud bi-syllabic cry, which has obtained for him his name of Ziczac.

Many were paired as early as February 1st.   Their evolutions in the breeding season are very curious.   Sometimes they assume the most laughable postures.   At this time they are often to be seen resting on the length of the tarsus, or sitting upon the sand.   I have gone up expecting to find a nest, but there never was one where a bird was sitting. The nests, when we found them, were generally empty— mere hollows in the sand.   Apparently, like Lapwings and Wrens, they make many before using one.   We obtained very few eggs.   Whatever bird or beast ventures near their nests they boldly attack with loud screams.   They are the greatest nuisance to anyone watching in a hole for crocodiles. I should say from my experience that the reptilian monsters were infinitely more indebted to the guardianship of the noisy Ziczac than to the Black-headed Pluvian, and for that reason I should side with those who suppose the former to be the *trochilus* of Herodotus.   His anecdote and its subsequent embellishments have formed the ground for some controversy ; but admitting that the story of the tooth-pick is one founded on fact, it is probable that Herodotus only wrote from hearsay, and knew no more which bird it was than we do.

The Spur-winged Plover is stated in the Zoologist to have occurred in England (Zool., 5041)—a mistake doubt-less.

161.   WHITE-TAILED PLOVER, *Chettusia villotæi* (Audouin).

I bought a skin at Alexandria, but the only example we met with ourselves was shot at Rackaba, near Damietta, on the 30th of January, and being mistaken for a young Ziczac (!) was thrust incontinently into a bag with other game.   A few years ago this was a very rare bird in collections.

162.   *Pluvianus ægyptius* (Linn.), (Hasselquist, 31.)

This is one of the most delicately-coloured birds in Egypt, and others like myself may call to mind the admiration which their first specimen evoked.   It is considered by many to be the crocodile bird of Herodotus ; and Gould, in his " Birds of Asia," makes it the faithful attendant on the monsters.*   I did not see very many in the Delta, nor for some days south of Cairo.   It was most abundant in Middle Egypt as far as Girgeh, after which it became scarcer again until we came to Silsilis.   In the breeding, or rather courting season, their actions are very amusing, and as I often got very near them I could observe their strange postures and attitudes.   I think their colours fade a little after they begin to breed, and their demeanour is sobered by the responsibility of having chicks ; their boisterous

---

* See my note under Spur-winged Plover.

rompings cease, and their emotions tone down as they sub-
side into the modest parents of a hopeful family. When
wounded they dive even better than *Totanus hypoleucos*,
shaking off the crystal drops from their glossy black backs,
and baffling the attempts of your attendant to retrieve them.

The "Pluvian," or Black-headed Plover, as it is more
correctly called, is a noticeable feature in the scenery of the
Nile. Hasselquist characterised it as the Egyptian Dotterel.
He says it is found in the plains feeding on insects, which is
hardly a correct statement ; and he includes it in his list of
migratory birds under the months of September and October, which is wrong again, as it is a resident. Nevertheless,
he was a good naturalist for his day. It is easy for men
who know better to carp at him now, but the wonder is that
he made so few mistakes.

I never noticed that the present species and the Spur-
winged Plover could raise the occipital feathers into the
kind of low crest represented in the plate of Savigny.

163. Stone-Curlew, *Œdicnemus crepitans*, Tem. (Hasselquist, 28, 32); "Karavan."

What would be the astonishment of a West Norfolk
gamekeeper to see the Stone-Curlews perching on houses at
Damietta? Our Diabeyha was moored near an ancient
"casern," now fast falling into ruins : the roof of this edifice
was their favourite resort. Twice we laid up for the evening
flight, but in vain, and we had to content ourselves with
listening to their shrill whistle, and watching their dark
forms against the sky. Up the Nile they were seen at
various places—always I think in pairs—and specimens obtained at Fechn, Minieh, and How. At the Faioum, also
the *Kiravan*, as it was there called, was rather common.
They are such swift runners that you have very little chance

with a winged one. I ought to say that those in Damietta were in flocks, but it is clear that they pair early.

164. AVOCET, *Recurvirostra avocetta*, Linn. ; *R. halebi*, Brehm, ; "*Helleby.*"

To have seen Avocets in a state of nature is alone enough to repay me for the long journey to Egypt. My first acquaintance with them was near Mansourah in the Delta on the 18th of January. We had been successful in shooting three out of four Teal, and had walked on some way when we came to a pond, the mud round which was so soft for a considerable distance that it would not sustain the weight of a boy. In this secure retreat were a magnificent flock of Avocets, and a flock of Shoveller-Ducks. They allowed us to come within seventy yards, and then the Avocets rose first in a compact phalanx of white and black.

On another occasion as we were returning from a village, we saw six, high in the air, coming towards us from the river, but they swerved before we could conceal ourselves. I have one or two other entries of having seen them in the Delta. When we went up the Nile we encountered Avocets for some time after leaving Cairo, and I never could sufficiently admire their gait, their re-curved bills, and their black and white plumage. The last shot above Cairo was on the 15th of March at Negardeh. It was in a state of change. The new feathers which had just come being pure black ; the old ones being dull brown. But the most interesting fact in connection with the Avocet—Captain Shelley having marked it as a winter visitant—was the discovery by Mr. Russell of a colony at Mareotis on the 19th of June, very tame, and apparently breeding.*

---

* The Avocet is one of England's departed glories. "May 12th, 1839. A man of the name of Gaffer says the Avocet used to be very

165.　STILT, *Himantopus candidus*, Bonn. (Hasselquist, 29) ;
"Abou magazel."

Of all the queer birds that Nature ever formed, this is
the queerest.　"At first sight," says Gilbert White, "one
might have supposed the shanks had been fastened on to
impose on the credulity of the beholder : " but Nature is
never wrong, and what seems to the superficial observer a
deformity, is a beautiful instrument adapted to the require-
ments of a wading bird which seeks its food in shallow
waters.　It is a strange yet elegant sight to see them bend
forward the body at each step, as they slowly pace along in
the water ; but when frightened, they rise up, they are only
grotesque.　With such unusual length of limb, it is needless
to say that they are slow fliers.　For some seconds their
legs hang down like a Flamingo's, and they are greatly
incommoded by them.　I have seen one go a hundred
yards with them dangling at right angles, which so re-
tarded his progress that my companions fired seven shots
at him before he was out of range.　Let me say that though
not shy, either the closeness of their feathers, or the small-
ness of their bodies, makes them a very hard bird to kill.
It was on the sandbanks between Thebes and Assouan
that they were most plentiful.　We only shot one in the
Delta, which I am rather surprised at.　Sometimes they
were single, but more often in pairs.　Once one of my
friends saw a flock of forty, but this was most exceptional.
Doubtless it is a resident.　I shot one at the Faioum in
June.　•

In "An Account of the Birds found in Norfolk," it is remarked that the changes of plumage to which the Stilt is

---

common [at Weybourne in Norfolk], and that he killed sixty-two at one
shot in the year 1814."

The above is a MS. note by the late Charles Buxton.

subject appear to require further elucidation.* They do not appear to have got it, as I cannot lay my hand on any work which explains why two adult black-backed males, shot in the spring, should have, the one a dark-brown head and neck, and the other those parts white ; but it is so in two of my Egyptian skins. I shot eight or nine Stilts, and I took some pains to unravel the mystery of their plumage, but all I could ascertain was that the black-backed ones were never females, though the brown-backed ones might occasionally be males.   Perhaps the white head is the summer plumage.† Mr. Blyth has some remarks on the colour of their heads in "The Ibis" (1865, p. 35), and he concludes by saying that the most likely explanation is "that differentiated races of this bird have been more or less commingled." This is probable, but not satisfactory.

The skin of the leg is scurfy, and the colour varies, the lightest birds having the lightest legs. The tarsus in the male is longer than in the female.

166. COLLARED PRATINCOLE, *Glareola pratincola* (Linn.) ; "Abou El Rusr."

Generally in flocks, but occasionally solitary. First shot on the 2nd of April. All naturalists have found a difficulty in saying to what family these birds belong. In their cry, flight, etc., I think they more resemble Terns than any other birds, and they are more often seen on a sandbank than inland. Four shot on the 9th of June out of a large flock had beetles in their crops with red backs and a peculiar smell. Their being in a flock looked as if they were not breeding.

---

* *Vide* Gurney and Fisher in "Zoologist" for 1846, p. 33.

† Against this view I must remark that Canon Tristram has a black-headed specimen, shot by himself in Algeria in June, and he informs me that others killed at the same time were black-headed also.

167. CREAM-COLOURED COURSER, *Cursorius gallicus*
(Gmel.)

On the 9th of March we saw a pair on the plain at Gow, and on the 27th of April I found a single bird at the same place.   He ran like a greyhound ; but, by making a stalking-horse of a camel, I managed to get a long shot.   He had been eating white grubs about 1¼ inches long.   Mr. Cory showed me a couple which he had shot, I think he said at Golosanah, but it cannot be considered by any means a common bird.   The legs are white.

OBS.   HOUBARA BUSTARD, *Houbara undulata* (Jacq.)

I hoped to have got this bird at the Faioum.   The overseer of the sugar factory there knows it well. He said they were not uncommonly brought in by the Arabs : he had one alive three months.

168.   CRANE, *Grus communis*, Bechst.
(Hasselquist, p. 207).

I am not positive what was the last date on which we saw the Crane.   We thought we saw two on the 17th of May, ; but if they really were Cranes, they were stragglers, behind the main body which had departed north some weeks before.   They are said to be common in winter, but I did not see one before February 14th.   He was on a sandbank with some Herons.   As he towered above his lesser brethren I felt no doubt of what he was, but we were just then scudding along before a famous breeze, and could not stop even for a Crane.   But at Gebel-Tair on the 28th of February, nineteen were counted.   Even this was nothing to what we saw afterwards.   At Siout and Gow great flocks were slowly sailing grandly round—in magnificent circles. This was in the second week in March. Their pinions were almost motionless, their necks were stretched a little downwards, and their whole appearance was majestic. Perhaps moved by curiosity, they came right over the Diabeyha, and I then saw that it was not a game of "follow-my-leader," but that each marked out its own circle and took its own separate course.

At other times they might be seen on the ground, marching off with great strides, like a much better drilled regiment of soldiers than any the Viceroy has. I believe it is considered a great feat to shoot a Crane, as they are notoriously shy and wary birds. Only once was it our luck to do so. On the 27th of February we had gone out for a long walk near Minieh, and we came upon a pair in an open field. They were standing still with their heads bent down to the ground, and really they looked such large brown creatures that it was difficult to believe they were birds at all. On one side of the field were some beans about three feet high, on the other a yellowish crop like mustard. Mr. Russell hid himself in the former, and I, taking a circuit, concealed myself in the latter. When plenty of time had been allowed us, the Cranes were put up and made straight for the beans. I heard two reports, and saw one bird go on : this was the cock. Mr. Russell had shot the hen. If he had killed it with his first barrel he would easily have got both. It weighed eleven pounds. We tied it to a large stick, and I fancy the Arab who carried it on board was not sorry when *that* job was over. The red skin on the head turned black next day, and red again after it was skinned. The length as noted down at the time was forty inches ; the expanse fifty-one. I looked for the ova of parasites on the axillaries which I had found in all my British specimens, but there were not any.

No doubt Hasselquist was correct in supposing that the

Crane came to Lower Egypt in autumn; but the statement made to him by some Egyptians that it came there from the south was wrong.

169.   HERON, *Ardea cinerea*, Linn.; " Balachoun."

The grey English Heron is a very common bird in Egypt and resident, but its numbers are probably diminished in the summer.   They are very fond of standing in parties of a dozen at the extremity of a sandbank when they are not fishing, where they can command a good view round. Upon these sands of Egypt they look almost white in the hot glare of the eastern sun.   I observed some about the lofty ledges of Gebel-Abou-Fœder, where the mountains rise in a precipice on the east side.   They are of stupendous height, and this is considered the most dangerous place on the Nile.   There were numbers more on the cliffs beneath the Coptic convent of Gebel-Tair (i.e. the mountain of a bird).   I dare say they breed there.   These cliffs are about two hundred feet high.   Those at Abou-Fœder are higher still.

We shot several specimens on the Nile, but none so fine as a very old bird which I shot at the Faioum.   I have often noticed some rusty yellow on the carpal joint, but in this one there was also a considerable amount of it on the lower portion of the fore-neck.   Two, got about the end of April, were still in immature plumage.   Fish is their general food: one fellow had eleven good-sized ones in his throat. It is possible that they themselves are occasionally made prey of by the crocodiles, as one was seen to snap at a Heron on the edge of a sandbank.   Vierthaler, in his Ornithological Diary on the Blue Nile, says that he and Brehm observed unmistakable traces of a quarrel between a Crocodile and a Crane, in which the former was victorious.

I shall have some remarks to make on the occipital plumes of the Night-Heron. In the present species Yarrell states that they are dark slate blue, which is true of mine; but a celebrated falconer told me that he once got one with a white centre. I have twice seen Herons with four plumes, once with five, and once with six; but in the last I will not be sure that they had not been stuck in, as it was at the shop of a birdstuffer rather clever at such tricks of the trade.

Mr. Rocke mentions getting a cock which at four months old exhibited the crest (Zoologist, ss., 81).

170. PURPLE HERON, *Ardea purpurea*, Linn.; "Hagaf."

This is a very handsome bird. It is of a more slender build than the Grey Heron, and more solitary in disposition, but it is not anything like so common. I only shot one in Upper Egypt, and two at the Faioum, one of which I could not find. I did not see as many at that lake as I expected. There were only two or three pairs, which were going to nest with the Buff-Backs, I have no doubt. The first we obtained went through some very funny antics. I did not see it myself, but it was described to me as squatting flat down on its stomach, with its neck extended to the full stretch, as if, Ostrich-like, it thought it could hide itself on a bare bank of sand.

171. GREAT WHITE HERON, *Herodias alba* (Linn.); "Ryti" and "Balachium abiad."

Seen only occasionally and at such a distance as fully warranted its reputation of being a very shy bird; but one at least—upon Lake Menzaleh—was sufficiently near to make its identification pretty certain.

172.   LESSER EGRET, *Herodias garzetta* (Linn.) ;
"Baiad."

It was not until March that we fell in with this exquisite wader.   I believe that it is comparatively scarce in winter, but that there is a northward movement in April.   On our return journey from Assouan a good many were seen and shot, some with a beautiful plume, others showing scarcely a trace of it.   Probably a few individuals do not assume it.

We found it nowhere so common as at the Faioum in June, where we shot some superb specimens, and others with no plume at all.   Nor is this a sexual difference, as the female has sometimes quite as fine a plume as the male. They were evidently about to breed with the Buff-backs. Two were seen with nesting materials in their beaks ; one was carrying a stick a yard long, but he appeared un- decided which nest to put it on, as after twice flying away and returning with it, he left the tamarisks in disgust, determined to sacrifice his long stick rather than let me see where the nest was.

The Egret is not invariably a solitary, for on the 21st of April I saw fifteen together with a flock of Spoonbills, and on the 1st of May four were killed out of a flock of nine. I have often seen them dancing, and supposed they were catching flies, but I never saw them set up the dorsal aigrette.

The cere is bluish in April, becoming much brighter in June; the beak is sometimes covered with a bloom, some- times not; the colour of the eye is yellow, but somewhat variable.   It would be easy to produce several instances of variableness in the iris of birds.   In the young Ring Dove* the iris is white, in the adult it is yellow ; but on the 3rd of June, 1871, I saw a Ring Dove which had the irides slate- coloured.

---

* *Columba palambus*, L.

173. BUFF-BACKED HERON, *Ardeola russata* (Wagl.).
(Hasselquist, 25); "Abu guirdan."

Is in some respects the most noticeable bird upon the
Nile, though far commoner below Cairo than above it.   I
shot one in winter with a good buff plume, but that is
very rare.   Nine-tenths of what the traveller sees are as
white as alabaster.   When he beholds them perched like
the purest of statuettes upon a gnarled old sycamore-fig, or
peering out from among the leaves of the Nabuk, he needs
no dragoman's prompting to convince him that now indeed
he has before him the veritable *Ibis religiosa*.   As in
England the Crane has bequeathed its name in certain
parts to the Heron, and the Bustard to the Stone-Curlew,
so the Buff-back has inherited that of the Sacred Ibis in
Egypt.

In the meadow land of the Delta they are very common,
and I have sat sometimes watching them by the hour.
Generally they will be in attendance on a herd of buffaloes,
pecking gnats off their legs, or scrutinising their foot-prints.
The cattle and their masters are so much indebted to them
that they become very unwary.   I have seen one almost
driven over by a man who was ploughing with two oxen.   I
think they prefer the fields very much to the river, indeed I
do not remember ever seeing them wading in the water like
other Herons.   In April we saw scarcely any except a few
large flocks on migration.   One of these was drawn up on
the Nile banks.   Another was on an uncovered sandbank
with some Ruffs and Caspian Terns.   Then for an interval
we did not see any, but in May I again found a few in a
field near Minieh.   They fly slowly with the neck and head
drawn in like a Little Egret.   If they come unexpectedly
on a concealed gunner, they stretch them out and utter a
cry which is dissonant, but not so loud as an Egret's.   I

never saw an Egret consorting with them, though I have occasionally seen the two species flying side by side. The Buff-back is the smaller bird, and may always be told at a distance by the shape and colour of his bill.

One of the most interesting sights at the Faioum was a breeding place of these birds—at that time (June)—in the most luxuriant plumage. A colony of, I should say, five hundred of them, had chosen a large bed of dead tamarisks for their breeding place. None had young, and a good many had not yet completed the process of building. Three was the commonest number in those nests which had eggs, but in one I counted seven. They stand from two to five feet above water-mark, and are made of branches snapped off dead tamarisks hard by, or picked up on the shore. One only had mud in its composition. Several were lined with a few reeds. They are not very large, the diameter being about a foot. Many of the old birds were carrying sticks about, which at a distance gave them the appearance of very long-beaked birds; albeit, all I saw near were carrying them crossways. At sunrise troops of them might be seen going south to forage in the fields as far as Medinet, or further; yet at nine o'clock they are not all off their eggs, and a visitor at eleven would find 100 or 200 which have already returned, or are perhaps staying there to keep guard and watch against other birds which might be tempted to steal from the nests. In the evening again it was very amusing to watch them like Rooks going home laden with locusts and beetles which they had caught in the fields of young sugar-cane and doura-corn, some following the sinuosities of the shore, some flying along the Bar El Wady canal (with the Cormorants and an occasional Egret), some passing straight over the tents, their white forms stand out clearly against the still blue water, all are bound for the same haven, a few, earlier than the rest, have their beaks open as if panting from the heat.

The first I skinned—which was shot at Boulac—contained eleven frogs. Another a green caterpillar and some grain. Another locusts. They, are said not to feed on fish (Ibis, 1863, p. 33).

Hasselquist (pp. 85, 195, 198) gives interesting particulars of the habits of a white Heron which he considered to be the Sacred Ibis, but which was in reality *Ardea bubulcus*; cf. Savigny's Histoire de l'Ibis, p. 6.

174. SQUACCO HERON, *Ardeola comata* (Pall.);
"Uak abiad zugaiar."

On the 25th January I shot a Squacco Heron at Damietta. It was wading in a reedy lake with some Red-shanks, but when I first saw it, it was alone. We did not meet with the species again until the 18th of April, when a second was shot from some rushes at the edge of the Nile near Keneh.

At the Faioum we saw some very handsome ones in June, among the tamarisks. I surmise that a pair or two were going to breed in company with the Buff-backs. They were very different in plumage from the brown-backed bird which I shot in January.

175. LITTLE BITTERN, *Ardetta minuta* (Linn.).

The only place where we met this bird was at the Faioum. I had expected to find it there, as I was told that I should, when at Cairo. It seemed however to be confined to one small odoriferous swamp, where the water was a foot and a half deep, and the reeds and bushes were above the height of a man; and I have no doubt it only comes here during the time of nidification. We put up at least fifteen pairs in a swamp of four acres. In spite of their slow ungainly flight they rise to some height, but they have not the power to go far.   They were always perched on the upper part of the reeds ; one, which was in the middle of a bush, when it saw me, commenced with deliberate steps and beak pointed upwards to ascend a slanting branch, with the object I suppose of getting to a clear place to fly away.   This unhealthy morass is on the south edge of the lake, about opposite Abouquisse.

I should add that the species is found at Damietta, as Mr. Hughes purchased a good specimen which had been obtained there.*

176.   BITTERN, *Botaurus stellaris* (Linn.) ; " Uak."

One, Damietta, January.   The eye turns downwards in its socket in this species.

177.   NIGHT HERON, *Nycticorax griseus* (Linn.) ; (23, *Alcedo ægyptia*, Hasselquist) ; " Uak sagar."

I presume the Night Heron is resident, though I cannot say I saw any during the latter part of my tour.   In the Delta we sometimes saw them singly, but generally in small flocks, upon the tops of trees ; never on the banks with the Common Herons.   On January 17th we saw about thirty— the largest flock we saw in Egypt—at Shibrue.   There were several adult birds, but for the most part we saw immature ones in the Delta ; whereas in Upper Egypt I believe we never met any except adults—single birds hiding themselves during the day in the umbrageous tops of the palms, which

---

* I have heard of several Little Bitterns being kept in confinement. A hard fate befel one of ours : it stuck its beak too far through the bars of its cage, and a malevolent Peacock wrenched off the upper mandible.   The same spiteful trick was played by a Parrot on one of its smaller brethren.

they would not quit until I was quite under them.   One fine specimen was shot upon a sandbank, but that was exceptional.

The flight of this bird is slow: when high up, battling against the wind, he makes no headway, but remains stationary: his short tail gives him an absurd appearance.

Two is the normal number of occipital plumes. I shot one with three, but they were short ones. My father has a Norfolk specimen with six.* A Night Heron weighs about 1¼ lbs.

Wilkinson, who was no ornithologist, thinks that "the Tufted Benoo" was the Buff-backed Heron, which he mixes up in his description with the Lesser Egret. I agree with Dr. Adams that the pictures are much more like a Night Heron. They vary, but one or two I think are unmistakably the Night Heron, which accordingly has the honour of being one of the four sacred birds of Egypt.

My father has determined this to be the *Alcedo ægyptia* of Hasselquist, in immature plumage, from the description in the Latin edition.

178. WHITE STORK, *Ciconia alba*, Bechst.; "Billerique."

Egypt is a famous country for collecting the Heron and Stork tribe: I doubt if any other country has a greater number of species or individuals. The subject of this note is familiar to everyone from boyhood as the household bird of the continent, emblem among the Germans of affection and constancy, whom it is pious to foster, impious to slay. But the feeling which protects it in Europe, (and in the Algerian "Tell,") does not yet extend to Egypt, and the

---

* At p. 4913 of the Zoologist, Mr. Rodd records the occurrence of a Cornish specimen with ten !

fellah will look on unmoved if you desire to shoot one. He will have a worse opinion of you for shooting the Buff-backed Herons, and he is right there, because the good they do is so very palpable and obvious.

With these preliminary observations, I will at once commence with my first experience of Storks in Egypt, which was about the end of March, and I dare say I shall not be believed when I describe the prodigious migratory flights which passed us. Armies of them would whiten the sand-banks at early morning, which had evidently spent the night there; and by day they were to be seen sailing round and round in countless myriads. It dazed the eye to look at them. The air seemed scribbled with their white forms. I am within bounds in saying that there seemed enough Storks to stock every church, and every tower, and every public office in the whole of civilized Europe. To those who deem me romancing, let me say this: no one should disbelieve a thing because he has not seen it. It must be borne in mind that Egypt, or at least the Nile valley (they are synonymous terms) is one of the greatest arteries, so to speak, by which feathered migrants seek a northern clime. Like man, they shun to cross the Great Sahara, where the sands are trackless and the elixir of life—water—is wanting. Hence their teeming thousands in the Nile valley. For the same number, which in another and a fertile land would perhaps be spread over 3,000 miles, are here compressed into a space which on a average is only three miles broad. And this will go on for ever. The channel which has been found so often will be found again; and unless their numbers are kept down by disease, each succeeding year will probably witness greater and greater droves, for few guns are employed against them, and they enjoy a comparative immunity alike from the real sportsman, the naturalist, and the pot-hunter.

The first time we saw a drove was very late in the

evening, and we did not discern them until a shot, fired at a passing bird, put them up. Then the whole air was peopled. Many were the conjectures which might have been heard on our Diabeyha as to what they were, and we finally resolved that they must be Numidian Cranes ; but this great flock was as nothing to what we saw on the 25th of March. On that day I was just thinking of getting out of bed—it was about 6 a.m., for I always rose early—when the waiter tapped at my door and pronounced the magic word *wiz*, which literally means a Goose, but which was employed by that functionary to designate any large bird which he thought we should like. I whipped on my clothes with something less than the speed of "greased lightning," and on coming up on to the deck beheld an extraordinary spectacle. On the sandbanks before me, motionless and still asleep, were three huge regiments of Storks, looking for all the world like great herds of sheep pasturing on the wolds of Yorkshire. I judged that in the largest of those "cohorts" there might be a thousand birds, but the others were not much less. I shot one with my rifle, and immediately the air was filled with them, each with his legs sticking out behind him, and a red beak appearing from between his great wings. After circling, one above another, in concentric rings (of which the highest seemed the smallest) for half an hour, during which the sky seemed alive with them, they took themselves off in a northerly direction to seek some safer quarters.

Besides these vast hordes, which I must say were even a greater phenomenon than the living islands of Ducks on lake Menzaleh, I now and then came upon much smaller flocks halting in the desert ; and very hungry and unsociable they appeared to be, each a hundred yards or so from his neighbour, and wrapped up in contemplation of the dreary scene around him.

The migration which I have attempted to describe was soon over, but long after the travellers had passed, we used occasionally to come across a solitary, which was no doubt some weakly bird which had been unable to keep up with the ranks. The first of these single ones, doomed to a life of celibacy, was by my note book observed on the 31st of March, watching some husbandmen at work by the edge of the cultivated ground. Its air bespoke a moody and despondent mind. After a little judicious stalking it was brought to bag, when it proved to have black beetles in its throat, and locusts in its gizzard. No doubt it sighed for the inundation, and the time when it should bear aloft in its terrible shears the juicy frog.

Other hermits we saw at Silsilis, Kom Ombos, Edfou, Erment, and Fechn. They had settled down into their summer tameness, and though cut off from their kindred, it is to be hoped they found some village mosque on which to perform the duties of incubation, and partners to aid them in its most important functions; but strange to say, I never saw a nest in Egypt, not even at Alexandria or Cairo; yet some must remain for the summer, as I saw a flock as late as June 12th, but I apprehend that Storks in full vigour do not find their northern limit in Egypt.

They appear from what has been written by some authors to have been met with in winter, but these may have been only individuals arrested on their southward journey by the same causes which stopped those we saw on their northward course. On the 19th of February I observed the first one that I am sure about, but my companions thought they saw some earlier.

Specimens pulled down the steelyard at from $5\frac{1}{2}$ to $6\frac{1}{2}$ lbs. I noticed that there were no tertials or feathers between the scapulars and secondaries, and that the bronchial tubes were over five inches in length, in spite of which the Stork is voiceless.*

179. BLACK STORK, *Ciconia nigra* (Linn.).

Rather common, but I believe we did not see any in the Delta. Mr. Buxton shot an immature bird at Erment, and an old one near Benisouef. The latter measured 38¾ inches from tip of tail to end of beak; expanse 53¼. A mass of half-digested fish was pressed out of its mouth. Captain Shelley says—"It is an unsociable bird, never congregating in flocks or associating with other species" *(o. c.,* p. 265*)*; but at Abou-Girg we saw twenty-four with Spoonbills, Herons, and Ducks in a flock. A single one is sometimes seen near a pool in the fields. I rather think it is not found in Egypt in the summer. We however saw one as late as May 17th, a very fine bird; it passed over me almost within gunshot.

180. SPOONBILL, *Platalea leucorodia*, Linn.; "Abu Malaka," or "Daouas," or "Midwas."

This singular bird was only seen twice in the Delta, but several were obtained up the Nile, and one at the Faioum. On one occasion a discharge of four barrels into a flock resulted in nine specimens, but they were mostly young birds, and got very dirty from the mud where they fell. In March I have counted as many as 103 in a flock. In April the numbers were generally smaller, but on the 22nd about a hundred were seen together. It is evidently migratory.

---

* The Stork is a rare bird in Norfolk. In 1861 one paid a visit to the parish of Northrepps and alighted in a large marl-pit, now disused, and close to a public road. The keeper went after it and would certainly have shot it, but a boy put it up. The bird then flew to Woodbastwick, where it was killed. It contained an egg ready for exclusion (cf. B. of Norfolk, II., 181).

We were very much mystified by the small size of some
we shot. It may probably have been that they were hens,
but the circumstance is also noticed by Von Heuglin (Ibis,
1859, p. 346). What made it remarkable was that they
were, with one exception, old crested birds with short dark
beaks, while the large-beaked specimens were immature.
The bill in the shortest I measured was $7\frac{1}{10}$,* in the longest
$9\frac{3}{4}$, a marvellous difference. The tarsus in the shortest $5\frac{1}{2}$;
in the longest $7\frac{1}{4}$. Captain Shelley gives the entire length
at 36 inches, but I have no doubt his system of measure-
ment is different from mine, as our biggest was only 29.
I measure from the forehead to the tip of the tail; and perhaps I ought to add, that wherever I give the length of a
bird it has been taken before it was skinned. Heuglin
(op. cit.) says the eye is yellow in the young, but in one
which I examined it was grey. Several specimens had the
thighs stained with buff, yet I never saw any wade above
the tarsus.

I should think that the White Herons set down as *Ardea
garzetta* with a query by Dr. Adams were probably Spoonbills.

A young Spoonbill in the Zoological Gardens used to
sit on its tarsal joints, with its feet raised an inch or two
into the air, so that no part of it but its knees (or ankles as
they are more correctly called) touched the ground. The
keeper told me that the Storks did the same.

181. GLOSSY IBIS, *Ibis falcinellus*, Linn.
(29, *Tringa autumnalis longirostris*, Hasselquist);
" Herres."

On the 13th of 'April I saw a Glossy Ibis in the water-
course, which one has to cross in going to the Memnonium

---

* In a young bird of the year shot at Yarmouth (Zool., 2871) it is
only 6.6.

or the Tombs of the Kings. It was standing near some Buff-backs. The next day we found it again in exactly the same place, but without the Buff-backs. When frightened by being shot at, it mounted very high, flying in circles with its neck extended.

At Damietta I was offered a pair which had been shot the previous spring. I took the larger and brighter one of the two, which I presume was the male. It is a fine bird, but not so good as an Alexandrian one of Mr. Allan's which I lately saw on sale at Mr. Gerrard's, and which may be the specimen referred to in the "Ibis" for 1863, p. 34. I saw another Alexandrian example at Mr. Mayers'.

Some remarks will be found about the Sacred Ibis (which we never met with) in chapter VI.

182. FLAMINGO, *Phœnicopterus antiquorum*, Tem.; "Bachirroch," or "Basharoos."

High praise has been lavished on the Flamingo, and the untravelled Englishman has always been taught that this is "the bird of all birds," and that nothing in nature is so surpassingly beautiful; while all writers have vied with one another in finding epithets to describe the spectacle of the pink tints of a band of them rising into the air "an animated rosy cloud." Having at last realised the ardent wish to see them, which I have ever had from childhood, I am bold to say that on the whole they are not overrated—their vaunted splendour is not a myth but a real thing, and nothing will ever dispel from my memory the feelings with which I first saw Flamingos. It needs not the halo of Afric's sun to illumine a splendour to which the gilded birds of the tropics must yield the palm. Marshalled, they stand in one long glittering line; some of them apparently with no head; others with but one leg; others with raised wing and extended neck, evidently enjoying what is denominated stretch. Their tall forms are mirrored in the glassy lake. They are silent and still. Perchance a distant boatman hails us. Perchance the word *backshish* is borne on the air with such bawling that the cautious Flamingos, fearful even in their security, are put up. Then what a delicious scene arrests the eye, as the black-pointed wings unfold and reveal the intense red scapularies, which, hidden before, appeared to be cream-colour, pale by comparison with their brightness now. They take several steps in the air,* half flying, half walking, and wholly awkward, for twenty yards or more; and then gathering themselves together they gradually let their long legs trail out behind. If a small troop, they perhaps fly away in Indian file; but if a large one, they go off in one bright mass, the vivid tints of which are visible afar off, and which no man who has seen it will ever forget. When the naturalist has got over his ecstacies he had better go to the mud where they were standing, as if, as is most probable, they have been preening themselves, he will be rewarded by some exquisite feathers.

It has been well said that the salt lakes in the north of Africa are the Flamingos' home. On the great waters of Egypt they breed so abundantly, that a birdstuffer at Alexandria told me that he got 200 eggs from Mariotis at one raid. What splendid opportunities might here be afforded to anyone sufficiently sun-proof to work out the imperfectly-known details of their nidification, and to fill up the blanks in our knowledge with regard to the posture which the sitting bird assumes and other points.

Up the Nile, travellers will very likely not see *one*. We only saw a few. They were between Cairo and Minieh, and were young birds. At the Faioum we did not see any at

---

* See Mr. Macgregor's picture of them taking wing on lake Menzaleh. (The Rob Roy on the Jordan, p. 80.)

all; at the same time I must say that the lake is large, and we only explored a portion of it.

✳183.   LESSER WHITE-FRONTED GOOSE,
Anser erythropus (Linn.).

I bought this small Goose of M. Eugene Filliponi at Damietta, where it had been killed in January, 1875, only a short time before our arrival. We neither of us knew what it was, but he was satisfied it was not the White-fronted Goose *(A. albifrons)*, which is very common. The following are the measurements :—

Wing	12.4 inches.
Tarsus	2.2 „
Culmen	1.3 „

For comparison, these are the measurements of a female White-fronted Goose, shot at Islay in Scotland.

Wing	17. inches
Tarsus	2.7 „
Culmen	2.1 „

And these of a female which I shot near Minieh in Egypt:

Wing	15.8 inches.
Tarsus	2.5 „
Culmen	1.9 „

The underparts in the Damietta example are brown without any barring. It is evidently a young bird. This is the first time that this species has been recognized in Africa.

My bird has been examined by Mr. E. C. Taylor, and Professor Newton, also by my father, who was the first to make out what it really was.

184. WHITE-FRONTED GOOSE, *Anser albifrons*, Gm.;
"Wiz" (Hasselquist, No. 36).

A good many were seen on the Damietta branch, particularly near Mansoura, where we fired at a large flock, which did not leave the neighbourhood, but returned again to the same sandbank. Between Cairo and Minieh we saw none, but on the 3rd of March we met with large flocks of *Anatidæ*, and obtained two of these Geese. After that, the sandbanks were entirely deserted by Ducks : no one should come to Egypt for that sort of sport later than January. Most Egyptian specimens of the White-fronted Goose, instead of being barred are nearly white on the under-surface, which has generally been supposed to be the immature plumage ; albeit, I have known one in confinement live five years and not get these bars.

185. EGYPTIAN GOOSE, *Chenalopex ægyptiacus* (Linn.).*

Not seen in the Delta, but very common south of Cairo; indeed we saw the first flock before we were clear of the town. On our return journey a portion of them had migrated, yet as late as the 20th of May over 150 were seen upon one sandbank at Zouyeh; and from the quantity of feathers and numerous tracks, it was supposed they had been there a long time. A dropped egg was picked up there. They were however generally in pairs, and were easily obtained by sailing on them in a punt. Mr. Buxton killed four couples, of which the heaviest one weighed 6¼ lbs.; but a pair which he shot on the 19th of May only turned the scale at 9 lbs., so that there seems to be a great

---

* I have seen a Pink-footed Goose (marked Bean Goose) in Lord Londesburgh's Egyptian collection at the Scarborough Museum, but whether really killed in that country I cannot say.

difference in weight. At Gebel-Abou-Fœder we found them nesting in cliffs. Of course we could not ascend to their nests, but there could be no doubt that they were breeding. One shot had a perfect egg ready for laying. These cliffs are very lofty; the lower stratum is devoted to Pigeons; on the tier above that the Geese; and still higher up a few Kites, Griffon Vultures, and a pair of Ospreys. It was very curious to see them looking down from their ledges. More wide awake then than the large flocks which, with beaks inserted beneath the scapulars, found balancing upon one leg conducive to sleep upon the sandbanks. They fly with powerful beats, but neither very high nor very fast.

The coloured pictures of them on the monuments are so bad that they are barely recognizable. The ancient Egyptians appear only to have known three or four colours. Most of their birds are only recognizable by the outline, which however is generally very correct and characteristic.

It would appear that opinions as to the edible qualities of this goose are conflicting. Mr. Blandford says it is in general excellent eating; but Dr. Kirk declares emphatically that this is the worst of all the Duck kind for the table, being in many cases quite uneatable. Where doctors disagree who shall decide?

186. RUDDY SHELDUCK, *Tadorna rutila* (Pall.) ; "Abu Ferona."

April 28th.—As I was waiting for the Diabeyha at Gow-Garbi, the sun having gone down, and it being nearly dark, I perceived a flock of large birds coming straight at me across the river. They made a loud noise like Egyptian Geese, which I at first mistook them for. However, on killing one it proved to be the somewhat nearly allied Ruddy Shelduck. Afterwards we saw them three or four times nearer to Cairo in May, always in flocks of about twenty.*

187. SHELDUCK, *Tadorna vulpanser*, Fleming.
(35, Anas damiatica, Hasselquist) ; "Chahraman."

My father considers, from the Latin description, that this is the Damiatic Duck of Hasselquist, and I accordingly quote it in deference to his opinion.

On the 3rd of June I saw two of these handsome fellows swimming on lake Faioum, at a short distance from where we were encamped. I could plainly see that they were male and female. I let fly at the drake, but he was too far for me, and I did not get him, and we never saw them again. The only other example I saw belonged to Mr. Cory, and was obtained by him in Cairo market.

Most naturalists are aware that the young of this species has a white face, but it is perhaps not so generally known that this mark of immaturity sometimes lasts to the spring, for I have seen a specimen with it on the 27th of March ; and I have known an instance in captivity of its breeding with a white face.

188. SHOVELLER DUCK, *Spatula clypeata* (Linn.) ;
" Hick."

Certainly a very common Duck. I shot four on the 27th of April ; two were drakes, and they were not in full plumage, but I considered that they were going off, and not that they had not yet assumed it. Its edible qualities

---

* Nine supposed occurrences of the Ruddy Shelduck in Great Britain are quoted in Harting's " Hand List," four of which I believe would not stand a proper sifting, viz., those said to have been killed at Caithness, Orford, Blackstakes, and Epworth.

are very second rate in Egypt ; but tastes differ, and I have heard it praised in England.   Indeed, a writer in the "Zoologist" says, "It is one of the best, if not the very best of the edible Ducks" (p. 6923) (cf., p. 3826).

189.   GADWALL,* *Chaulelasmus streperus* (Linn.).

Markets at Alexandria and Cairo.

190.   PINTAIL *Dafila acuta* (Linn.) ; "Balbul."

The Pintail is the commonest Duck on the Damietta branch of the Nile, and we certainly saw huge flocks of them.   Yet I dare say there would be thousands more, and other Ducks too, if it were not for the annual slaughter which takes place at Menzaleh.   We shot some at flight, but the only time when they seem to be approachable on the river is the early morning.

We kept the drake alive which our boatman took on Menzaleh (see p. 94) eighteen days, and then let him go at the Barrage, but I doubt if he would live, as he was very thin, and his wings cramped from being tied together. When our captive was roused he hissed, but he was an apathetic bird.

There is to some extent a separation of the sexes, as I often noticed a flock all males.   In our voyage up the Nile we still found it the commonest of the tribe, but not in coming down again.   I shot five females the first week in March, and after that date very few Pintails or Ducks of any kind were seen on the river, except the Garganey Teal, which came later.   The last Pintail shot by us was on the 8th of

---

* Yarrell gives "*Grey Duck*" as a synonym of the Gadwall.   On the coast of Durham I have often heard it applied to the common Mallard.

May, but there were some at Birket-El-Kairoun (the Faioum) in June.

191. WILD DUCK, *Anas boschas*, Linn.; "Kodari."

Previous writers state that the Wild Duck is everywhere plentiful. On the contrary, we found it so scarce that we only shot one all the time we were in Egypt. It is just another instance of the variableness of Egyptian Ornithology—a variableness which has in it a promise of new facts for new observers. Hasselquist informs us that they appear "on the tables" about the beginning of November.

*192. MARBLED DUCK, *Anas angustirostris* (Ménétr.); "Miniet."

When Captain Shelley published his "Birds of Egypt," this species was unknown to him as occurring in the country. It was therefore with no little surprise that we found it to be quite common on Birket-El-Kairoun (the Faioum) in June. We are however forestalled in the discovery by Canon Tristram, who it appears, some time ago, when out in the neighbourhood of the marshes near Alexandria, bought one, fresh and bleeding, of an Arab. It was certainly the most plentiful Duck at the lake. I saw most the day I went over to the north side. On the sand by the brink of a neighbouring pond, there were both single birds and small flocks. On the lake I saw it in couples near the shore or near an island, but I never saw it far out upon the water, or at a distance from the reedbeds. The specimens shot were all drakes. No eggs were found: I think it very likely that the ducks were sitting.

193. GARGANEY, *Querquedula circia* (Linn.);
"Arraeh."

Was first met with on the 10th of April, and not far from
El-Kab, the same place mentioned by Captain Shelley.
Between then and the end of the month several were shot
in the plashes of water which are left by the receding Nile.
They were evidently on migration. The males appeared
to be going off in plumage.

The young Garganey is just the colour of a young Teal.
It differs from it in having no speculum, and the neck and
bill are both rather larger. Yarrell gives 16 inches as the
length of the Garganey, and 14½ for the Teal, but persons
not versed in ornithology would be sure to confound the
young birds.

194. TEAL, *Querquedula crecca* (Linn.); "Charchir."

I cannot understand how this can be called the most
abundant Duck in Egypt—vide "Shelley's Birds of Egypt,"
p. 286. We found it particularly scarce, only shooting
three couple all the time we were in the country ; yet I do
not mean to say that my predecessor has been guilty of a
mistatement respecting it. The explanation probably is
that the *Ornis* of Egypt is peculiar, and birds which are
common one season are scarce another. When observers
are multiplied in that advancing country, and we can take
the mean of many observations, we shall arrive at the truth.

195. WIGEON, *Mareca penelope* (Linn.); "Sarvai."

We saw the Wigeon in the markets at Alexandria and
Cairo, but I should have reckoned it one of the rarer Ducks,
had we not seen so many on lake Menzaleh. When we

were within an hour or two of Geut-El-Nosara (the port of that lake) flock after flock crossed our bows, all Wigeons, and chiefly drakes. There was no mistake about them, even if I had not examined four or five which had been caught. The only one we shot ourselves was a female, on the 3rd of March, near Minieh. Hasselquist says,—"This kind was brought alive in great numbers (to Cairo) about the middle and latter end of November; they are caught in nets at night, just before the water is entirely returned or dried up."*

196. POCHARD, *Fuligula ferina* (Linn.); "Homr."

Of all the myriads of Ducks at lake Menzaleh, Pochards seemed the commonest. I saw acres and acres of them. In one place an immense flock, which I believe were chiefly Pochards, extended three miles as they sat upon the water, without any visible break. The Pochard is occasionally subject to a white patch on the foreneck. I have seen two drakes and a duck thus marked.†

197. WHITE-EYED DUCK, *Nyroca ferruginea* (Gm.).

We only got this in the winter. It was not uncommon then in the Delta, and we shot six, but only one was a fine old drake.

---

* A tame Wigeon of my father's began to shed its plumage on the 17th of June, and completed the moult on the 20th of August. It began to reassume the male plumage on the 19th of September, and finished the process November 10th, having been nearly four months of the year in a state of change. In the above instance I do not think the period was lengthened by confinement, for I have often noticed what a long time the drakes of this and other species are in getting their perfect dress.

† My father kept a drake Pochard thirteen years. Once, when he was carrying it from one pond to another, its red eye changed to yellow from fright, but rapidly recovered its original colour after being released.

198. Tufted Duck, *Fuligula cristata* (Linn.); "Zurk."

Two were shot in the Delta.*

199. Little Gull, *Larus minutus*, Pall.

Mr. Russell saw what I have no doubt was a bird of this species with some Terns at the Faioum.

Sharpe and Dresser have referred the *Larus Dorbignyi* of Audouin, figured in the "Description de l'Egypte," to the Little Gull. I believe it to be the Black Tern, for the following reasons. It agrees in size; the toes are so divided that there is but very little web; the tail is more forked than a Little Gull's; and the back is much blacker. It is a young bird of some sort or other, and the description "red legs" would not apply to a young *Larus minutus* more than to a Black Tern. Neither species is common in the country. My father, however, thinks that it is more likely to be a young White-winged Tern.

200. Black-headed Gull, *Larus ridibundus*, Linn.

A great many seen in Lower Egypt, but I am not sure whether they were all of this species. It was only positively identified at Menzaleh and Benha.

201. Great Black-headed Gull, *Larus ichthyaetus*, Pall. ; "Hin."

I must say I was disappointed with this royal Sea-Gull when I saw him at Pelican-point, Damietta. To my mind

---

* Since returning to England I have heard from M. Filliponi that he obtained a pair of the White-headed Duck (*Erismatura leucocephala*) on lake Menzaleh.

he is not near such a fine bird on the wing as the Greater
Black-backed Gull; and he is quite as shy, for we never
obtained so much as a shot. By the 23rd of January this
species had already partly put on its summer plumage, and
in connection with this, I may mention, that I have frequently known the English Black-headed Gull* to have a
nearly black head in winter.

✻202.   COMMON GULL, *Larus canus*, Linn.

We found this common in the Delta. We first certainly
identified it at Damietta on the 23rd of January, when five
specimens were shot. Near Samanhoude a sixth was shot,
and I am sure several flocks were seen between those places,
yet it has been considered very rare.

203.   MEDITERRANEAN HERRING GULL, *Larus
leucophœus*, Lict. ; " Norasa."

A good many were seen in Lower, and I believe a few in
Middle Egypt. A young one, obtained at Damietta, had
the legs white, tinged with flesh colour. Compared with
some young English Herring Gulls, its plumage was whiter.

204.   LESSER BLACK-BACK GULL, *Larus fuscus*, Linn.;
L. fuscescens (Licht.) ; " Goka."

This Gull is a resident in Egypt, though where it breeds
I cannot say. They were to be seen in the harbour at
Alexandria on the 7th of January, and again on the 20th of
June. I met with them at the Faioum, and in Upper
Egypt also ; this species was very frequently shot in the
beginning of May. I do not know a bird of more unsullied

---

* *Larus ridibundus.*

beauty. Sometimes one might be seen floating beside the diabeyha ; and I remember there were more than a score of them swimming within gunshot of the place where we anchored at Cairo. Though so pure to look at, they are foul feeders. I shot one beside the stranded carcase of an enormous Nile fish: it contained scales larger than a shilling. On comparing five adult Egyptian skins with three English ones, it is seen that the back is darker by many shades ; legs yellow, beak ditto, inferior angle red, eyelid red, eye yellow ; length 21 inches.

Obs. Skua Gull.

June 17th, Alexandria, observed a bird which has not been noticed in Egypt before, viz., a Skua, but of what species I cannot say. It appeared too big for Richardson's Skua. It was teasing the Gulls in the harbour.

205. Caspian Tern, *Sterna caspia*, Pall ; "Abou Belaha," i.e., Father of Dates: so called because of its red beak.

A fine one obtained, January 23rd, at Damietta, where they are not uncommon, and may occasionally be decoyed within gunshot by whistling in imitation of their note. Always intently searching the surface of the water, they fly at a somewhat greater altitude than the other Terns, from which they may be distinguished afar off by their magnificent red bills. We saw several in Upper Egypt, and shot three splendid specimens near Gebel-Silsilis the first week in April, besides one at the Faioum on the 2nd of June. The last seen on the Nile was on the 12th of May. They weigh about $1\frac{1}{4}$ lb. Feet black, mottled with yellow. The specimen shot at the Faioum was much more backward than the Silsilis specimens, having the head still profusely mottled.   The Caspian Tern* breeds in January in the region of the Zambesi (Ibis, 1864, p. 337).

OBS. COMMON TERN, *Sterna fluviatilis* (Naum.).

At Menzaleh I observed some small Terns which may have been *S. fluviatilis*. Hasselquist gives a long description of a Tern which comes to Trajan's canal in great flocks in the beginning of January, but I cannot satisfactorily make it out.

206. WHISKERED TERN, *Hydrochelidon hybrida* (Natt.).

I confess I doubt this being a resident species (cf. Heugl. Syst. Ubers, No. 734), though it became excessively common after the 26th of April. In many parts the Nile was covered with them, as they slowly beat up against the north wind, which prevailed very much in the beginning of May, and which was no doubt detaining them. I recollect one evening at dusk I observed these Terns feeding upon the yellow-dun fly in company with hundreds of Bats. The intensity of colour on the breast varied much, the darker being of course in summer garb.

---

* In the Dover Museum there is a very young Caspian Tern with some down on the head. It was brought quite fresh to the Curator (still in the flesh I believe), and must have been killed not very far off. He told me that the man who brought it was a foreigner. It is possible that it came from Sylt; if on the other hand it was a British-killed one, it was very interesting in that state. It is not the example mentioned at p. 265 of "The Note-Book of a Naturalist," by E. P. Thompson, who I believe started the Museum at Dover.

207. GULL-BILLED TERN, *Sterna anglica,* Mont.

January 26th.   A few on lake Menzaleh, half a mile from the village of Geut-El-Nosara.   They flew round our boat in large circles, sometimes darting down as if to catch a fish, and sometimes checking themselves as they thought better of it.   Occasionally they came within gunshot, when I could see that they were in winter plumage.   When near us they moved the head sideways, but in the distance—as I could see with the telescope—they kept steadily looking down into the water.   We afterwards obtained specimens at Manfalout and Bibba, and saw a flock at El-Bab (the 1st Cat.).   I believe we did not see any on the Faioum, but I did at Alexandria on the 20th of June, so the species must be resident.

✻208. LESSER TERN, *Sterna minuta,* Linn.

I am disposed to think that this fairy-like Tern should be considered a summer visitor rather than a winter one. It would seem to be not nearly so rare as has been hitherto supposed.   In the first part of May we several times saw small flocks, and obtained specimens.   In particular a great many were seen between Bibba and Cairo.   At the Faioum also it was rather a common bird, and one was seen carrying some building materials.   When we returned to Alexandria we saw them again there, on the 11th and 17th of June.   I was also shown a skin at Damietta by M. Filliponi, who said that they were not very rare there.

I watched their actions with great attention, as I have often done before in Norfolk.   They are just the same in Egypt.   Precisely the same discordant cry strikes upon the ear, and one looks everywhere for their small white forms, so like in hue to both sky and water, to discover one at last close to the boat.   He passes on with slow, aimless flight, his pinions gently waving rather than flying, but all the while with head and beak pointing downwards intently scanning the limpid lake, whose glassy surface mirrors him again and again. His tail is on the move continually. It is the governor or rudder by which he steers. Every now and then, as he flies along, he shakes himself up with a kind of shiver. What this is for I do not know, but I describe him as I have seen him in that glorious country, which I shall always look back to as a naturalist's paradise. Now his wings seem to go back with the force of the air, and he strikes the water aslant. Without an effort he rises again and passes on, but seeing a fish, or some floating matter which he had nearly overlooked, pauses, checks himself, turns downwards at right angles, and plunges into the water with a splash.

✳209. WHITE-WINGED TERN, *Hydrochelidon leucoptera* (Meisn).

This is much scarcer than the Whiskered. We shot four at the Faioum where I suspect it breeds, and one on the Nile. The latter was on the 1st of May; it was with two others. The gizzard was full of flies. I also was shown three which had been killed at Damietta, and one which had been killed at Alexandria. This is the handsomest of all the Terns. Von Heuglin seems the only writer who has met with it. He says that this species and the Whiskered Tern are common all the year in Egypt and Nubia, and that in July he has often shot young birds which had evidently been hatched there (Syst. Ueb., p. 70).

210. SCISSORBILL, *Rhyncops flavirostris*, Vieill.

A sight of this strange bird is a gain which those have who visit Egypt late in the season. Ours was, I believe, the last diabeyha on the river, which accounts for our getting the Scissorbill and sundry other species not met with by Messrs. Adams and Smith.   Its novel beak is an eccentricity of nature which no one who confines himself merely to British birds has any idea of, the mandibles being flattened perpendicularly, and the lower one projecting beyond the upper a long way—$1\frac{1}{8}$ inch in one specimen, which I shot.   That, it is true, was the longest.   It varies much, and in another the projection was only $\frac{5}{8}$ of an inch; but I refer the reader to Captain Shelley's picture, which will give a much better idea than any description of mine.

We were lucky enough to see a great many, and to watch their habits under very favourable circumstances, especially at Erment, Silsilis, and Keneh.   The first appearance was on the 20th of March, near the spot mentioned by Captain Shelley.   We had landed to shoot some fowl on the sand-bank, and the reports put up a flock of about a dozen Scissorbills.   We at once left the fowl to take care of themselves, and after some manœuvring I succeeded in shooting three of the coveted birds.   Their unusual length of wing makes them look so much larger than they really are, that they easily pass between large shot.   Terns are generally easy birds to get near, and the Scissorbills, however different in other respects, proved to be no exception.   When we afterwards met them at Silsilis five were killed at one shot; and that day a curious thing happened.   A Scissorbill was shot at about thirty yards' distance, and when I picked it up a gunwad was sticking to its wing.

There is good reason to believe that they follow the course of the Nile as far as the Delta.   I obtained confirmation of the occurrence of one at Damietta (Ibis, 1864, p. 243), and they were seen by us at various points as far north as Minieh, and again two were shot at Benisouef, and two more were seen on the 21st of May, within twenty miles of Cairo.   They fly very low over the water, every now and then just shearing it with their beaks, in play or in feeding. They make marks with them in the sand, deep and slightly curving, some nearly two inches long. What those hieroglyphics mean I cannot say. Possibly they find there some small sand worms. I never saw any swimming ; they appear to be as averse to it as the true Terns ; but they settle on *terra firma* much more than they do. At night they are as active as by day. Occasionally you may see them raise their wings until they nearly touch over the back. The expanse is about 39 inches, but of course among many specimens there was a good deal of variation. Eye almost black ; beak coral red at the base, shading off into light straw-yellow at the tip. I think the females have rather shorter beaks than the males. At the same time our shortest was a male according to Mr. Hughes' dissection.

Von Heuglin says at the end of autumn these birds collect and travel in immense flocks (Syst Uebers, No. 727).

*211. CINEREOUS SHEARWATER, *Puffinus kuhli*, Boie.

This was the last bird I saw. It was about an hour after leaving Alexandria harbour, on the 20th of June, that the first was seen ; afterwards I saw a good-sized flock or two. After my return to England, M. Filliponi obtained a specimen. He writes that it was killed at the mouth of the river, a few miles north of Damietta, and that two fishermen who plied their trade at the place informed him that it was a scarce bird, but that one or two were seen every year in the autumn, that it always appeared at sundown, and that they called it *Oum-Gournaya,* which means hiding mother.

212. WHITE PELICAN, *Pelicanus onocrotalus*, Linn.;
(Hasselquist, pp. 85, 208, 210); "Bagah."

The Pelicans which we saw on lake Menzaleh were pre-
sumedly of this species. There is a neck of land called
Sayal, an hour and a quarter's walk from Damietta, over
which Pelicans not infrequently pass, and in tempestuous
weather they may be got by lying up, but their feathers are
such a tough armour that many are hit for one that is killed.
At this place they flew very low, but we did see some flocks
at a far greater height, and one bird afterwards circling
right over the town of Damietta. I do not remember seeing any Pelicans from the time we left Damietta until the
11th of March, when six rosy ones were descried on a sandbank near Girgeh. I do not know how long it takes for a
Pelican to arrive at maturity, though it might easily be
ascertained from the numerous specimens kept in confinement, but certainly in the same flock you may see some far
larger than others, and much rosier. The roseate colouring
of the adult Pelicans is probably more intense during the
breeding season. We were too late to see many on the Nile ;
occasionally we met with a single one or a pair migrating
north, and once, on the 16th of May, I counted about fifty-
seven high up and going in the same direction, but we
never had the good fortune to come across such an immense
flock as Captain Shelley tells of, although we were near the
same place at about the same period of the year. On
enquiry we were told that we had come much too late for
Pelicans, and that they were only common in the winter.
This I dare say was true, as I know that other boats had
obtained them ; possibly they go to the large lakes in the
Delta in April to breed. Hasselquist says that some remain at Damietta and on the islands of the Delta in
summer.

- As it was we were content to get one specimen—a fine

salmon-tinted bird, measuring 108 inches from tip to tip. It was shot on the 9th of April. The tarsus was 5½ inches, carpus 26½, culmen 18, length 59. Legs yellow, eye brownish red—not so bright red as in the examples at the Zoological gardens. The *whole body*, wings included, was covered with large air-cells.

Pelicans do very well in confinement, and I was told at Menzaleh that they could be caught alive more easily than shot.

Hasselquist says, " The inhabitants of Damietta make a vessel out of the upper part of the beak, with which they bale the water out of their boats." I should have thought the lower part more adapted for the purpose.

Before leaving Egypt I purchased a young Pelican which had been shot at Suez. It is dark brown all over, and appears to me to be hardly full grown. The bill is 14½, and the wing 26 inches.

✳213. *Pelicanus minor*, Rupp. ; *P. mitratus*, Licht.

On the 15th of April a pair of Pelicans were discovered sitting upon a sandbank near Thebes, and Mr. Buxton shot the smaller of the pair. It measured—length 48 inches, culmen 12, wing from carpus 26, tarsus 5, expanse 104. It was pure white in colour without any tinge of roseate, but it had the usual yellow feathers on the breast, and two of the secondary quills were white. The crest was nearly four inches long. The living specimen of *P. minor* in the Zoological Gardens has at present no crest (September, 1875). The one we got had the usual air-cells over the whole body, and in its pouch a parasitical worm.

214. DALMATIAN PELICAN, *Pelicanus crispus*, Bruch. ;
"Bagah."

Possibly some of the Pelicans we saw at Damietta were

of this species; I cannot say, as we never shot one. I found a dead one one day, but it was too far gone to examine. We met a Diabeyha returning from the second cataract with some skins on board. The only one we were fortunate enough to get was a small grey bird at the Faioum. When the breast was cut open it was found to have bled so profusely, that a spoon had to be used to ladle out the blood. Its beak was $11\frac{3}{4}$ along the ridge, carpus 22 inches. There were a good many on the lake in similar plumage. They had white backs, and a white pouch and legs, and beak very pale. We judged them to be birds of last year. Several persons asserted that they did not breed on the lake, but I should think that they would probably be found to do so if it was well searched, especially as some old ones were also seen there.

It was the most absurd sight possible to see a Pelican sitting in a leafless tamarisk bush very little bigger than himself, yet that was their favourite perch. How the splay feet manage to hold on I cannot think. They are withal a cautious bird, for long before the punt has got within shot the Pelican has slipped off (without any commotion), and is sailing away nearly as fast as you can row. With his head turned he steadily looks back at the pursuer, while he breasts the waves, he calculates the distance to a nicety, and then he very leisurely raises his wings (leaving the water with none of the Flamingo's awkwardness), gives two or three flaps, and sails, and then two or three more flaps low over the water, you think he is going to alight every time he glides, after his great flaps; the tamarisks have their roots deep down in the water, and a good many fish may be seen basking near with their backs above water. Probably these are the attraction to the Pelicans. We thought that they minded the sail of the punt, as the native boats have no sail, so I tried to get near them in a large fishing boat, but they minded that still more.

B B is the only shot for Pelicans. A loose charge is no good. A No. 4 shot will drill a clean hole through the big wing bone without breaking it.

I observe that the example in the Zoological Gardens at London has a greater power of moving the eye than most birds. On stating to the keeper that I had seen these birds sitting in tamarisk trees, he said that one perched on one occasion on the iron rail which divides their·cage down the middle.

215. CORMORANT, *Phalacrocorax carbo* (Linn.);
" Agag."

We saw a few at Damietta and some more in Middle Egypt as we were going up, but in the Faioum none.

Captain Shelley, Mr. E. C. Taylor, and Dr. Adams, are of opinion that they stay to breed. I, however, do not believe they breed either at the cliffs of Gebel-Abou-Fayda, or of Gebel-Tair.

*216. LONG-TAILED CORMORANT, *Graculus africanus*
(Gm.) ; Sav. Desc. de l'Eg., ois. 8, fig. 2 ;
Carbo longicauda, Swains ; Westafr, II., p. 255, pl. 31 ;
Finsch and Hartlaub, p. 847.

This is one of the commonest of birds at lake Faioum in June. Some we shot were in immature, or perhaps still in winter plumage, with all the underparts, except the vent, white ; others were curiously mottled black and white ; and others were in full breeding plumage. Some of the latter had the flesh of the forehead raised in a very singular manner, but on looking at my skins I see that it has much sunk down. These birds had also crests. But the strangest thing about them is a sharp bone, about half an inch long, at the back of the head, which you can feel projecting under the skin.

It was great sport shooting them in the evening, which may be easily done as they come flying down the Bar-El-Wady canal, which unites the Bar-Joseph to the lake. Here one of us would hide up behind the stunted bushes, and as they were very regular we knew exactly what time to look out for them. It is necessary to see them a long way off, as they are rather shy withal, and then to keep well hidden; but sometimes the specks which were taken for Cormorants turned out to be only Buff-backs, though generally they flew in a more straggling flock. Now and then one comes stealing low over the water, or a pair pass out of shot. They are going to a bed of tamarisks a mile out in the lake, where they intend nesting with the Buff-backed Herons. We saw a few sitting upon nests, but they had evidently not begun to lay. Indeed they may only have been using empty nests as a convenient perching place. They took up a position on higher boughs than the Buff-backs—often seven or eight on the top of the same tamarisk. All the nests there seemed to me to be the same, and to be built of the same materials, so that I judge they were all Buff-backs' or Herons' nests of some kind. I saw a Buff-back settle upon one, on which a moment before there had been a Cormorant. They are such good divers, that of the first six shot (by my friend) only one was bagged. They are very easy to skin when not fat.

Hartmann found the *P. africanus* at Gebel-Tair, (J. F. O., 1863, p. 300) and either this species or the Lesser Cormorant was formerly common at Damietta, and known by the name of "Fessek," as I am informed by M. Filliponi, who however has not seen one this seven years.

R

217. LITTLE CORMORANT, *Phalacrocorax pygmœus*, Tem.

The Little Cormorant is probably far rarer than the Long-tailed African Cormorant at the Faioum, as I only shot one—a male, on the 1st of June. We at once noticed it as something different, from its entirely black bill and pouch, dark brown eye, and brown head. All the African ones we shot—amounting to fifteen in number, had red or reddish eyes and yellow bills. The rest of the plumage was also very different. In *P. pygmœus* it was more silky, and the scapulars and wing coverts, instead of being grey, broadly tipped with black, were nearly as dark as the rest of the back, and each feather was rimmed, not tipped with black. The only white upon the bird was a certain number of hair-like feathers very sparsely scattered over it.

The two Little Cormorants shot at the Faioum in February, which Captain Shelley describes at p. 296, (o. c.) were correctly named I have not a doubt. Perhaps the Long-tailed one is only a summer inhabitant. Von Heuglin says that *P. pygmœus* was only met with by him in Lower Egypt in winter and spring (Syst. Ueb., No. 752).

218. GREAT-CRESTED GREBE, *Podiceps cristatus* (Linn.) ; ? "Chaer."

On the desert side of Birket-El-Kairoun, there is a piece of water which I suppose forms part of the great lake in winter. It is fringed with a luxuriant growth of reeds, the very place for a pair of Great-crested Grebes to nest ; and here on the 8th of June I saw two beauties, but so expert are they in diving at the flash, that though I got within twenty-five yards I failed to shoot one.

✱219.   EARED GREBE, *Podiceps nigricollis*, Sundev.

Von Heuglin seems not only to have found this in winter (Shelley's "Birds of Egypt," p. 313), but also breeding.   I ·have not Petermann's "Geographische Mittheilungen," but the reviewer in the "Ibis" (of his list at p. 311 of part VIII.) says, he found it breeding at the lake of Tamieh in Faguin (Ibis, 1862, p. 81, cf., p. 195).   I do not know where these places are, but I saw a Grebe on Menzaleh which appeared, from its size to be this species, on two occasions, first from the shore, and afterwards from a boat.

**220.✱   LITTLE GREBE, *Podiceps minor* (Linn.) ;
 "Zah-ut."**

Three times I came across them in the Delta on inland waters, and once in the Faioum on the same pond with the Great-crested Grebes, but they are equally quick with them in diving ; and unless you get a shot when they are not looking at you, you have not much chance.   The 17th of January was my earliest date.   The pair at the Faioum, which were in full summer plumage, were observed on the 8th of June, so we are justified in concluding that it is resident in the country.†

---

* The Lesser Kestrel, Sand-coloured Dove, and Coot, were omitted by error in the numbering, which makes the total 223.

† A marshman, named Rich, informs me that about 1860, in the depth of a hard winter, some two hundred Dabchicks made their appearance at Surlingham Broad, Norfolk, which was frozen over.   The following Sunday, idle fellows from Norwich attacked them on the ice and drove them into the dykes, and before the expiration of a week they were nearly all killed.

A somewhat similar visitation took place at Worthing in November, 1868 (Zool. ss. 1482).

UNDETERMINED SPECIES.

On the 12th of June I saw at the Faioum a very long-tailed bird, rather larger than a White Wagtail, and somewhat similar in colour, flying over a garden of trees near our camp. I do not believe it belonged to any species, or even to any genus described in the "Birds of Egypt," and I am totally unable even to hazard a guess as to what it may have been.

ADDENDUM.

Since the foregoing list of Birds of Egypt went to press, my father has received the following, collected at Damietta, a few miles from the shore of the Mediterranean, from Mons. E. Filliponi.

GREATER SPOTTED EAGLE, *Aquila vittata*. Nine specimens killed in December. Of this fine series, three are nearly adult and six immature.

OSPREY. December 19th.

SWAINSON'S HARRIER.

MARSH HARRIER.

SCOPS EARED OWL, *Scops giu*, male. September, 1875.

COMMON GOATSUCKER, *Caprimulgus europæus*, male. September, 1875.

ORIENTAL SWALLOW, *Hirundo savignii*.

ROLLER.

CURLEW, *Numenius arquatus* (Linn.). May, 1875.

GREAT BLACK-HEADED GULL, *Larus icthyaëtos*. Two fine specimens ; one in full breeding plumage was killed at the end of February *(vide antea)*, the other, which has no ticket, is in change. .

GREAT CRESTED GREBE, *Podiceps cristatus*. December 31st.

CINEREOUS SHEARWATER, *Puffinus kuhli.*   February 25th.*

NOTE—Lesser White-fronted Goose *(Anser erythropus).* I find from a translation of Heuglin's "Ornithologie Nord-ost Africas," by Dr. Bree (Field newspaper, November 22nd, 1873), that our party was not the first to discover the Lesser White-fronted Goose in Egypt, it having been got before in the Delta.

* This is the same specimen already alluded to.

PASSING NOTES

ON

THE BIRDS OF ITALY.

ON the 30th of December, 1874, I was ensconced in a railway carriage between Macon and Turin. We kept passing continually rivers—affluents I suppose of the Rhone, and at one place the waters swelled into a majestic lake. Here I saw several hundred Ducks, all of which were gone when I traversed the margin of the lake again in the summer. Some which were nearer than the rest, I could see to be common Wild Ducks.

Shortly before entering the famed tunnel of Mount Cenis, which took us twenty-five minutes to pass through, my attention was directed to some flocks of Alpine Choughs, looking exactly like Jackdaws, which I thought they were, until one came near enough for me to see its yellow bill.

I will now say something about the Natural History of Turin, which Bradshaw describes as a brand new city. So it is, and a very good one; capital shops and good hotels. The completion and opening of a new arcade was celebrated while I was there, to be called the "Galleria subalpina." Perhaps I cannot give a better idea of its avifauna than by a list of the birds in the market.

Kestrel	Green Woodpecker
Song Thrush	Jay
Missel Thrush	Magpie
Redwing	Alpine Chough
Ring Ouzel	Cornish Chough
Fieldfare	Quail
Blue Thrush	Greek Partridge
Grey Wagtail	Red-legged Partridge
White Wagtail	Grey Partridge
Water Pipit	Pheasant
Meadow Pipit	Woodcock
Meadow Bunting	Snipe
Cirl Bunting	Water Rail
Italian Sparrow	Coot
Tree Sparrow	Shoveller
Chaffinch	Pochard
Hawfinch	Wigeon
Stonechat	Goldeneye
Robin	Mallard
Alpine Accentor (eight)	Red-breasted Merganser
Great Titmouse	Black-headed Gull

Though some of the birds herein named would be hard
to an English digestion, for all this miscellaneous collection
purchasers would be found.   I forget if it was at the market
that I saw a Snow Bunting, a fine old cock, but tailless, or
at the birdstuffer's, Carlo Bonomi, Via D'aorgennes, No. 41,
at whose shop I was shown a good many birds.   Among
the rarest ones, which I was assured by him had been killed
in the vicinity, I have jotted down Temminck's Stint, Ring
Dotterel,* Lesser Ring Dotterel, Black Tern, Smew, (adult
male and female), Waterouzel, Penduline Titmouse, Scops
Owl, Rock Thrush, Little Crake, Little Bittern, and Nutcracker.

There was another birdstuffer, and I may as well give

---

* The following fact I had from Mr. Bates of Eastbourne.   An egg
of a Ring Dotterel lay seven days on a shelf in his house, and on the
seventh he heard the chick begin to break the shell.

the addresses for future convenience—M. Grasselli, Via di Po, No. 19.

With the Museum, founded by Bonelli, I was especially pleased, both on account of the superb collection of Egyptian remains, and on account of the birds. They are displayed in excellent galleries, but I was sorry to see some of the specimens ticketed wrong. There was a very good Great Auk, and a melanism of a Woodcock, being the fifth melanism that I have seen, though so rare.* The "Ibis" says that the whole of the Marchesa Antinori's Abyssinian collection is here, (Ibis, 1864, p. 410,) and I noticed some hybrids between *Corvus cornix* and *C. corone*, to which allusion is made in the "Ibis" for 1870, p. 450.

From Turin to Bologna was but a short journey. As soon as I was installed at my hotel I went to visit the bird market, where I saw nine species which I had not seen at Turin,—Yellow Hammer, Crested Lark, Wren, Nuthatch, Starling, Rook, Teal, and Pintail. Here, to complete my list of market birds, let me give the names of the live ones which I saw for sale in cages at Turin and Bologna. Barn Owl, Little Owl, Nightingale, Goldfinch, Greenfinch, Serin, Brambling, Linnet, Ortolan, Hoopoe, Magpie,† Greater-spotted Woodpecker, and Turtle Dove.

Bologna is remarkable for its leaning towers. There are

---

* I think if any further argument was needed for Sabine's Snipe not being a good species—and there are still a good many sanguine people who stand up for it—we have it in the discovery that the Woodcock is liable to melanism, and I believe also the Great Snipe and the Jack Snipe.

† How many interesting birds may be discovered even in grimy London by those who know how to use their eyes. In Regent's Park I have more than once seen the shy Magpie, a bird I may remark· which is not included in a list of thirty-eight species by Mr. H. Smith in the "Field," (November 28th, 1874,) nor in another of fifty-seven in the P. Z. S. (1863, p. 159).

two of them ; one leans nine feet, the other five.   They are said to have been built by ancient noblemen, in the days when a nobleman was not considered a nobleman without a tower.

In the afternoon, having nothing better to do, I took a guide to the Cemetery, said to be the best in Italy.   It is very costly and elaborate, many of the beautiful sculptures being by noted artists.   The best are those of pure white Carara marble.   Others of the second and third quality are veined with grey.   The place has received the name of the Catacombs—spacious galleries, having three rows of vaults on either side.   For the smallest a man pays five pounds ; for a larger one much more.   These galleries are built in the form of squares, and the plot of ground within is about two acres.   This is called "common ground," and the poor are buried here (gratis) in trenches ; the males by themselves, the females by themselves, and the children by themselves.   After a lapse of not many years, their bones are dug up and committed to great cave-like vaults, and the ground is trenched and sown again, until a fresh crop of these ghastly remains is ready to be harvested.   In working some excavations it was discovered that on this very site there was, hundreds and hundreds of years ago, a necropolis, or Etruscan city of the dead.

From Bologna by Ancona to Brindisi is the well-known route of all travellers for and from Egypt and India.

The cultivated land was no longer divided into fields. Rows of mulberry trees took the place of trim fences, garnished with drooping vines, and these further south gave way to the olive.   What a different aspect the country presented when I returned in the last week of June.   Then it was all waving fields of yellow corn, and scores and scores of Italian husbandmen were coming down by train to put the sickle to it.

For miles the iron road skirts the shore of the Adriatic

Sea. It could not have been more placid and calm since the last Doge of Venice stood on the deck of his gilded barge and wedded it, amid the plaudits of his nobles by dropping in a ring. Here and there a few fishing smacks with parti-coloured sails of various bright hues, and here and there a few stake nets, and a fisherman's house, were all that was to be seen. For a long time I scanned the sandy shore and the limpid water without being rewarded by the sight of a sea-bird of any kind. At length I perceived a man with a long gun, hiding behind a heap of seaweed, in the hope that a flock of Gulls would come within shot of his ambush. Afterwards two more flocks of Gulls and one Lapwing appeared, and barring Crested Larks nothing else whatever.

Probably birds are more plentiful in summer, as when returning in June I saw the following from the railway carriage, as well as a Manx Shearwater and some Mediterranean Herring Gulls, which I observed as we approached the harbour of Brindisi.

Kestrel	Magpie
Swift	Redbacked Shrike
Swallow	Goldfinch
Sparrow (*Passer italiæ*)	House Martin
Titlark	White Wagtail
Common Sandpiper	Starling
Little Owl	Hooded Crow (2)

I was rather surprised to see Hooded Crows on the 24th of June, but writers on the ornithology of Italy say they are resident.

Several instances have come to my knowledge of their being seen in summer near Cromer in Norfolk; for example last July, one was seen from the 12th to the 27th, and the keeper at Trimingham picked up seven young Pheasants of its killing.

ANALYSIS

OF THE

CLAIMS OF CERTAIN BIRDS

TO BE

ACCOUNTED BRITISH.

A VERY useful attempt to put together all the recorded occurrences of our rarer British Birds has recently been made by Mr. Harting in his "Handbook of British Birds," but it was not within the scope of his work to examine minutely into the claims upon which each individual rested. Believing that many of these would turn out to be purely imaginary, I have applied myself to this task, and I now present the results of my analysis of seven of them. It is by no means in the interest of science that fictitious records should be perpetuated and copied from one book into another,—until the original authorities being dead or lost sight of, it is too late to verify them.

I intend to go on working at the subject, so I will only here say that if any reader should chance to be in possession of valid disproof of any of the occurrences here given, I shall be greatly indebted to him to inform me of the same for my future use. The truth, the whole truth, and nothing but the truth, is what we wish to arrive at, and with regard to British Birds that is not always easy.

EAGLE OWL.

Few indeed are the number of times that the Eagle Owl has really been killed in a wild state in this country, yet many are the supposititious records of it. Mr. Harting (op. cit.) gives a pretty fair list of them, to which I can add a few others, having noted down for some time any which I came across. I wish to premise that though some are obviously incorrect, and others presumably so, I think this noble bird of prey has indubitably occurred in one or two instances, and it may once upon a time have been not very infrequent in Shetland and Orkney, according to the opinion of the best authority upon those groups—the late Dr. Saxby; but unfortunately it is so often kept in confinement that nearly all the cases—the more recent ones especially—are open to the suspicion of being escapes.

In Norfolk an Eagle Owl* was taken alive in 1853, according to the Rev. G. Jeans (Naturalist, 1865, p. 258), and a second in Mr. J. Tomlinson's collection was shot at Somerton in 1864. I believe these would not stand a careful enquiry, which at present has never been made, but would speedily find themselves in the category with our tame bird, which escaped at Northrepps in 1869, and was recorded in more than one journal with much pomp and parade.

A fourth seems to have been got off Flamborough, *fide* Mr. P. Hawbridge, in 1837 (Wood's Naturalist, III., p. 155); while a fifth was seen at North Sunderland in October, 1872, *fide* Mr. J. Sutton ("Birds of Northumb. and Dur.," p. 22); and again another, supposed on "very good

---

* In the "Field" of December 13th, 1873, this example is stated to have come from Norway.

authority" (Selby, B. B., I., p. 83,) to have been killed in Durham, is said to have been in Mr. Bullock's collection, but there is no Eagle Owl entered as British-killed in his sale list.

According to the Rev. F. O. Morris, an Eagle Owl was shot at Bedale in March, 1845 ; and another at Horton, near Bradford, in 1824 ; and a third occurred near Harrowgate in 1832 (B. B., I., p. 184).

Another was taken, in 1848, in Lincolnshire, but according to Mr. Cordeaux was an escaped bird (Cordeaux's "Birds of the Humber," p. 12), which being the case, I do not quite see why my friend has included it in his work.

Mr. Harting (op. cit.) has not mentioned four asserted by Mr. Stewart (Mag. of N. H., V. p. 579) to have visited Donegal, and in truth it is so improbable as to be hardly worth serious consideration.

In the Isle of Sanday, Baikie and Heddle say one was killed in 1830 (Nat. Hist. of Orkney, p. 31) ; and in Shetland Mr. Saxby has two to notice, the first on the faith of a Mr. Nicholson, who saw it sitting on a stone in dignified solitude in the autumn of 1863 ; and the second at Balta in March, 1871, seen by himself, in which on that account, knowing what an accurate and conscientious naturalist he was, I should be ready to place confidence.

To conclude, the latest occurrences which I have to notice, are one at Bridgnorth in 1873 (Zoologist, 3997) ; and one or two in the same year, I believe, on the Tummel in Perthshire (see " Pall Mall Gazette " and " Land and Water " of February 15th, 1873) which had come from the stock of Mr. Fountaine, the noted breeder of these birds, and had been purposely set at liberty on an estate in that county.

RED-THROATED PIPIT.

The Red-throated Pipit must be the subject of a note,

as I am going to show that it has no title to be included as a British bird, and to prove that, I must quote some extracts from a pamphlet or paper, professing to be "A list of the birds that have been observed to breed in the island of Arran, Scotland, since the year 1835, by Dr. Martin Barry."[*] The bird has been admitted into our lists, as most naturalists are aware, on the faith of a skin labelled "Unst., 4th May, 1854," in neat characters by an unknown hand. The mysterious interloper was lot 401, at the sale of the collection of Mr. Troughton of Coventry, and its purchaser was Mr. F. Bond. I turn to the list I have just spoken of, and there I find the Red-throated Pipit, and at the end the following remarkable sentence: "I have received a nest with the old birds from Uist (sic), taken May 4th." I have not the smallest doubt that here we have the identical bird, the date agreeing and the locality also, though the latter appears to be misspelt; and the obvious explanation is that Mr. Troughton had bought it at the sale of the collection said to have been formed by Dr. Barry. It only remains for me to show that this list, of which I have never seen but one copy, is untrustworthy, and from the tissue of misstatements contained in it I will select as follows :—

"I believe that this is the first time the Aigle Jean-le Blanc, *Circaetus gallicus* (Vieillot), has occurred in Scotland. I have several times seen specimens in Ireland; the last one was nailed up to warn the smaller fry not to steal poultry.

"The Great Black-headed Gull, *Larus ichthyaetos*, was obtained by myself on the island of Arran, June 5th, 1844, with the eggs.

"It is strange to find the slender-billed Tern, *Anoüs tenuirostris*, breeding so far north—my pair of birds were shot on the Island of Arran, and three eggs obtained June 10th, 1844."

---

[*] A recent, and I need hardly say, a trustworthy list of the Birds of Arran, with notes, appeared in 1872 from the pen of Mr. Robert Gray. As a matter of course the Red-throated Pipit is not admitted.

SPOTTED SANDPIPER.

Some time ago I set myself to collect all the recorded instances of the Spotted Sandpiper in Britain, and a most extraordinary task I found I was in for. I was indeed astonished at the number of occurrences, but still more at the feeble foundation on which most of them rested. I ended by collecting such a tangled skein of conflicting evidence, that I laid the job aside in sheer despair, but have now gone through it again, and present a careful resumé with all the proof and all the disproof that I obtained. The 277th plate of Edwards' "Gleanings of Natural History," to start with the original offender, represents the Spotted Sandpiper from Pennsylvania. This distinguished naturalist and talented draughtsman fancied that it was also found in England, and in the accompanying letterpress he mentions a specimen from Essex, which "differed in no respect from the American Tringa, but *in being without spots on its under side*, except on the throat, where it had a few small, longish, dusky spots down the shafts of the feathers" (VI., p. 141).

Of course the want of spots shows it to have been a Common Sandpiper, but I have still further proof. I have found a MS. note in the handwriting of Donovan, in a copy of Montagu's Dictionary (in the possession of Canon Tristram), saying that this bird, after standing in the Leverian Museum twenty years, passed to him. Therefore it is a fair surmise that Plate CLXXXIV. of his "British Birds" is its portrait, and no one would want to be told after looking at it that it represents the Common, not the Spotted Sandpiper.

And now we come to the so-called Spotted Sandpiper of Bewick (B. B., 1st ed., II., p. 111), which is the specimen mentioned in Wallis' "History of Northumberland." His admirable woodcut, which is much too accurate to leave any doubt about its being the common species, has been the means of misleading many. Once more the bird had to be resuscitated, see Yarrell, B. B., 1st ed., II., p. 545, where a certain birdstuffer professes to have received one unskinned from Cromer. What is become of the valuable (!) specimen I cannot say, nor does it signify. Mr. Stevenson having gone into the case some time ago, and satisfied him·self that it was set up from a foreign skin (B. of Norf., II., p. 234).

After this, a variety of spurious records found their way from time to time into print, for the most part based on a misapprehension of the correct coloration. I will take them *seriatim*. The first has reference to Shetland (Zool, 1844, p. 462), but is explained away in the "Birds of Shetland" (p. 195). The second to Whitby, and is not explained at present. It was an adult female, (?) stated to have been shot on the 29th of March. Mr. E. T. Higgins saw it in the flesh (Zool. 2456), but the intestines had been removed. Doubts having been raised, I enquired if it could have been "drawn" and packed in salt, and sent over from America (cf. Zool., 1293), but Mr. Higgins says it certainly was not salted. Twelve months previously he had thought that he had seen one at Bridlington (Zool., 2147), which is about thirty miles south of Whitby.

A short period elapsed, and in July, 1849, an announce-ment appeared from Mr. J. Duff (Zool. 2499), that within a few days of the occurrence at Whitby, one had been taken at Bishop Auckland; and after a brief interval a second was reported from that locality: but they proved on a more critical examination to be only examples of the Green Sandpiper. (Hancock. B. of Northum. and Dur., p. 123.)

Mr. Hogg quotes Mr. J. Grey for its occurrence on the river Tees, (Zool. 1173), but I saw, I believe, the very bird. in Mr. Grey's collection at Stockton, and I am sorry to say that this again was a Green Sandpiper.

Nor have we yet done with Durham, for it is set down in Sir C. Sharp's "History of Hartlepool," (app. XVII.) and in Cumberland in a list by Mr. Robson (Zool., 4166), but in my opinion both are obvious mistakes.

In September, 1863, a man of the name of Emerson shot at Epworth in Lincolnshire a Sandpiper, which was pronounced by the local birdstuffer to be a Spotted Sandpiper, and as such it was recorded, together with a Ruddy Shelduck and a Bittern by Mr. S. Hudson (Zool., 9291); but serious doubts having been expressed about them, it was suggested that they should be examined by a competent naturalist, when the Ruddy Shelduck proved to be something very different; and I cannot help thinking that the same fate would have befallen the Spotted Sandpiper had it been forthcoming, but its owner had discreetly sold it to a commercial traveller at a public house, and I have traced it no further.

About this time two were shot at Retford (Notts.), according to a provincial newspaper, but I can say nothing about them as I have not seen them or the newspaper.

The "Yorkshire Post" likewise makes mention of one in some "Miscellaneous Rural Notes for 1867," by Mr. Roberts, giving I believe Scarborough as the locality, but this was certainly a case of mistaken identity, as was in all probability the other.

A Spotted Sandpiper is stated in Harting's "Birds of Middlesex," p. 180, to have been shot at Kingsbury reservoir, a large sheet of water near London, considering its inland situation much affected by waders. Its possessor was Mr. Milton, and at his sale in 1852 at Stevens' it was bought by the well-known collector, Mr. Bond. It was lot 75, and entered as killed at Kingsbury. Mr. Bond traced the specimen, which he has kindly permitted me to see, to a person named Crane, who formerly worked for Mr. Ward the taxidermist, and who he believes stuffed it, but no facts were elicited, and I cannot now ascertain Crane's whereabouts.

Under the date of August 7th, 1854, Mr. J. Cavafy writes to the "Naturalist" to say that Mr. Swaysland had shown him, among other rare birds killed at Brighton, "several Spotted Sandpipers." Brighton is noted for rare birds, but if the above were really procured there, it is singular that we should have heard no more of them, and accordingly I think we may take it as pretty certain that there was some mistake which further enquiries or a more critical examination revealed. In the case of another which I saw at Mr. Swaysland's shop in 1871, I am now satisfied that there was a mistake. He said—doubtless in perfect good faith—that it was killed between Worthing and Little Hampton by a Mr. Gringer, whose letter he showed me as proof. He had bought it of Mrs. Wells, the widow of the late trustworthy and intelligent birdstuffer at Worthing, and with her I had some correspondence on the subject, the result of which was to leave no doubt on my mind that a mistake had been committed by somebody.

I have further to name another pair marked "Sussex" in the sale catalogue of the collection of Mr. Byne of Milligan Hall, near Taunton, and I think I remember that gentleman showing them to me, and saying they came from the birdstuffer at Brighton. I have not the least doubt that here also there was some mistake, though after a lapse of several years it becomes not easy to ferret it out.

In Mr. Ecroyd Smith's "Notabilia of the Mersey District," Mr. C. S. Gregson says (p. 51):—

"Edwin Lord, of Warrington, shot two specimens on the Mersey below that town in May, 1863, one of which I possess."

I have been obliged by a photograph of this bird. There is no mistake about it. And Mr. G. vouches for its authenticity to me, in a letter, in the following words:—

"It was shot on the Mersey by E. Lord, skinned by him under the wing, given to me by him, and set up by myself after being shown to various friends fresh."

But though willing to give credence in this instance, I should for the present withhold it from an example which I am told is stated in Byerley's "Fauna of Liverpool" (p. 19)—a work I have not seen—to have occurred on Formby shore, *fide* Mr. Mather, a birdstuffer, not now living.

In a foot-note to his "Handbook," p. 140, Mr. Harting informs his readers that he procured a Spotted Sandpiper of Mr. Burton, the well-known birdstuffer in Soho, which was said to have been shot with another on the coast of Kent. This other I purchased, and at the same time learnt from Mr. Burton that the name of the person who obtained them was Bromley, but from his conversation with me he appeared to be exceedingly doubtful of either of them being British.

My father has a specimen obtained from Mr. Mummery, the curator of the Museum at Margate, who averred that it was killed in that part of Kent. I do not believe a word of it ; not that I would insinuate that he could be guilty of intentionally deceiving, but a mistake is possible, and may have been, and no doubt was committed.

I am sorry I cannot abbreviate this long tale. It is a necessary part of my scheme to quote every instance that has come to my knowledge, no matter how improbable, no matter if it be disproved already, no matter that I am morally satisfied of its not being a sound case.

Professor Newton, who has taken a great interest in the subject, and for whose assistance I beg to return my best thanks, feels convinced, after looking over my evidence, that some more cases might still be refuted ; and several other able ornithologists deny the right of the subject of this essay to British citizenship. As the lawyer said, "I leave it in the hands of an intelligent jury;" merely observing that there surely never was a bird about which so much misapprehension has existed,—a misapprehension which I read extends even to the continent. My next reference will be to the "Zoologist," (p. 2684) where Mr. T. J. Tuck has recorded one at Mildenhall in Suffolk. He saw it soon after being mounted. It was shot, as he has informed me, about February, 1869, and the possessor of it is Mr. Gregory Sparke of Bury. Then I hear that it has a place in Rowe's "Perambulation of the Forest of. Dartmoor," but I have not the book to refer to. There is no mention of it in his catalogue published in 1863, so I pass it by as suspicious and go on to those figured in Mr. Selby's splendid folios, which are equally doubtful. I could not see them in the Twizell collection which I went over shortly after his death.

With regard to Scotland, there is an air of probability about the pair* recorded in Gray's "Birds of the West of Scotland," (p. 299) to have been obtained in August, 1870, at or near Aberdeen, which no one can deny, and I must say that all the careful enquiries which I have made from Mr. Angus and Mr. Mitchell, have not shaken the authenticity of these specimens, but have entirely tended to confirm them. I am assured on all hands of their genuineness, that they were left while in the flesh at the Museum, that the stomachs were sent to Mr. Gray for dissection, and that they really were killed where stated. The species is also in the statistical catalogue of Wick in Caithness, but Mr. W. Reid, who has examined the bird for me, writes that it is not a Spotted Sandpiper, and from his description I have no doubt that he is right in considering it to be a Spotted Redshank, a very different bird with which it has more

---

* A photograph of them was obligingly sent to me, and I have since had an opportunity of examining one of them at Mr. Gray's house.

than once been confounded. This is believed to be the individual alluded to by Shearer and Osborne in the Trans. of the Phys. Soc. of Edinburgh. Again I should say that the example referred to by the late Professor Macgillivray, as "observed near Montrose," (B. B., IV., p. 358) was the same which I learn from Mr. Gray is mentioned by Messrs. Molison and Brewster in their list of the Birds of Craig in Forfarshire. I have no evidence about it, but Mr. Gray thinks that a mistake may have been made. Mr. Molison was a collector and birdstuffer, and I have ascertained that he possessed "Bewick," the picture in which may have led him into error.

Ireland may be dismissed with a very few words. Dr. J. D. Marshall, at p. 395 of the 2nd vol. of the Mag. of Nat. Hist., says: "One specimen was shot near Belfast in July, 1828, and another in September." I have no doubt they were among the instances investigated by Thompson, who, though a discursive writer, was a most conscientious naturalist (N. H. of Ireland, II., p. 216).

And now to conclude, after having mentioned so many other people's Spotted Sandpipers, let me mention my own. In the course of my enquiries I learnt that Mr. B. Bates, the birdstuffer at Eastbourne, was in possession of a pair which he received in the flesh from a gasfitter named Lee some day in the beginning of October, 1866; and as Mr. Borrer and others were kind enough to make enquiries for me with a satisfactory result, and as I found that Mr. Lee remembered the afternoon when he shot them at what is called the Crumble pond, about a quarter of a mile from Eastbourne, a place where a good many rare birds have been killed, I bought one of them, and have since seen the other. I carefully examined both and made further enquiries without shaking the testimony of any one concerned in the matter, and I can only say that I now

most fully believe in them.* The circumstance of a pair
being got together is no argument against them: I apprehend we have several instances on record of two examples
of an American bird being obtained in England at the same
time.

Here my long list of twenty-six cases terminates. To
give a summary of them I should say that at least fifteen
have been cases of mistaken identity, but the remaining
eleven I believe to have been correctly named; albeit, I
am persuaded that five were foreign skins, though it is not
for me to say that they were wilfully palmed off as British.
But it must be as clear as daylight to anyone, that it would
be very unfair to doubt all on that account; and I would
indicate as those most deserving of credence the examples
at Aberdeen, Warrington, Eastbourne, Whitby, Kingsbury,
and Mildenhall. Other American Sandpipers have occurred
dozens of times in England and not been doubted, why
then the Spotted?

GREAT WHITE HERON.

British authors have wavered a good deal about the
Great White Heron, but it is now pretty well established.
It certainly has not been for lack of records, for besides the
sixteen enumerated by Mr. Harting in his Hand List, I can
name six.

Firstly. A specimen supposed to have been killed in
Norfolk, *teste* Mr. Thurtle (B. of Norf., II., p. 149); a very
poor one, with all the appearance of having been stuffed
from a skin.

Secondly. A specimen in the sale of Mr. Stephen Miller's
collection, lot 47, bought for seven and sixpence, but by

---

* Probably the above was the authority for including the species in
the list in Gowland's "Guide to Eastbourne."

whom is not known.   Mr. Stevenson possesses a letter—or at least a copy of one—written in 1831 by Mr. Dawson Turner to Mr. Selby, in which he considers that a reference is made to this bird by the writer, who offers the loan of pictures of Norfolk-killed specimens of this and other rare birds.

Thirdly.   The Rev. F. O. Morris says that one was shot at New Hall by John Townend (B. B., IV., p. 115).   No further particulars.

Fourthly.   An example, seen and shot at, on Romney Marsh by moonlight, about February, 1849 (Zool., 2419). If this was what it purports to have been, it may have been the same which the late Dr. Strong obtained a few months afterwards at Thorney, *teste* Messrs. Forster and Little.

Fifthly.   Sir Wm. Jardine remarks that during the winter of 1840 a "White Heron" was, according to the newspapers, seen several times on the Solway (Nat. lib., Birds, III., p. 135), and it is conjectured that this may have been the example which was afterwards killed in Haddingtonshire.

Sixthly.   Mr. R. Gray has found in a copy of Baikie and Heddle's "Nat. Hist. of Orkney," a MS. note made therein by one of the authors, which states that two were met with on the island of Damsay (Birds of W. Scotland, p. 277).

Long admitted on sufferance, this fine species must now be considered as having been fully installed by Strickland and Macgillivray, but most of the other records must be taken *cum grano salis*, it being very likely where the bird has been only seen and not obtained to have been a Spoonbill or some other species.

HARLEQUIN DUCK.

The Harlequin Duck is without doubt one of the very scarcest of our accidental visitants, yet of our leading Ornithologists, one remarks that it has "been frequently captured," and another merely says that it is " more rare than the Long-tailed Duck." It may not therefore be labour in vain if I proceed to show that Messrs. Yarrell and Gould were not alive to its real scarcity, by bringing together the various supposed instances of its occurrence, and showing how little all of them were worth on investigation; but as Professor Newton and Mr. Harting have already been over the same ground (Ibis, 1859, p. 165; Hand-book of B. B., p. 160), it is not to be expected that I should have much new matter to bring forward, and I have not. For the sake of expedition, I may as well dismiss the cases already disposed of by Professor Newton, and commence with 1802, when Mr. Montagu published his " Ornithological Dictionary," and this Duck was introduced on the authority of Mr. James Sowerby, who had received a pair from Lord Seaforth. No doubt these are what Mr. Mudie refers to when he says (B. B., II., p. 354) that the Harlequin has been seen in Lewis, as I understand that this island was Lord Seaforth's estate. For the following note by the late veteran naturalist J. E. Gray, I am indebted to Professor Newton :—

"The Sowerby Museum was in Meade Place, Lambeth, near the Orphan Asylum. It became in a bad state from neglect, and some specimens were sold privately, and the rest at the auction rooms, now Stevens'. I do not know what became of the Duck. I think I recollect it in a separate glass case as was then the fashion, but rather baddish in condition."

The above does not furnish us with much information, nor am I more fortunate in regard to Mr. Simmons' young female from Orkney, about which I have nothing fresh to impart, though I should say *prima facie* that its being a young female is against it, for as will be seen in the sequel, the young of this species and the young of the Long-tailed Duck have been several times confounded. It is not very likely to have been the specimen in Mr. Bullock's sale (15th day, lot 59), which, according to a MS. note in Professor Newton's copy of the catalogue, was killed in the Orkneys and bought by Dr. Adams for a guinea ; though this latter may be one of the three or four incidentally mentioned by Selby and Donovan.

In 1858, Major W. R. King shot a fowl which he is convinced was a Harlequin—and a drake in good plumage—at Buchan in Aberdeenshire (The Sportsman and Naturalist in Canada, p. 231).   He has been so obliging as to inform me that he shot it after several days' storm from the northeast, that it was swimming a short distance only from the shore, and that it appeared to be either wounded or much exhausted.   It was stuffed, but during a temporary absence from home was unfortunately so injured by damp and moth that it had to be thrown away.

Mr. Gray says, "The Harlequin Duck has since been included in a catalogue of the Birds of Caithness, prepared by Mr. E. S. Sinclair (B. of W. Scotland, p. 394).   No doubt on the same authority it finds a place in Osborne and Shearer's "Birds of Caithness," (R. Phys. Soc., Edin., II., p. 340) but as Mr. Sinclair has been found to be wrong in the case of the Spotted Sandpiper, there seems to me a probability of his having been mistaken here as well.   His collection has been sold to the Thurso Museum, as Mr. Reid informs me.

In the "Naturalist" for 1854, p. 242, Mr. Edward relates the death of a Harlequin at the hands of a rabbit-catcher of Loch Strathbeg, who—abandoned wretch that he was— for the sake of a "paltry sum" sent it "away south," to the great indignation of the local magnates; and by doing so effectually closed the door against incredulous people like myself, who would have made further enquiries.

Having now done with North Britain, I will begin again with Norfolk.   Nobody knows what has become of the specimen which Mr. Wigg bought in Yarmouth market (Nat. His. of Yarm., p. 12, Intr. XII.). Uncharitable people insinuate that he consigned it to the spit, like the Red-breasted Goose which he bought there on another occasion. We cannot be expected to credit a bird which was eaten; and if a man calling himself a naturalist could not get the better of his unfortunate gastronomic tastes, he must pay the penalty of not being believed.

There is a note in the series sent by Mr. Joseph Clarke to Mr. Stevenson, for the use of his work, upon this Duck, as follows:—

"One shot at Yarmouth in 1833.* Harvey sold it to Mr. Hoy."

Now 1833 was the year before the "Nat. Hist. of Yarmouth" came out, and I think I may take it for granted that this was not Mr. Wigg's bird; but if it were another one, how came it that the Messrs. Paget who, as is evident from their introduction, were familiar enough with Harvey the birdstuffer, pass it over in silence? and how also can we account for there being no mention of it by Mr. Hoy in his article on "Rare Birds killed in Suffolk and Norfolk in 1832—3" (London Journal for 1834; see also Mag. of N. H., VII., p. 52), save by the supposition that they disbelieved in it?

There is also a drake in the Norwich Museum said to have been killed near Yarmouth (Zool., 1380). I find that it was presented in 1839 by my father, who does not believe in it. Neither do I, for it was remounted, and Mr. Knight, who took the stuffing out, told me that it had the appearance of having been set up from a skin. I am sorry I have not made out a better case for Norfolk, but such a rich county can afford to spare one species; I have no bias for or against it, and only wish to get the unvarnished truth.

---

* Mr. Clarke informs Mr. Stevenson that he saw it in the flesh, and that it was a young male.

Mr. Gatcombe has seen the supposed specimen recorded by Dr. Moore as killed at Plymouth, (Mag. of N. H., 2nd ser., I., p. 365) as no doubt it was, seeing that it turns out to be a young Long-tailed Duck. In his "Sketch of the Nat. Hist. of Exeter," Mr. D'Urban notes that several immature specimens have been obtained on the Exe, (p. 122) but in a later edition he has wisely omitted this, and I hear from him that they turned out, as I expected, young Long-tails again.

Mr. Yarrell bought two "young females" in the London market, as he informs his readers (B. B., 1st. ed., III., p. 263), but he did not know the bird from the young Long-tailed Duck, as his miscalling the one killed by the Duke of Richmond proves (Ibis, 1859, p. 165), therefore his evidence must be rejected. Mr. Bond is also very sure that he once saw three or four young birds there, but even such a good naturalist as he is may have been mistaken, and as he did not take the trouble to preserve one, I cannot admit that he has proved his case.

Again, I have very little doubt that Mr. Yarrell was mistaken when he adds, that the keeper at Sir Philip Egerton's shot a female in Cheshire in 1840. Great author as he was, he did not know what a rare bird the Harlequin was. At this distance of time I cannot attempt to disprove it ; but the following are a few additional details with which Sir Philip has favoured me. He writes that he believes the underparts were not dark, which they ought to have been, that it was a bird of the year, and that it was never preserved. Its occurrence was only communicated to Mr. Yarrell on the authority of Professor Agassiz, who chanced to be staying at his seat at Oulton Park.

Professor Newton has given me a reference to a page in the Zoologist (p. 145), where Mr. J. D. Banister records a young female killed in Lancashire, and I have investigated it and find that it was a mistake.

A female is said, in Morris' "British Birds" (V., p. 258), to have been shot on the Don near Doncaster, and I have tried to do the same by that, but all the information I could get was that it was procured a little above the town by a Mr. Cartwell, that Mr. Reid the well-known birdstuffer was guarantee for its being correctly named, and that the Rev. W. E. Strickland purchased it, and there I lost the clue ; but the locality assigned, so distant from the sea, is against its having been a Harlequin.

A Duck which Mr. J. Cordeaux shot at Bridlington is described in the Zoologist (ss. p. 23) as a Harlequin, which he thought it was at the time, but is now inclined to believe that it was a young Long-tail, and hence has excluded it from the "Birds of the Humber." It was not preserved.

The author of the "Birds of Bucks and Berks" (p. 206) tells us of a Harlequin killed at Maidenhead. I had my suspicions about it as soon as I read the passage, and they were well founded, for Mr. E. Andrews, in whose possession it is, writes me that it has "a beautiful black-and-white top-knot lying down the neck similar to a horse's mane." This settles the question as far as the Harlequin is concerned, and though not a very precise description, applies tolerably well to the American Wood Duck, and I will hazard a guess that this is what it is.

I scarcely care to make any allusion to two, said to have been taken in the island of Arran, for I know them to have been so utterly unworthy of credit—one in 1844, the other in 1856.

Not one whit more trustworthy is the account quoted from the Times by Mr. Simeon (Stray Notes on Fishing, p. 209) of a too-confiding "Harlequin," which visited the pond of a "Naturalist" and became "quite domesticated there," though all will agree with his protest against its subsequent fate.

And here I bring to an end this bloodstained roll of

would-be Harlequins, only regretting that the tragical
deaths of so many innocents should have done so little for
the cause of science.   Out of the whole twenty-two I could
have dispensed with twenty.   Eight are in my opinion
clearly mistakes, and the rest are all doubtful except two—
those being the original Lewes specimens, and the recent
Aberdeen one.

RED-BREASTED GOOSE.

The Red-breasted Goose being such a rare bird at home
and abroad, I am delighted to have it in my power to give
any additional particulars about it.   It is a species which
most ornithologists have always viewed with peculiar interest, perchance because it is so high-priced, and so
seldom comes into the market; perchance because of its
beauty; perchance because it is by some supposed to be
moribund, though with this I do not agree.

A list of no less than ten reputed British specimens are
given in Mr. Harting's most useful handbook, though I
would deduct four of them, and references to five local cata-
logues are added.

The fine specimen which was shot near London in 1776—
the locality must not be taken too literally (Fox's "New-
castle Mus.," pp. 96, 212)—is still in good order.   It would
seem from external appearance to have the breast-bone in,
which was the old mode of stuffing.

Of the Yarmouth specimen recorded by Paget, and Shep-
pard and Whitear, Mr. Stevenson is going to give a full
account, and I will not anticipate him further than to say,
that he has not been able to get any actual proof of its
having been correctly determined by Mr. Lilly Wigg, who
being, as I have hinted before, afflicted with an unfortunate
penchant for tasting rare birds, cooked this valuable Goose,
which, skinned and sold, would have laid him golden eggs of

the right sort ; but in a fit of remorse he saved some of the feathers, which he handed to Mr. Sparshall, who afterwards gave them to my father, but we cannot find them now.

Accounts differ as to whether the slayer of that one killed at Berwick was a Mr. Burney or a Mr. Innes of Oserwick ; but it does not much signify, as I consider it well established that it really was killed there.

Mr. Moore, in his first catalogue of Devonshire birds, sets it down among the birds not hitherto noticed in the county, but in his second (Mag. of N. H., 1837, p. 266) he has two to bring forward, the first shot at Kenton Warren in 1828, and in the possession of the late Mr. W. Russell of Dawlish; the second, shot February 21st, 1837, on the Teign marshes. I cannot verify them by ascertaining into whose hands they have now passed, so I can only hope that the next historian of the birds of that part of England will take the subject up and be more successful.

I am sorry that I can place but little confidence in the example affirmed by Mr. Hogg, to have been shot at Cowpen near Teesmouth, by a man named Hikely (Zool., p. 1178) ; but when I lived at Darlington I saw Hikely's son, and the account he gave me was so very much the reverse of reassuring, that I am constrained to let it go to the limbo of the doubtful.

Mr. T. Amherst possesses a specimen, said to have been killed at Hastings, in 1866, but I have my suspicions about that also.*

It is a bird which has always commanded a long price. I have tried more than once to obtain a specimen, but until this month (Dec., 1875) I never got an offer of one at a lower figure than eight pounds. This is a small sum to what some of the British specimens have fetched.   Mr. Hunt

---

* Two Red-breasted Geese are believed to have been once killed near Garstang (Zool., ss., 3236.).

tells us (B. B., II., 234) that Donovan's, which had been in the Leverian Museum, was knocked down to Mr. Foljambe for fifteen and a half guineas; and the Berwick specimen (which is not in perfect plumage) was sold for the still larger sum of twenty-seven pounds to Dr. Leach. This is confirmed in an old MS. note in the library of Professor Newton, but both these high figures pale before the thirty-one pounds which was offered and taken for the Maldon specimen—the latest and the best authenticated, which is now the property of Mr. Marshall of Taunton.

BRUENNICH'S GUILLEMOT.

I supplied the author of the Handbook before quoted with several of his references to Bruennich's Guillemot. I see that most of them refer to Scotland and its isles, or to Ireland. I should dismiss the Emerald isle with very little ceremony, for the example found floating off Dublin (Zool., 2609) had been dead many days, and as the recorder remarks, is hardly a fair Irish bird, assuming that it really was the species in question, and the cases which Thompson gives (B. of Ireland, III., p. 213) would never do to fall back upon, they being something more than doubtful.

In the same manner I should set aside Shetland, where we have no later authority than Captain Ross for it, and that open to grave doubts; which leaves me no choice but to turn to Orkney, and all that can be said for Orkney is that we are informed by Professor Macgillivray (B. B., V., p. 316) that the only British specimen he ever saw was among some skins from Orkney, which had belonged to Mr. Wilson, Janitor of the Edinburgh Museum. This is no doubt the same individual alluded to in the "Nat. Hist. of Orkney" (p. 86).

On the mainland of Scotland we have a slight discrepancy. Mr. A. G. Moore says (Ibis, 1865, p. 449) :—

"Brünnich's Guillemot is included by Sir W. Milner in his list of the Birds of Sutherland, published in the Zoologist; but Mr. Henry Milner has kindly informed me that the bird was not found breeding there, and only a single specimen was purchased on that occasion."

This has been requoted by Mr. Gray and Mr. Harting, but I have turned to Sir William's list (Zool., 2014) and cannot find any mention of it. I conclude, however, that in some way confusion has arisen with his later records in the same volume, (pp. 2059, 2061) in which he speaks of a Brünnich's Guillemot and egg at Soa, a little island close to St. Kilda.

It has been "once met with" in Banffshire, *fide* Mr. T. Edward (Zool., 6971), and once in Caithness.

In England I have no remarks to offer on one killed at Rosemullion Head, in Cornwall, by Mr. G. Copeland ("Cornish fauna," p. 39), except to say that Mr. Rodd in his more recent catalogue takes no notice of it; nor any to make on a specimen obtained at Freshwater on the 7th of February, 1860, by Mr. Rogers, (Guide to the Isle of Wight, p. 434).

On the whole I do not believe in any of them, and I think that unless further evidence is forthcoming, this Guillemot might really be withdrawn from the British list.

MISCELLANEA ORNITHOLOGICA.

ADDITIONS TO THE AVIFAUNA OF DURHAM.

In his remarkable but somewhat lengthy paper on the Birds of Durham, read before the British Association at York, and reprinted in the fourth volume of the Zoologist, Mr. Hogg enumerates 202 species. From this number I should deduct the Ringed Guillemot, (three or four have been taken, but I deduct it as not being a good species,) Golden Eagle, Scops-eared Owl, Chough, Great Black Woodpecker, Ptarmigan, Spotted Sandpiper, and Red-breasted Goose, which leaves 194 well authenticated. Mr. W. Backhouse's additions (Zool., 1261) bring it up to 212, and I shall now preceed to quote from various sources twenty-five more very rare species, making a total result which will compare favourably with most counties, and which I trust will be putting a spoke in the wheel of some future faunist.

GREENLAND FALCON.

I will commence with that splendid species, the Greenland Falcon, though I insert it, I am sorry to say, with some doubt, albeit Mr. Green, naturalist of Stockton, avers positively that he met with one at Teesmouth chasing some Terns, and shot it.

T

I have seen the young male Peregrine which lamed itself against a floating-light, and was recorded as the present species ("Naturalist," 1853, p. 60) though the mistake was afterwards corrected (p. 135). It is a very fine bird, but not the rarity we could have wished.

RED-FOOTED FALCON.

A mature male near Marsden Rock, October, 1836, *fide* Albany Hancock (Mag. of Zool. and Bot., I., p. 491).

SNOWY OWL.

Helmington, near Bishop Auckland, November 7th, 1858, *fide* Mr. H. Gornall (Hancock, Cat. of the Birds of Northumberland and Durham, p. 20).

EAGLE OWL.

I receive with some doubt the statement of an Eagle Owl being got on the moors, (Selby, Brit. Orn., I., p. 83,) but I am assured that one was seen at Seaton Carew.

TENGMALM'S OWL.

Near Marsden, October 11th (cir.), 1848 (Zool., ss. 1799, 2765) (Hancock, op. cit., p. 20).

WHITE'S THRUSH.

Castle-Eden dene, January 17th, 1872. Full particulars of this fine addition to the *Ornis* of Durham are given by Mr. Sclater (Zool., 3019, 3041).

GOLDEN ORIOLE.

I have no other authority than Mr. Proctor's list in "Sketches of Durham."

BLACK REDSTART.

This must be added to the list. Indeed it is said to have nested at Durham, and I am surprised not to see it among the instances cited in the 4th edition of Yarrell, B. B.

LAPLAND BUNTING.

Durham, January, 1860 (Hancock, op. cit.)

ALPINE SWIFT.

One seen at South Point, near Durham, July 24th, 1871, by Mr. G. E. Crawshall (Field newspaper, Aug. 5th). During the preceding month examples had been observed in Kent, Essex, and Norfolk.

GREY-HEADED WAGTAIL.

Has been obtained once at least.

SHORELARK.

Has occurred on two occasions.

BLUE-TAILED BEE-EATER *(Merops philippensis)*.

Seaton-Snook, Teesmouth, August, 1862, *fide* Rev. T. M. Hicks (Hancock, op. cit., 28). I should like this specimen to be compared again, as I think it may turn out to be *Merops ægyptius*, Forsk., the Blue-cheeked Bee-eater, which is more ·likely to occur, because it is a much more western species. Seaton-Snook is not the place where I should have expected to meet with a Bee-eater, though I remember being shown a bird of equal brilliancy which was found there, a Jacamar, already skinned too. The skin of a Patagonian Penguin was picked up on the "slake" at Jarrow (Fox's Neuc. Mus., 233). It was supposed to have been thrown overboard by a whaler, but I have read of one coming in a consignment of guano, and being picked up in a mummified state on the land.

> Certainly the Cedarbird has no claim to be admitted in a list of Durham birds, if indeed it be right to receive it into a British list. I asked Mr. Heaviside, one of the birdstuffers at Stockton, about the examples recorded at p. 3506 of the Zoologist, and he remembered nothing about them.
>
> The other supposed occurrences are one—hitherto unrecorded—in the late Mr. Newcome's collection, said to have been shot at Highgate, *teste* Mr. Holford.
>
> A second in the possession of Mr. Batson of Horseheath, Lincolnshire, Zool., 3277, 3506.
>
> A third, shot in Fifeshire in 1841, in the late Sir William Feilden's collection. Gray, B. of West Scotland, p. 109.

CRESTED TITMOUSE.

This is again a doubtful bird, but I give the published evidence for what it may be worth. First, three or four were seen near Witton Gilbert, *teste* Mr. P. Farrow (Ornsby, p. 197; Hancock, op. cit., p. 76, note). Second, a male shot on Sunderland Moor, January, 1850, *teste* Messrs. Calvert and Duff (Zool., 2766).

STOCKDOVE.

In May, 1866, I discovered this species at Castle-Eden dene. I think it was not before known to be a Durham bird. Mr. Sclater has since found it rather common there. The following winter I obtained specimens at Darlington and High Coniscliffe, and I have no doubt, that as a resident species, it will before long become abundant in the county.

PALLAS' SANDGROUSE.

Durham shared to a small extent in the visitation of 1863. There was a rumour of them again in 1872 in Northumberland (Ibis, 1872, p. 334).

RED-LEGGED PARTRIDGE.

I am surprised to see no mention of this in Mr. Hancock's catalogue. In 1866 I was offered a specimen at Darlington. It is true it had been shot at Richmond, which is over the Yorkshire border, but I have no doubt of its sometimes occurring in Durham. Though its numbers may be diminished where it was once plentiful (and no wonder, considering the means taken to destroy it,) it has been extending its area for many years past. Some years ago one was shot at Stockton, but this may have been one of a bevy which I learn from Mr. Grey were turned out at Wynyard and bred at Cole Hill.

CRANE.

Mr. Newman is the recorder of a Crane at Hartlepool

(Zool., 8005), but he omits the date which, when the exact day is lost, is always worth giving approximately.* Possibly by some strange mistake it may have been confounded with the Black Stork next to be noticed ; for there is no mention of it in Mr. Hancock's catalogue.

BLACK STORK.

Hartlepool, 1862, *fide* Mr. W. C. Horsfall, Zool., 8196. Here again the exact date is wanting, though I know there is no mistake about the bird, some of my friends having seen it. The same year one was got at Otmoor (Gould, B. of G. B.).

SQUACCO HERON.

A Squacco Heron was got on the "Glasgow" canal in October, 1852, *fide* Mr. W. Martin (Morris' Naturalist, 1853, p. 61). Where the "Glasgow canal" may be I cannot say, as I am unable to find it in the map. The bird had no plumes, and the owner showed his sense of the value of it by exchanging it for a case of two Bramblings.

PINK-FOOTED GOOSE.

Has been obtained by Canon Tristram and others. This turns out to be the commonest Goose in many parts of England, now that the distinctions are better understood.

---

* I may here remark that correspondents of the Zoologist and other periodicals devoted to Natural History, often say a bird was killed "last week" or "yesterday," which conveys nothing if a letter is not dated ; and dates after a signature are so frequently omitted that they should always be put in the body of the letter, which is the only way of insuring the insertion.

EGYPTIAN GOOSE.

I saw some in October, 1866, which had been shot at Tees-mouth. They have been recorded (Zool., ss. 525). Whether they were "escapes" I know not, but one which I examined in the flesh presented no signs of domestication. They struck me as being a sedentary bird in Egypt.

NYROCA DUCK.

Mr. Rudd records a specimen at Coatham (Zool., 2773). This Duck has several English names, but it is perhaps most generally known as the Nyroca or White-eyed Duck.

WHITE-WINGED TERN.

A specimen in Mr. Hancock's collection was shot at Tees-mouth (op. cit., p. 144).

PELICAN.

The last on my list is the Pelican which Canon Tristram found dead upon the shore (Zool., 5321). It is conjectured that it may have died on board some passing vessel. It was *Pelecanus onocrotalus*, so far as Canon Tristram could judge from a specimen minus its head.

NETTING SEA-BIRDS ON THE WASH.

IN 1873 I saw nets for the first time at Blakeney for catching birds at night on the muds; long, large-meshed nets, supported by poles. I had always thought before that they were only used in the Wash. Charles Hornigold was the first man to use them there, that is to say of recent years, and the art has been carried to perfection by Mr. F. J. Cresswell of Lynn. One of the best day's wild fowling I ever had was in company with that gentleman on the 18th of December, 1862. Well protected with wraps, for the cold was intense, I went on board the "Wild Duck," which is the name of his yacht, and all night we rode at anchor in a sea so tempestuous that she lurched like a drunken man, in order to be early at the nets in the morning; but it was well worth the trouble to see the singular spectacle which so many varieties of birds dangling in the meshes presented. There is nothing like a pitch-dark, blustering night, and the catch was good.

Woodcock - - -	1
Curlew -	3
Knot - - - -	15
Golden Plover -	3
Gray ditto - - -	3
Bartailed Godwit -	1
Redshank - -	1
Oystercatcher - -	2
Dunlin - -	34
Gulls of different species, including the Greater Black-backed - -	17
Total	80

The success was not quite so great the next night, which was calmer, but about forty Plover, Curlew, etc., were taken.

Mr. Stevenson, who gives his readers some interesting particulars (B. of Norf., II., 376)—in part supplied by me— enumerates twenty-one species as having been taken in these nets, but the number is below the mark. I will select a day in proof from Mr. Cresswell's gamebook, in which three additional ones are mentioned.

Dec. 1st, 1869.	Dunlin	40
	Knot	19
	Grebe	1
	Guillemot	1
	Razorbill	1
	Gulls	5
	Golden Plover	1

I suppose a high tide laid the nets under water, which would account for the diving birds. Coots are now and then caught in the same way.

Mr. Stevenson (l. c.) remarks that sixty Dunlins have been taken in one night: I think that is very likely. Thirty-six Knots have been, and on one occasion sixty Oystercatchers, and nothing else; but the best haul was seven Grey Geese at one swoop, which rolled themselves up in one little bit of net into such a ball, that it had to be cut to pieces to get them out.

With Mr. Cresswell's permission I will give the total take for eleven consecutive years :—

1859		132	Birds.
1860	-	292	,,
1861	-	192	,,
1862	-	313	,,
1863	-	267	,,

1864 1865	-	493	,,
1866	-	614	,,
1867	-	631	,,
1868	-	486	,,
1869	-	273	,,

These statistics are pretty good evidence that the sea-fowl do not all sleep at night. Grey Crows will rob the nets when they get the chance; so will another sort of two-legged poacher. One of the latter kind forgot he had a Prince of Wales' feather on the sole of his boot, which left an ·impression at every step, and led to his ultimate detection.

The nets, which are about five feet high, are generally placed at high-water mark. All of them together reach at least a third of a mile. They are fatal to everything between a Lark and a Shelduck. If a Dunlin so much as touches with the tip of his wing it is wound round in an instant, and there he hangs until he is taken out and killed. The majority of the birds are taken out alive, and many small waders so caught, especially Knots, have been presented by Mr. Cresswell to the Zoological Society, and have lived for some years in the cage at the south end of the fish-house.

SHORT NOTES ON BRITISH BIRDS.

RED-FOOTED HOBBY.

As it is a point of interest to know where rare birds are to be found, I think that this is the time to mention that I have recently ascertained a young male Red-footed Hobby in my father's collection, to be the same specimen recorded in Paget's "N. H. of Yarmouth." It was shot at Breydon, not as Messrs. Paget say in 1832, but on the 1st of May, 1830. In all probability it was the first killed in Britain. Mr. D. B. Preston of Catton, to whose notes I am indebted for clearing up the confusion, says it was killed behind the "Vauxhall Gardens," and he saw it shot. He adds that Mr. Lombe of Melton, on hearing of the circumstance, sent an artist to draw it. On referring to some MS. notes left by that gentleman I find that "drawings were sent to the Linnean Society"—drawings that is to say (I suppose) of my father's bird and his own killed at Horning in the same year.

AVOCET.

In April, 1867, I had a pair of Avocets from Leadenhall Market. I was told it was a great thing to get a pair; but in April, 1871, I saw no less than seven there. I think they came from Dort or Dordrecht in Holland. It was a sight not to be forgotten.

LITTLE EGRET.

This is the most beautiful bird I ever saw in a state of nature, and I should say the handsomest on the British list. Books would have us believe that it has been killed twenty times in this country, but this is not true. There are only five of them, which, like Cæsar's wife, are above suspicion. I would not give much for the specimen in the Wisbeach Museum, though the inscription on it says that it was killed at Sleaford, Anwick, (South Lincolnshire) in December, 1851. Its history, as far as Mr. Cordeaux and I can learn, is that it was given as a skin by the Rev. F. Latham* of Helpringham. I think that the explanation may be that in a general cleaning it has changed tickets with some other bird, but there it stands. It is in winter plumage, and is marked a male.

GREAT-CRESTED GREBE.

It appears that this ornament of the waters is apt to be aggressive at times. A friend was one day in his punt among the mudflats and shoals of the Wash, and he chanced to wound a Grebe. Without more ado the bird came right at him, and would have attacked him he thinks if he had not instantly struck it down with his paddle.

I once read a parallel case in " Land and Water." I have found up the paragraph, which is as follows:—

" On February 18th, 1870, just at daybreak, a bird attacked a man who was walking along a wood; it gave several harsh screams and rushed at his waistcoat. With difficulty he managed by kicking it to kill it. He said he was very much frightened. He

---

* Who informs Mr. C., *in. litt.*, that he thinks he got it in Hampshire.

brought me the bird; it is a fine specimen of the Great Crested Grebe."

GOSHAWK.

I think it was in the autumn of 1864, that a Goshawk, which is a rare bird in Norfolk, was trapped in our woods at Northrepps, but broke loose, the spring being too feeble. The bait was the remnants of a Cushat Dove, which he was eating when first seen, and oddly enough he went into the trap by moonlight.

POCHARD.

At Lynn, as I learn from a friend, the name "Pochard" is pronounced "Pocka," and it is applied to the Scaup Duck, while the true Pochard goes by the name of "Red-headed Pocka," and the Tufted Duck is dubbed the "Whiffling Pocka." Provincial names are very confusing.

GREY WAGTAIL.

There is a certain curious fact in the economy of the Grey Wagtail, for which I have never seen a satisfactory explanation given. It has happened over and over again, that one of these birds took an extraordinary fancy for, or dislike to, a window, and by way of giving vent to its feelings was found perpetually charging the glass with its beak until the panes were smeared with marks. One naturalist actually declares that this kind of thing went on for three months, and the tapping of the infatuated Wagtail never apparently stopped for ten consecutive minutes all day.

WOOD-PIGEON.

I have taken 440 ivy berries out of a Wood-Pigeon's

crop, besides trefoil leaves and sundry indigestible bits of wood. It has often struck me what indigestible things birds eat. With us in East Norfolk the food of the "Cushat" in November and December would appear to be almost exclusively acorns, and the number they can stow away in their dilatable crops is very great.

GREATER-SPOTTED WOODPECKER.

A Greater-spotted Woodpecker dissected by me, and which proved to be a male, had almost entirely shed the red crown of immaturity, without in the least assuming a red occiput. Mr. Plant has recorded an instance of its quite doing so (Zoologist, 2824), and his bird was going to nest. So it appears that there is a period—though a very brief one—in which the sexes of this species are not distinguishable.

SNIPE.

December 7th, 1875. Saw five Snipes which were killed at one shot flying.

PEREGRINE FALCON.

It has been doubted if a Peregrine in its wild state will tackle a Heron, but the following extract from a letter from Mr. A. D. Stark to my father, dated December 15th, 1852, respecting a young female Peregrine which he gave to him, would seem to show that this is occasionally the case :—

"It was shot on the river wall between Thorpe and Rockland by a wherryman, who was on board his wherry at the time. It had struck a Heron to the ground, and appeared so far to have cowed him that he dare not move, and it was enabled to make two subsequent strikes. Whilst it was in the act of making a third strike, the man fired at it and injured the tendon, as you perceive. Being thus disabled it was carried by the wind (which was blowing tolerably hard at the time) out of a direct line from its prey; and the Heron seeing his opportunity, availed himself of it and took to wing."

Though quite winged, this bird lived some years in confinement.

ROCK DOVE.

Mr. Bailey tells me that, in the winter of 1870-1, hundreds of Rock Doves were picked up on the rocks at Flamborough Head dead through stress of weather, and I certainly saw very few when I was there the summer following. Another observer adds that some people make a practice of netting them, as they can get a great price from pigeon-shooters for them, but that those who want them for the "pot" generally shoot them by lying up at the fresh-water springs which go over the rocks. They come inland most when the corn is cut and the seed is sown. Tons and tons of their dung have in former years been taken out of a large cavern, called Bempton Pigeon-cote.

OYSTERCATCHER.

I never but once saw a "pied Oystercatcher"—as some people term them—which really was pied. It was shot at Tees-mouth, and was for some time in my possession.

Mr. F. Bond has or had an Oystercatcher with the white neck ring going quite round. This is unusual, but I have seen one in Leadenhall in which the same mark, though not so far continued, was an inch in depth.

SHRIKE AND GOLDEN ORIOLE.

I possess a dilapidated and tail-less specimen of a hen

Golden Oriole, which I bought of Mr. Baker of Cambridge, who accounted for its condition by telling me that it was killed and mutilated by a Grey Shrike. The affair happened in this wise. Both birds had nests at Falkonswaerd, in North Brabant, and close together, and jealousy, the destroyer of amity, crept in between the two mothers: at least I can only suppose it was this which incited the butcher-bird, in a moment of vindictive malice, to rip up the Oriole, so that the King of the Netherlands' falconer and Mr. Baker actually saw the unfortunate bird's entrails hang out upon the ground.

NUTHATCH.

April 24th, 1872. Led by her clamour, I detected the tail of a Nuthatch sticking out of a hole forty feet up the bole of a Scotch fir tree. A pair of Starlings were looking on. April 30th, one of the Starlings was in the hole and the Nuthatch had gone. Three days before I had seen what I think was a Nuthatch's nest only *two feet* from the ground. It was a small hole in a beech, plastered around with the customary mud, and lined with flakes of Scotch fir bark. I took note of another beech tree in which a small crack or crevice had been filled with mud, evidently by a Nuthatch, but for what purpose I cannot divine, as it was far too small for a nest. There was a Starling's nest underneath it. A similarity in breeding habits often brings the Starling and Nuthatch into juxtaposition. I have seen holes which were alternately the property of Starlings, Nuthatches, and Bats. One such was in a large ash tree at Braconash; and in a second hole in the same tree I caught the Barn Owl and Stock Dove.

At Hethel I have found and taken the egg of the Nut-hatch from a hole in a brick wall; and I am credibly informed of a case in which a nest was found in a common pump.

These notes refer to Norfolk.

HAWFINCH.

The Hawfinch is sometimes not uncommon in Norfolk. I have seen it at Braconash, Northrepps, Gunton, Hethersett, and Barningham.

SABINE'S SNIPE.

There seems to be a growing belief that all Sabine's Snipes are young birds. Mine certainly is.* The head, neck, and thighs, have or had a good deal of down on them, and the underpart of the wing was all young stubs, and the legs were thick below the tarsal joint, like the young Stone Curlew. That the bird is a variety I have not a shadow of a doubt.

GREEN WOODPECKER.

My father lately obtained a Green Woodpecker at Norwich—a male, shot in the neighbourhood. The crown and occiput are of the usual brilliant red, but the nape is black, and that colour runs from the eyes to the termination of the red on the occiput. A constant and somewhat analagous variation has given to the Spanish Woodpecker the name of *Gecinus sharpii.*

TAMENESS OF THE COOT.

Coots feed with the Ducks and Waterhens in St. James' Park, and are so tame that I have had them come within two

---

* Shot at Wareham (Zool., ss., 1293.)

U

paces of me for a piece of bread. I dare say they would take it from the hand if the Ducks did not drive them about.

WHITE GULLS.

At p. 9784 of the "Zoologist," a description is given of a White Gull shot at Lytham, and I should like to offer a few remarks upon it, as the bird has since passed into my possession. It is not correct to speak of it as pure white, for there are some dark feathers on the occiput, and on the underparts faint remains of the broccoli-brown, which characterises the immature plumage of the Glaucous Gull, and that the recorder was correct in referring it to that species I have little doubt, but I do not at all agree in his conclusion that it must be a very old one. I should rather judge it to be in the intermediate stage between old age and immaturity. Although he says he has never seen or heard of one, there are such things as albino Gulls. My father possessed two, and in each of them I discovered a dark feather on careful examination, which proved to me that they were not the Glaucous.

GREATER WHITETHROAT.

It is well known that the autumn plumage is different from the spring. Among other points is the head, which turns from brown to grey, but it would appear that some carry the brown head—like certain cock Blackcaps—into the ensuing spring, for a female sent from Cromer lighthouse, which it had flown against, in May, 1872, was in that state of plumage. Of course I am well aware that there are numerous instances of other birds which should in the normal course of thing, be adult by Christmas, carrying their immaturity into the spring succeeding, and I think all such cases are very interesting. In my introductory chapter on the Birds of Egypt I have alluded to the theory, supported by Kirk and other observers, that many birds—*Insessores* particularly—breed to the south of the equator in our winter, which is their summer; and it may be their young which are got in England in spring in immature plumage.

RAZORBILL.

On the 2nd of August, 1871, Mr. Cordeaux saw only six Razorbills at Flamborough Head—where he had gone on purpose to study the sea-fowl—in three days; but when I was there a few weeks before, viz., on the 21st of June, every fourth bird I saw on the rocks was one. This shows that they had shared in the benefits of the recently-passed Act, and it was some other cause which occasioned their scarceness in August. They appeared to me to be quite as numerous as the "Parrot" or Puffin.

I only saw one young one, which was about half-grown; all the rest were adults. I was told that the Jackdaws got their eggs very much; but what amused me was a story which was told to me of an overbold Jackdaw who ventured to worry one of the old birds. The Razorbill bore it until it could stand it no longer. There was a limit to endurance, and exasperated beyond measure by such unprovoked assaults, it at last seized the tormenting Jackdaw and bore him into the sea.

The Razorbills come quite over the top of the Flamborough cliff when the wind is high. Several nearly flew against me, appearing almost unable to check themselves.

RICHARDSON'S SKUA.

A man at Lynn saw a Gull, which he said was a Great

Black-backed, attacked by a Richardson's Skua. It must have been ravenous to venture against such a large bird. The Gull turned upon its puny assailant, struck him, and knocked him down on to the ground as a reward for his overweening ambition. The man then picked him up and found that one eye was struck out, notwithstanding which painful injury, he eat some food which was offered to him, after which he was taken to my informant who sent him to the Zoological Gardens, but I do not know how long he survived his injuries.

KITTIWAKE.

When I visited Flamborough soon after the passing of the Sea-birds Act, I found that the poor Kittiwakes were getting up their numbers very slowly. I did not see above a hundred. It was of course the plume trade which had thinned them so. Parties always shot at them in preference to the Guillemots, because they paid part hire of the boat. Mr. Bailey informed me that they were called "Petrels," and in their second year "Mackerel birds."

BLACK-HEADED GULL.

In 1860, on the day of the great gale—the memorable 28th of May, I visited Scoulton Mere, in Norfolk, with my father, the largest Gullery of its kind in England. About 16,000 eggs had been gathered. In 1872, when I went again, only 4,000 eggs were taken. This sad falling off was due to dry seasons. Brown, the keeper, told me that once the farmers spread the fields in the neighbourhood with manure sown with salt, which poisoned the worms, etc., upon which the Gulls fed, and that a great number died in consequence. He said that they suffer from Stoats and Rats. He had on one occasion 150 of the nestlings and eggs just chipping destroyed by a Stoat which swam across to the "hearth," as the island which they nest on is called.

It is surmised that "Scoulton" means "School town," which I think doubtful, though one might naturally expect it to take its name from the great colony of Gulls which have nested there from time immemorial. The place belongs to Mr. Weyland, and intending visitors will do well to remember that an order from his agent at Norwich is requisite to go upon the island.

There is another much smaller and more recent Gullery at Hoveton Broad, in Norfolk. It is divided into four little colonies, which in 1872 barely numbered 400 birds. The owner, Mr. Blofield, started with sixteen pairs, which were supposed to have come from the Martham district, and may have been the descendants of the old colony at Horsey.

WILLOW WARBLER.

I have observed this species in the winter (Dec. 25th) at Bayonne, which looks as if it was within the limit of its winter migration. The Willow Wren* and Chiff-Chaff are exceptions among the Sylviads, which as a rule go further south than was supposed in Mr. Yarrell's time. Neither in Egypt nor in Algeria could I find a vestige of several species said in books to winter in North Africa.

---

* The Willow Wren goes to South Africa but not the Chiff-Chaff, as far as my father knows.

GIBRALTAR.

. THERE are few better places for birds than Gibraltar. The number of species enumerated in Irby's recent publication— the "Ornithology of the Straits of Gibraltar"—proves it. No doubt this is in a measure from its geographical situation. Hoopoes, Bee-eaters, and other birds, halt here for a few hours on their passage. Some meet a premature death by coming in contact with the panes of the lighthouse on Europa point; others pass north and spread themselves over Spain, France, and England; others again may settle down in the vicinity.

In January, 1870, I was detained some days by an overdue steamer, and found plenty to do in rambling over the rock, and making notes on its zoology.

PORCUPINE.

One stuffed specimen killed on the Rock.

MONKEY.

I saw nine Monkeys at the back of the Rock, which I was told was about all there were. They are strictly preserved. I was very fortunate in seeing them, as many visitors hunt the Rock for them in vain.

BONELLI'S EAGLE, *Nisaetus fasciatus (V.)*.

From that noble look-out—the signal station—many a

sportsman must have seen this Eagle, and noted the white patch on the back, alluded to by Colonel Irby (op. cit., p. 44).

KESTREL, *Cerchneis tinnunculus* (Linn.).

One was seen to fly into a hole in the old Moorish tower.

SPARROW, *Passer domesticus* (Linn.).

BLACK WHEATEAR, *Dromolæa leucura*, Gm.

Seems to keep chiefly to the top and eastern side of the Rock.

ALPINE ACCENTOR, *Accentor collaris* (Scop.).

BLUE THRUSH, *Petrocossyphus cyanus* (Linn.).

Rather solitary, perching upon rocks and rough ground.

BLACK REDSTART, *Ruticilla titys* (Scop.).

Favier says that the immature birds keep together (Irby, op. cit., 82), but the old ones are solitary. I certainly saw more in the adult male plumage than in the female, which the above may in part explain.

BLACK-HEADED WARBLER, *Sylvia melanocephala*, (Gm.).

See "Zoologist," February, 1875.

BLACKCAP, *Sylvia atricapilla*, (Linn.).

This warbler would not appear to winter so far south as some of its congeners.

ROCK MARTIN, *Cotyle rupestris* (Scop.).

Is the species alluded to in the fifteenth letter of the White-Marsham correspondence (Norw. Nat. Soc., Trans. ii., 181).

BARBARY PARTRIDGE, *Caccabis petrosa* (Gm.).

Bought one in the market with its throat cut, indicative of its Moorish origin.

STONE CURLEW, *Œdicnemus crepitans*, Tem.

One in the market. As it was with the Partridges, it may have come from Africa also.

CURLEW, *Numenius arquata* (Linn.).

I saw two which a man had shot.

JACK SNIPE, *Lymnocryptes gallinula* (Linn.).

RING DOTTEREL, *Ægialitis hiaticula* (Linn.).

KENTISH PLOVER, *Ægialitis cantiana* (Lath.).

I found that I could distinguish these from the Ring Dotterels by their speed in running, and greater disinclination to take wing.

SANDWICH TERN, *Sterna cantiaca*, Gm.

At St. Roque.

GREAT OR COMMON SKUA, *Stercorarius catarractes* (Linn.).

This bold bird was swimming within about sixty yards of

the steamer. When it got up, its flight was just like a Gull's.

BLACK-HEADED GULL, *Larus ridibundus*, Linn.

Hovering about the military slaughter-house.

LESSER BLACK-BACKED GULL, *Larus fuscus*, Linn.

GANNET, *Sula bassana*, (Linn.).

Several seen between Cadiz and Gibraltar.

PUFFIN, *Fratercula arctica* (Linn.).

I· was shown a young one at a chymist's, being stuffed.

EARED GREBE, *Podiceps nigricollis*, Sundev.

A Grebe was swimming in one of the moats, which I am nearly sure was of this species.

Military strictness reigns at Gibraltar. At 5.45 p.m. a gun is fired, the band begins to play, and the gates of the town are closed for the night; after which no one is allowed to pass the lines on any pretence, and benighted travellers must find their way back to St. Roque, or sleep on the sand.

THE BITER BIT.

Terns, Sandpipers, and Crows, are known to have been caught by cockles and mussels, and to have suffered a lingering death by starvation. Instances are recorded of the Pewit, Water-rail, and Razorbill having met a like fate. Made bold by hunger, they incautiously inserted their beaks into the juicy bivalves, which closed upon them with a fatal tenacity ; others, which had inadvertently stepped into the trap, were caught by the toe, and in like manner perished.

THE FIRST EDITION OF YARRELL.

THE late Mr. Yarrell adhered to the laudable practice of devoting a paragraph under each species to its geographical distribution. With reference to Egypt, he has been singularly unfortunate in the sources whence he drew his information. I find that country accredited with possessing a number of species which are unknown to it, or only very rare stragglers ; and on the other hand, no mention is made of a still larger number which do inhabit it.

HYBRIDS.

IN June, 1870, I saw at the Bayonne Museum a hybrid between a male Peacock and a hen Pheasant. In June, 1875, I saw what appeared to be another hybrid Peacock alive in the Bois-de-Bologne at Paris. I have also seen a Peahen which had in a great measure assumed cock's plumage, strutting about in a yard in Norfolk.

MISPRINT,

ORNITHOLOGISTS suffer much from misprints. The worst I ever saw was *cyruscrayers* for Sarus Cranes. In bringing my book to a close,* let me express a hope that my readers will find nothing so bad as that in the preceding pages.

---

* THE SACRED IBIS.—Since the preceding pages went to press, I have learnt from Mons. Filliponi that he has lately obtained a Sacred Ibis near Damietta, and seen three others. His description of the bird leaves no doubt on my mind that he has correctly named it, and there is nothing remarkable in its occasionally occurring in Lower Egypt as a straggler.

INDEX.

JARROLD AND SONS, PRINTERS, NORWICH.